Contemporary African American Women Playwrights

"*Contemporary African American Women Playwrights* powerfully reminds readers of the capacity of theatre, drama, and spectacle to stimulate audiences toward the establishment of community and the pursuit of social change."
Joycelyn Moody, University of Texas at San Antonio, editor of African American Review

"Philip Kolin has managed to put together a comprehensive collection that not only reminds us of the historically significant contributions of African American women playwrights but also connects us to their contemporary relevance."
Valerie Curtis-Newton, University of Washington

"For students and scholars of American theatre and drama generally and African American theatre and drama most particularly, this is an extremely valuable critical source."
Harry J. Elam Jr, Stanford University

In the last 50 years, American and World theatre have been challenged and enriched by numerous female African American dramatists. *Contemporary African American Women Playwrights* is the first critical volume to explore the contexts for and influences of these writers, and their exploration of black history and identity through their diverse, courageous and visionary dramas.

Editor Philip C. Kolin compiles a wealth of new essays:

- David Krasner provides an in-depth background study on the dramatic legacy of Lorraine Hansberry, Zora Neale Hurston, Marita Bonner and Georgia Douglas Johnson.
- Individual chapters devoted to: Alice Childress, Sonia Sanchez, Adrienne Kennedy, Ntozake Shange, Pearl Cleage, Aishah Rahman, Glenda Dickerson, Anna Deavere Smith and Suzan-Lori Parks.
- An original essay and accompanying interview with Lynn Nottage.
- Comprehensive discussion of attendant theatrical forms, from chore-opoems and surrealistic plays, to documentary theatre and civil rights dramas, and their use in challenging racial and gender hierarchies.

Contributors: Brandi Wilkins Catanese, Soyica Diggs, James Fisher, Freda Scott Giles, Joan Wylie Hall, Philip C. Kolin, David Krasner, Sandra G. Shannon, Debby Thompson, Beth Turner, and Jacqueline Wood.

Philip C. Kolin is Professor of English at the University of Southern Mississippi. He is a widely published poet and academic, whose works include *Understanding Adrienne Kennedy, Othello: New Critical Essays* (Routledge 2002), and *The Tennessee Williams Encyclopedia*. He was the founding coeditor of *Studies in American Drama, 1945–Present*.

Casebooks on Modern Dramatists
Kimball King, *General Editor*

Peter Shaffer
A Casebook
Edited by C. J. Gianakaras

Simon Gray
A Casebook
Edited by Katherine H. Burkman

John Arden and Margaretta D'Arcy
A Casebook
Edited by Jonathan Wike

August Wilson
A Casebook
Edited by Marilyn Elkins

John Osbourne
A Casebook
Edited by Patricia D. Denison

Arnold Wesker
A Casebook
Edited by Reade W. Dornan

David Hare
A Casebook
Edited by Hersh Zeifman

Marsha Norman
A Casebook
Edited by Linda Ginter Brown

Brian Friel
A Casebook
Edited by William Kerwin

Neil Simon
A Casebook
Edited by Gary Konas

Terrance McNally
A Casebook
Edited by Toby Silverman Zinman

Stephen Sondheim
A Casebook
Edited by Joanne Gordon

Horton Foote
A Casebook
Edited by Gerald C. Wood

Samuel Beckett
A Casebook
Edited by Jennifer M. Jeffers

Wendy Wasserstein
A Casebook
Edited by Claudia Barnett

Woody Allen
A Casebook
Edited by Kimball King

Modern Dramatists
A Casebook of Major British, Irish, and American Playwrights
Edited by Kimball King

Pinter at 70
A Casebook
Edited by Lois Gordon

Tennessee Williams
A Casebook
Edited by Robert F. Gross

Beth Henley
A Casebook
Edited by Julia A. Fesmire

Edward Albee
A Casebook
Edited by Bruce J. Mann

Joe Orton
A Casebook
Edited by Francesca Coppa

A. R. Gurney
A Casebook
Edited by Arvid Sponberg

Neil LaBute
A Casebook
Edited by Gerald C. Wood

Contemporary African American Women Playwrights
A Casebook
Edited by Philip C. Kolin

Martin McDonagh
A Casebook
Edited by Richard Russell

Suzan-Lori Parks
A Casebook
Edited by Alycia Smith-Howard

Contemporary African American Women Playwrights

A Casebook

Edited by Philip C. Kolin
University of Southern Mississippi

Routledge
Taylor & Francis Group

LONDON AND NEW YORK

First published 2007
by Routledge
2 Park Square, Milton Park, Abingdon, Oxon OX14 4RN

Simultaneously published in the USA and Canada
by Routledge
270 Madison Ave, New York, NY 10016

Routledge is an imprint of the Taylor & Francis Group, an informa business

© 2007 Taylor and Francis Group, LLC

Typeset in Sabon by
Keyword Group Ltd
Printed and bound in Great Britain by
Biddles Ltd, King's Lynn

British Library Cataloguing in Publication Data
A catalogue record for this book is available from the British Library

Library of Congress Cataloging in Publication Data
 Contemporary African American women playwrights / [edited by] Philip Kolin.
 p. cm. – (Casebooks on modern dramatists)
 Includes bibliographical references (p.) and index.
 1. American drama–African American authors–History and criticism. 2. American drama–Women authors–History and criticism. 3. American drama–20th century–History and criticism. 4. African American women–Intellectual life. I. Kolin, Philip C.
 PS338.N4C66 2007
 812′.52099287–dc22
 2007017379

ISBN10: 0-415-97826-2 (hbk)
ISBN10: 0-203-93354-0 (pbk)

ISBN13: 978-0-415-97826-2 (hbk)
ISBN13: 978-0-203-93354-1 (ebk)

Contents

General Editor's note

For over 50 years, African American women playwrights have transformed and reinvented the American theatre. This volume is the first critical study that explores the work of these artists; focusing on ten of the most influential.

Every one of these figures has made a powerful contribution to American theatre. Each essay devoted to one of these playwrights examines themes and techniques as well as studies the contexts and connections between these writers. Key ideas cycling through the works of these playwrights include performing blackness, challenging racial and gender hierarchies, rescuing feminist visions, and creating a new dramatic territory for the production of African American history. Significantly, the volume closes with an original interview with Lynn Nottage, who addresses many of these central concerns of African American women playwrights.

The editor of this important volume is Philip C. Kolin, Professor of English at the University of Southern Mississippi. Kolin is a widely known scholar of modern and contemporary American theatre. He has published books on Edward Albee, David Rabe, Adrienne Kennedy and Tennessee Williams. He is regarded as an international authority on the plays of Williams, especially because he edited *The Tennessee Williams Encyclopedia*. His more than 150 essays on American playwrights (and Shakespeare) in major journals further attest to his scholarly preeminence.

Kimball King
General Editor

Contributors

Philip C. Kolin, Professor of English, at the University of Southern Mississippi, has published more than 30 books, including *Conversations with Edward Albee, Williams: A Streetcar Named Desire, The Undiscovered Country: The Later Plays of Tennessee Williams, Othello: New Critical Essays* (Routledge), *Understanding Adrienne Kennedy,* and *The Tennessee Williams Encyclopedia.* Kolin has also published more than 150 scholarly articles and notes, most recently a study of the formation of Kennedy's canon for *CLA Journal* and an interview with Billie Allen in the *African American Review.* He is the General Editor for the *Routledge Shakespeare Criticism* series and was the founding coeditor for *Studies in American Drama, 1945–Present.*

Brandi Wilkins Catanese teaches in the Theatre and the African American Studies Departments at the University of California, Berkeley. Her published work includes an essay on George C. Wolfe's *The Colored Museum.*

Soyica Diggs, who was a Postdoctoral Humanities Fellow at Stanford 2006–2007, is an Assistant Professor of English at Dartmouth. She is currently preparing a book that examines modes of black performance in African American drama and literature through historical, cultural, and psychoanalytic readings.

James Fisher is Chair of the Theatre Department at the University of North Carolina at Greensboro, and the author of several books, including *The Theater of Tony Kushner: Living Past Hope* and the editor of *Tony Kushner: New Essays on the Art and Politics of the Plays.* A widely published critic, Fisher is also a director and actor. He was named Indiana Theater Person of the Year in 1997.

Freda Scott Giles is currently Associate Professor of Theatre and African American Studies at the University of Georgia. Her most recent publication is "From *A Raisin in the Sun* to *Venus*: Embodiment of and Re/union with the Lost Home," *New England Theatre Journal* and is at work on a book dealing with African American drama during the

Harlem Renaissance. Giles was a member of the Owen Dodson Lyric Theatre and performed in *Magic* and *Lions*, both under the direction of Glenda Dickerson.

Joan Wylie Hall, who teaches at the University of Mississippi, is the editor of *Conversations with Audre Lorde* and the author of *Shirley Jackson: A Study of the Short Fiction*, in addition to numerous articles on American women writers. She is currently working on a book on local colorist Ruth McEnery Stuart.

David Krasner is the former Director of Undergraduate Theatre at Yale University and is currently Associate Professor and Head of the Acting Program at Emerson College. He has numerous publications and has twice received the Errol Hill Award from the American Society for Theatre Research.

Sandra G. Shannon, Professor of Drama at Howard University and coeditor of *Theatre Topics Journal*, is a leading authority on the works of August Wilson. She has published *The Dramatic Vision of August Wilson* and *August Wilson's Fences: A Reference Guide*. She has also coedited *August Wilson and Black Aesthetic* and serves as the President of the Black Theatre Network.

Debby Thompson is an Associate Professor of English at Colorado State University. She has published articles on contemporary drama, African American playwrights, and racial identities in a range of journals, including *Theatre Journal*, *African American Review*, *Contemporary Literature*, *Studies in Twentieth-Century Literature*, *MELUS*, and *Mosaic*.

Beth Turner is the founding editor and publisher of *Black Masks*, a journal on Black performing arts. She retired from NYU's Tisch School of the Arts where she taught dramatic literature and history and is currently enrolled in the Ph.D. program in theatre at the University of Georgia, working on a study of the impact of post-traumatic slave syndrome on the work of women playwrights and filmmakers of the African diaspora.

Jacqueline Wood, who teaches at the University of Alabama at Birmingham, has published essays on Sonia Sanchez and Adrienne Kennedy, and has had an interview with Sanchez in *African American Review*. Wood's edition of Sanchez's plays is forthcoming.

Acknowledgments

I am grateful to many individuals for their goodwill and assistance as I prepared this volume. Straightaway, I want to express my thanks to the African American women playwrights in whose honor this volume was conceived and developed. For over 50 years their collective canons have reshaped and reinvigorated American and world theatre. I also thank my contributors for their stalwart dedication to this project and for their impressive participation in the evolving body of scholarship on these playwrights.

To Harry Elam and David Krasner go my thanks and profound respect for their steadfast friendship and vast knowledge of African American theatre, past and present, that they generously shared with me and with several of my contributors.

Kimball King, the august General Editor of this Modern Dramatists series, deserves kudos on earth and crowns in heaven. For many decades I have been the beneficiary of Kimball's wide ranging knowledge of American drama, his keen academic advice, and his unstinting kindness. Editing this volume in his Series is, beyond doubt, a blessing. Working with Ben Piggott and Minh Ha Duong, my editors at Taylor and Francis, has also been a sincere pleasure, and I am grateful to them for their commitment to this volume and their help in stitching it together.

At the University of Southern Mississippi I am particularly grateful to Michael Mays, Chair of the Department of English, and Denise von Herrmann, Dean of the College of Arts and Letters, for their sustained and enthusiastic support of my research. They are model administrators and scholars. My thanks also go to my research assistants Benjamin Geddes and Maria Englert for their diligent cooperation throughout this project.

God has blessed me with a loving extending family—my spiritual mother and father Margie and Al Parish, Deacon Ralph and Mary Torrelli, Sister Carmelita Stinn—and with my children Kristin, Eric and Theresa, and my grandchildren Evan Philip and Megan Elise who wonder why Pop is always busy. Finally, my gratitude goes to Nancy Steen for her lifelong devotion to civil rights and for her sustaining friendship and sagacious counsel.

Philip C. Kolin
University of Mississippi
September 2007

1 Introduction

The struggles and triumphs of staging gender and race in contemporary African American playrights

Philip C. Kolin

Black male playwrights historically have had a commanding voice in American theatre. In the 1930s, Langston Hughes's *Mulatto* (1935) was the longest running play by an African American playwright on Broadway. In 1941, Richard Wright adapted his widely known novel *Native Son* (1941) for the stage. In the 1960s, the protest plays of Amiri Baraka and Ed Bullins received resounding critical attention and productions. In 1970, Charles Gordone's *No Place to be Somebody* was the first play by an African American dramatist to receive a Pulitzer, and in 1981 Charles Fuller's *Soldier's Play* also won this prestigious award. The plays of August Wilson (twice a Pulitzer winner), beginning with *Ma Rainey's Black Bottom* (1984), earned him "the stature of premier theatrical mythographer of the African American experience" (Marra 123).

But African American women playwrights are also taking their place as the leaders of the American theatre, creating their own theatrical space, history and mythos. While they are the heirs of Lorraine Hansberry's legacy, perhaps the most widely taught and staged African American woman dramatist, most of the playwrights represented in this collection have radically departed from her realistic techniques and boldly interrogated and amplified her protests against racism and classism. The racial prejudices these playwrights have fought against as African Americans and as women have pyramided in the last third of the twentieth century. Gender politics and gaps have also intensified their searching for or proclaiming their identities. Each playwright in this volume has not been afraid to assert, assault, and to discover the complexities of survival of self in the process. Their politics are aesthetic; their aesthetics are political. As Anna Deavere Smith proclaims:

> Yes, my entry into the theatre is political. Largely because of my race and gender. I am political without opening my mouth. My presence is political. The way I negotiate my presence becomes political. If I tried to deny my politicalness, I would be even *more* political.
>
> ("*Not So Special*" 80)

Their works challenge and attempt to change an oppressive ideology, whether it be a white patriarchy, an institutionalized theatre culture, or a dominating African American male surety. Glorifying the battle, Pearl Cleage calls herself one of "the African American Urban Nationalist Feminist Warrior Women" (Alexis Smith 39).

Combating the snares of the status quo, these playwrights also are heavily invested in experimentation, oftentimes rooted in earlier cultural movements (e.g., Harlem Renaissance; Black Arts Movement) as well as dramatic and musical techniques (e.g., minstrelsy, spectacle). The name of playwright Ntozake Shange translates the creative selfhood of these playwrights—"She who brings her own things." Their plays explore the frontiers of signifying and often take audiences across horrifying dramatic terrains, physical, and psychic. It is hardly coincidental that so many of the playwrights whose work is studied in this collection are responsible for actually creating performance—as dancers, actors, composers, scenographers, directors, producers. They preside over the age of performativity. Their canons range from realistic, well-made plays to daring experimental performance pieces to moving dance montages. The triumph of their creations are reflected in Alice Childress's subversive well-made plays, Sonia Sanchez's radical protest dramas, Adrienne Kennedy's mind-chilling nightmares, Shange's choreopoems, Glenda Dickerson's mythopoetic works, Suzan-Lori Parks's decolonizing history plays, and Anna Deavere Smith's documentary monologues. These original, revolutionary most times, scripts have taken American theatre into one of its most powerful eras.

The eleven original essays, and one interview, here attempt to chart the evolutionary history of these contemporary black women playwrights and to assess their contributions to American stages. These playwrights represent a widely diverse group of writers whose voices have and will continue to shape American drama. The essays are arranged in roughly chronological sequence, although in a few instances the order has leaped chronology to group or link complementary playwrights and scripts. Thematic continuity seems more crucial than strict chronological order which, because of the overlapping productivity of these dramatists, would have been less effective, e.g., separating Kennedy's plays from Shange's which are so indebted to hers.

In the opening essay, David Krasner discusses three significant playwrights of the Harlem Renaissance, or earlier, and their impact on Lorraine Hansberry. The achievements and themes of these four black women writers serve as a bridge to the contemporary dramatists in this collection. The Harlem Renaissance, which trumpeted the cultural affirmation of the arts, emerged from the 1920s and empowered writers, according to Langston Hughes, "to express our individual dark-skinned selves without fear or shame" (694). This is exactly what later generations of black women writers have done. For Krasner, Georgia Douglas Johnson, following the footsteps of Alain Locke, laid the groundwork for folk drama found in the plays of Dickerson, Cleage, or Lynn Nottage. Zora Neale

Hurston's love of performance and theatre, for example, compelled her to write plays with vivid theatricality, thereby establishing a positive view of performance that later playwrights emulated. In Krasner's view, Marita Bonner, one of the most unappreciated playwrights, paved the way for a black avant-garde with her expressionistic dramas, precursors to the works of Adrienne Kennedy and Suzan-Lori Parks. Krasner also stresses how these three playwrights anticipated Lorraine Hansberry (1930–1965) whose landmark play *Raisin in the Sun* (1959) was a paradigm of social realism.

The plays of Alice Childress (1920–2004), the subject of the following essay by Soyica Diggs, also foreshadowed the themes, characters and culture clashes of more contemporary black women playwrights. Although vastly understudied, Childress's canon spans over 40 years with more than a dozen plays, ranging from savage social criticism to a celebration of comic Jackie Mable in *Moms* (1987). Childress was the first African American woman to have her work performed Off Broadway—*Gold Through the Trees* (1952)—and won an Obie for her *Trouble in Mind* (1955). Praised for creating the "well-made play," as Hansberry was, Childress, according to Diggs, generated the tensions about gender and race that were to be highly productive in more contemporary drama. Beginning with Childress's early play, *Florence* (1949), and analyzing her other work of the civil rights period (1949–1969), Diggs argues that Childress wrote dialectal dialogues that transformed what audiences had known about the performance of blackness, or the changing status of signifying blackness, one of the central debates of the Black Arts Movement (1965–1975). Childress's most influential (and anthologized) plays are *Wedding Band* (1966) and *Wine in the Wilderness* (1969), which also focus on the performance, and acceptance, of blackness. The former play, about an interracial couple during World War I, was aptly subtitled, *A Love/Hate Story in Black and White*, thus looking forward to the identity struggles found in Kennedy's *A Movie Star Has to Star in Black and White* (1976) as well as to numerous plays and films, including Lanford Wilson's *Gingham Dog* (1969), Spike Lee's *Jungle Fever* (1991), and Mira Nair's *Mississippi Masala* (1991) starring Denzel Washington, on miscegenation. *Wine in the Wilderness* continues Childress's valorization of the strong black woman, in this case a ghettoized street person, Tommy Tomorrow, who is rejected by a smug black middle-class that finally learns to appreciate her honest earthiness and natural beauty.

Though more widely known as a highly prolific black revolutionary poet, Sonia Sanchez (1934–) as a resistance dramatist is the subject of Jacqueline Wood's essay. Wood emphasizes Sanchez's unique position as the only female dramatic voice within the cadre of black militant playwrights of the 1960s and 1970s, the period of the Black Arts Movement with which she was closely associated. Sanchez was also affiliated with the Nation of Islam, even writing a children's play, *Malcolm Man Don't Live Here No Mo* (1972), on the death of Malcolm X. In acknowledging Sanchez's understudied dramatic works, Wood examines her theory of poetic voice as it articulates her political vision of theatre, its value as weapon and revelation. Exploring four of Sanchez's published plays as well as one of her unpublished scripts (*I'm Black When I'm Singing, I'm Blue When I Ain't* 1982), Wood identifies the central themes of Sanchez's plays, particularly her uniquely self reflexive interrogation of the black militant community and her efforts to privilege the issues and struggles of black women searching for their identity, most powerfully revealed in the monologue *Sister Son/ji* (1969) whose words and clothes symbolize her conflicts.

The next two essays concentrate on playwrights who have dominated the black avant-garde in the American theatre—Adrienne Kennedy (1931–) and Ntozake Shange (1948–). My study of Kennedy stresses that for over 40 years she has been writing shocking, surrealistic plays that have radically departed from realistic/naturalistic conventions. Her plays are nightmares about a chaotic world of shifting locations and selves. While not denying that Kennedy maps the landscape of the unconscious, I suggest a new way of reading her plays as cultural artifacts reflecting the tumultuous times during which they were written—especially the 1960s. Contextually, through her black and mulatta characters we enter a world of civil rights atrocities and legislation that often failed to contain such horrors. In *Funnyhouse of a Negro* (1962), Sarah is haunted from the opening tableau until her tragic death by the spectre of the lynching rope that tropes many racial prejudices, historical and contemporary. In *Rat's Mass* (1966), Kennedy analogizes white supremacists of the 1960s to Nazis, underscoring hate crimes against black children and the heinous process of racial flagging. The bombing of the Sixteenth Street Church in Birmingham in 1963 offers a further historical context in which to interpret the stage horrors and bloody imagery in Kennedy's play. Seen in historical perspective, *A Lesson in Dead Language* (1964) also reflects the racist opposition to desegregation, by metamorphosing the schoolroom into a torture chamber of shame. But Kennedy's political message is not limited to the 1960s; it can be traced across the trajectory of her canon to include racial profiling, or highway apartheid, as in *Sleep Deprivation Chamber* (1996).

In the following essay, James Fisher argues that among black women dramatists Shange holds a unique position as a creator of experimental works merging theatrical and poetic traditions with music and dance, an amalgam that played a major role in exploring black identity in the American theatre. Yet Fisher claims that Shange's signature "choreopoem," *for colored girls who have considered suicide/when the rainbow is enuf* (1976), was inspired by such diverse sources as the writers and performers of the Harlem Renaissance, Hansberry's social dramas, and, of course, Kennedy's surrealistic nightmares. As Fisher points out, Shange can boast of a career-long examination of the emotionally painful transition from adolescence to womanhood, a preoccupation which has also set her apart from her contemporaries. Acclaiming Shange's exploration of identity, Anna Deavere Smith begins *Fires in the Mirror* by interviewing Shange who proclaims: "I am part of my surroundings/ ... / and what's inside our identity/ is everything that's ever happened to us." Fisher concludes that Shange is wary of success in the mainstream commercial theatre and prefers to experiment with small ensemble casts in performances that reject the spectacle and linear dramatic structure of traditional theatre while emphasizing the emotional experiences of the young women whom she has typically depicted.

Like Sanchez, Atlanta-based Pearl Cleage is a poet and an activist, championing strong and creative black women. In fact, all except two of Cleage's widely produced plays have been commissioned either by the Women's Project in conjunction with the Southeast Playwrights Project of Atlanta or by Atlanta's Alliance Theatre. In studying Cleage's plays beginning in 1983, Beth Turner sees Cleage as one of the foremost African American dramatic voices of contemporary American theatre in large part because of her portraits of valiant women put in a position of having to defend themselves. In Cleage's articulation of feminist opposition to the interlocking oppressions of sexism, racism, and classism, Turner finds that her work also resonates with the spirit of both Alice Childress and Ntozake Shange. Focusing in detail on one of Cleage's most well known plays, produced by both prominent Black and white theatres, Turner carefully explicates *Flyin' West* (1992) with its four nineteenth-century African American women who settled in the all-black town of Nicodemus, Kansas. Turner also closely reads Cleage's *Bourbon at the Border* (1997) and *Blues for an Alabama Sky* (1995), set in Harlem in the 1930s, which was selected as the official theatrical presentation of the USA at the 1996 Olympic Festival of the Arts in Atlanta.

Turning to Aishah Rahman (1936–), Brandi Wilkins Cantanese explores the ideas and dramatic techniques of a writer who has been an enduring and prolific presence in contemporary African American theatre as both an author and educator/mentor to younger generations. Rahman's work, according to Cantanese, has helped to shape the way we understand African American woman and culture in general. Her essay conducts an overview of Rahman's published, full length works, concentrating on such recurrent themes as the use of a jazz aesthetic, her recourse to intertextuality, her repeated staging of narratives that resurrect black cultural icons, her explorations of interracial and intraracial gender politics, and her interest in African-based spiritual practices. Exploring these themes, Cantanese insists that Rahman centers African American aesthetics and values rather than allowing them to remain on the cultural margins. Accordingly, Rahman's decision to work outside of the aesthetic tradition of dramatic realism allows her to depict aspects of African American life that defy reductive stereotypes found elsewhere in the American theatre. Rahman is an important link to other African American dramatists who engage the same issues and travel the same dramatic landscapes, such as August Wilson, Glenda Dickerson, Suzan-Lori Parks, George C. Wolfe, and Anna Deavere Smith.

Perhaps Rahman's closest contemporary spirit might be Glenda Dickerson who, like her, often uses a realistic situation as a springboard into a symbolic/mythic world. Freda Scott Giles points out in her essay on Dickerson that she has conceived, constructed, and mounted well over a dozen performance works. She has directed more than 50 plays as well. According to Giles, Dickerson's works enter into a dialectic with contemporary history, politics, and feminist thought. Dickerson has placed these works into two general categories—"miracle plays" and "performance dialogs." Dickerson's "miracle plays" may be described as a mythopoetic theatre framed in the reality of black women's experiences while the "performance dialogs" are designed to bring underrepresented discourses involving women of color into the academy. Giles stresses that Dickerson has created a theatrical language that reflects her feminist, theatrical, and teaching philosophies. Influenced by poet and playwright Owen Dodson as well as by Georgia Douglas Johnson, Eleanor Traylor, and Ruby Dee, Dickerson continues the legacy of a highly poetic black theatre. Though she has often been compared with Shange and Anna Deavere Smith, Dickerson's plays are uniquely hers, documentary testimonies by women combined with music, poetry, and movement. Giles shows how Dickerson has created a theatrical canon far less abstract and deconstructive than either Kennedy's or Parks's.

Anna Deavere Smith, whose plays Joan Wylie Hall assesses, occupies a crucial place as a contemporary performance artist. Like Shange or Cleage, she is an actress–playwright but her trademark is the solo performance of her own work. Like fellow dramatists Adrienne Kennedy, August Wilson, Suzan-Lori Parks, or Dickerson, Smith examines African American identity in a national context, but her works are neither impressionistic nor do they adhere to the formula for the well-made realistic play. Instead, Smith writes raw documentary scripts about American cities in crisis. For her Obie award-winning *Fires in the Mirror* (1993) and *Twilight in Los Angeles 1992* (1993) she created a montage of conflicting monologues from interviews with hundreds of individuals—gang members, rabbis, activists, police officers, truck drivers, teenage girls, etc. Playing more than 25 roles in *Fires*, for example, Smith (re)presented African American, Hasidic, Hispanic, and Anglo characters, male and female, young and old. Performing this widely diverse cast of characters, Smith challenged audiences to follow her lead in bridging differences. As she claimed, "gender, race, space, and acting" lead to the "travel of self to the other." Applauding Smith, Hall emphasizes that her theatre goes far beyond the categories of white and black and reminds us that *Fires* and *Twilight* are installments in Smith's larger theatrical project, the performance series *On the Road: A Search for American Character*. The greatest test of Smith's art, though, came with *House Arrest: A Search for American Characters in and Around the White House* (2002), a play that pushed the documentary form to its limits, according to many critics. In a 1993 speech before the Association for Theatre in Higher Education, Smith articulated her poetics underlying her plays: "What I am proposing is creating theatre that juxtaposes worlds that are far apart in order to create an aesthetic contrast out of a politically explosive interaction. We could then capture a raw natural, genuine modern drama which could ultimately influence how societies negotiate differences" ("Not So Special" 88).

Unquestionably the most prolific playwright in this volume, and possibly in all African American drama, is Suzan-Lori Parks (1964–). She won two Obies in the 1990s and was the first black woman playwright to win a Pulitzer Prize for her *Topdog/Underdog* (2002). From November 2002 to November 2003, Parks wrote a play a day for an entire year, resulting in her collection of *365Days/365 Plays*, which was performed in 2006–2007 by more than 800 theatres/acting companies divided into 52 hubs around the country. Each theatre or troup took an individual week of plays, allowing for multiple world premieres. Without doubt, *365* is the most ambitious theatre experiment in the history of American (and perhaps world) drama. In her essay on the "Diggin the Fo'-Fathers: Suzan-Lori Parks's Histories," Deborah Thompson explores the way Parks uses history, not actual history but "myths of history." Like Anna Deavere Smith, Parks moves history forward in our consciousness. Indebted to jazz (with its variations, responses, and repetitions), Parks "digs up" the remains of history to uncover, as Thompson argues, contemporary discourses of African American identity, masculine and feminine. Thompson acknowledges that some of Parks's discursive "digs" occur on the level of words, through etymologies both true and false ("fo'-fathers" = forefathers, or oppressive white patriarchs). Parks situates African American characters in freakish settings from white history and literature to decolonize and deconstruct expectations. In *The American Play* (1994), carnival customers shoot at a black actor who looks like Lincoln. In *Topdog* (2002), a character named Booth shoots his brother named Lincoln. *In the Blood* (1999) and *Fucking A* (2000) dig up two black Hesters from Hawthorne's *Scarlet Letter*. Focusing intently on *Venus* (1995), about an African American woman taken to London to play Venus Hottentot in a freak show, Thompson traces Parks's contemporary discourses on race through exploration and imperialism, religious moralism, freak shows, jurisprudence codes, medical anthropology, and romantic heterosexual love. Like other Parks's plays, *Venus* also performs an archeology of contemporary theatre, Thompson maintains, attacking it as a dangerous product of the society of surveillance.

In the concluding essay in this volume, Sandra Shannon interprets the works of Lynn Nottage (1964–), zeroing in on her two best known plays to date (*Intimate Apparel* [2006] and *Crumbs From the Table of Joy* [2004]) and conducts an original interview with the playwright as well. Placing Nottage's work in the company of fellow playwrights such as Shange and Parks, Shannon identifies her major themes, most important being the rescue of voices of neglected black women from history and the artifacts they carry forward with them. In Shannon's interview, Nottage reveals the process by which she became a playwright, the ways in which she developed her art of storytelling, critical to her aesthetic as one of America's most proactive contemporary playwrights, and the context in which she sees her art in relationship to African American male authors.

As these overviews indicate, the critical essays in *Contemporary African American Women Playwrights* survey a wide range of playwrights, dramatic techniques, and racial/gender issues. In investing both background and foreground, this volume offers readers an informed history of and vital appreciation for a major group of playwrights whose works are defining the American theatre today—and for tomorrow as well.

Works cited

Gener, Randy. "One Nation, Under Suzan-Lori Parks." *American Theatre* (April 2006): 20.

Hughes, Langston. "The Negro Artist and the Racial Mountain." *Nation* (June 23 1926): 692–4.

Marra, Kim. "Ma Rainey and the Boyz." *August Wilson: A Casebook*. Ed. Marilyn Elkins. New York: Garland, 2000.

Smith, Alexis. "Pearl Cleage." *Women Who Write Plays: Interviews with American Dramatists*. Hanover, NH: Smith and Kraus, 2001. 24–55.

Smith, Anna Deavere. "Not So Special Vehicles." *Performing Arts Journal* 17 (1995): 77–89.

2   "Something's going on down here that concerns me"

Johnson, Hurston, Bonner, and Hansberry

David Krasner

Lloyd Richards, director of Lorraine Hansberry's *A Raisin in the Sun*, said of the 1959 production that/it "not only tells you a story; it tells you about the times and what people were concerned with and interested in at that moment in time."/He added: module

> I was standing in the lobby of the theatre looking at the people lined up to buy tickets. There was a woman who was at the ticket window who gave the treasurer one dollar. The treasurer told her the ticket is $4.80. She exclaimed, "$4.80? I can see Sidney Poitier [the star of the production] around the corner in a movie for ninety-five cents." She went into that pocketbook and got out the rest of her money and bought a ticket and started walking into the theatre. It was only 3 pm, so the treasurer tells her that she couldn't go in now, she'd have to come back at 8.30. I stopped her and asked her why she was paying $4.80 to see Sidney when she could pay ninety-five cents around the corner. She said "the word's out in my neighborhood that something's going on down here that concerns me, so I had to come down here to find out what it was about." At that moment I knew why I was in the theatre, and what I was doing here (2).

In many ways this story summarizes African American theatre history. The phrase "something's going on down here that concerns me" echoes W. E. B. Du Bois's oft-quoted 1926 statement outlining four fundamental principles of a "real Negro theatre": "About us, By us, For us, and Near us" (134). Building on Richards's story and Du Bois's manifesto, my aim is to examine precursors to the authors examined in this collection. In the following, three representative authors of the Harlem Renaissance— Georgia Douglas Johnson, Zora Neale Hurston, and Marita O. Bonner— will be discussed. Their impact on one of most important dramatists of the twentieth century, Lorraine Hansberry, will remain central in my essay. Though it would be a mistake to portray these three playwrights with a uniform brushstroke, each knew the others and each conveys a deep "concern" over the conditions of black women. All contribute themes essential to African American theatre—Johnson, folk drama; Hurston, theatricality; and Bonner, the avant-garde—and these themes eventuate in Hansberry's *A Raisin in the Sun*. All four set the stage for the dramatists analyzed in this anthology.

Georgia Douglas Johnson and the folk

The female dramatists of the Harlem Renaissance (sometimes referred to as the New Negro era, c. 1916–1935)—Angelina Weld Grimké(1880–1958), Georgia Douglas Johnson (1877?–1976), May Miller (1899–1995), Eulalie Spence (1894–1981), Mary P. Burrill (1884–1946) and Alice Dunbar-Nelson (1875–1935)—indicted a system of racial oppression. The moral rhetoric of American democracy pitched during World War I (and again during World War II) was blunted both in tone and content amidst the fact of lynching. The Harlem Renaissance playwrights challenged the American way of life as a paradigm of social virtue. Their plays depicted black men under siege and black women choosing childlessness or infanticide over their children succumbing to lynch mobs. In her notes to her play *Rachel* (1916), one of the earliest dramas by an African American woman to deal with race violence, Grimké remarked that if anything can make all women sisters "it is motherhood." She added: "If I can make the white women of this country see, feel, understand just what [effect] their prejudices ... were having on the souls of the colored mothers everywhere," then "a great power to affect public opinion would be set free and the battle would be half won" (Grimké Papers).

Georgia Douglas Johnson, like Grimké, was committed to social change. Already an accomplished poet by the time she turned to playwriting in the mid-1920s, her one-act *Blue Blood* received honorable mention in the 1926 Urban League's *Opportunity* playwriting contest. In the following year her play *Plumes* took first prize. During the 1930s, Johnson submitted five plays to the Work Project Administration of the Federal Theatre. Her biographer Judith Stephens, speaking broadly, observes that "As a prolific playwright of the New Negro era, Johnson participated in, and was undoubtedly energized by, ongoing debates concerning the nature and goals of a 'real' Negro theatre, the use of dialect, the portrayal of black characters, and the role of white playwrights in the Negro little theatre movement" (11).

Alain Locke was Johnson's close associate. Locke, a Howard University Professor and editor of the landmark 1925 book *The New Negro*, was an influential scholar who often served as her advisor. Their relationship was, in fact, personal: they became close friends following the deaths of Locke's mother and Johnson's husband. Their mutual admiration and the fact that they both resided in Washington, D.C. helped forge a close bond (see Stewart). By the early 1920s Locke regularly critiqued Johnson's work and in 1928 he wrote the foreword to her third book of poetry. In 1927 Johnson opened her home on Saturday nights to black artists and intellectuals, including Locke, Du Bois, Hurston, Bonner, and others. Gwendolyn Bennett would dub the group the "Saturday nighters of Washington, D.C." (212). Most importantly, Locke influenced Johnson's ideas of folk theatre.

According to Locke folk theatre should raise black consciousness, provide a focal point around which the popular imagination might be awakened, and unify the community through imaginary situations in drama having concomitant relations to the real world. The "folk play," Locke insisted, is drama "of free self-expression and imaginative release," yielding "beautifully and colorfully the folk life of the race" (1926: 704). Drama for Locke should be popular, not in the Broadway-laden sense catering to stereotypes, but rather as representative of what the early-nineteenth-century German scholar J. G. Herder called "*das Volk.*" As I have mentioned elsewhere, folk drama for Locke and Johnson, "being the dramatic enactment of text, music, dance, and shared myth, had the characteristic of a collective religious performance, binding the community together as participants in a ritual rather than as mere spectators at the theatre" (Krasner 139). In countering Broadway's black musicals emphasizing fast hoofing, show-girl attractions, and buffoonery, "Locke's concept of drama exalted a counter-primitivism grounded in folk drama, devoid of the misconception that black people are happy-go-lucky dancers and nothing more" (139). For Locke, African American drama ought to depict folk life realistically and passionately. Instead of propaganda advocated by Du Bois, Locke viewed the situation in the 1920s as a "dilemma of choice between the drama of discussion and social analysis and the drama of expression and artistic interpretation" (Locke 1926: 703). Drama, he believed, should "grow in its own soil and cultivate its own intrinsic elements; only in this way can it become truly organic, and cease being a rootless derivative" (1926: 703). Folk theatre ought to be an indigenous and vibrant African American drama. In his unpublished "Notes on Drama" (c. 1926), he says that "a peasant folk art pouring out from under a generation-long representation is the likeliest soil known for a dramatic renascence" ("Notes on Drama," n.p.). From this fecund ground, "the supporters and exponents of Negro drama do not expect their folk temperament to prove the barren exception." ("Notes on Drama," n.p.). Drama was to be modeled on Yiddish theatre and the Abbey Theatre of Ireland; specifically playwrights should emulate the Irish playwright J. M. Synge. As Locke said: "Somewhat under the inspiration of the Irish and Yiddish theatres, but also in part under a momentum of its own, our drama is reaching out toward two new channels of expression—the realistic folk-play, of which we have instances in the work of [Willis] Richardson, and the poetic-folk play, of which we have as yet just the merest beginnings" ("Notes on Drama," n.p.).

Johnson's play *Plumes* exemplifies Lockean folk drama. It comes nearest to the spirit and form of Synge's *Riders to the Sea* (1904): both Synge and Johnson consider illusion, poetry (dialect), and the need for poor people to make compromises. Like Synge, Johnson's folk play concerns the conflict between dreams and reality in a peasant setting. *Plumes* takes place in "The Kitchen of a two-room cottage" (74). Charity Brown's daughter is dying offstage. Charity must decide whether to pay for an expensive operation likely to fail or use the money for a dignified funeral. Johnson exposes ancient myths of rural, lower-class African Americans in their relationship to death. Many low-income people consider burial a matter of pride. They desire a dignified funeral for themselves and their relations. Despite its cost, the black lower class place great emphasis on a pricy send-off. Johnson tapped into this longstanding tradition and deep feeling about last rites, funerals as homecomings, and suspicion of doctors. During slavery and into the reconstruction era many women created mutual aid societies to guarantee respectful burials. These folk experiences, like folk songs and legends, were communicated within an underground culture. The concept of death and the one-set kitchen milieu of the "folk" will reappear in *A Raisin in the Sun*. The matriarch of Hansberry's play, like Charity, must decide the best way to use the insurance money for her family. The kitchen space in *Plumes* likewise comprises a social relations grid in *Raisin* that informs a poetics of domestic architecture elaborating familial bonds.

Zora Neale Hurston: Theatricality and the black experience

In a letter to Constance Sheen (February 2 1926), Zora Neale Hurston (1891–1960) wrote, "You know how interested I am in the theatre, and I am just running wild in every direction, trying to see everything at once" (2002: 80). Notwithstanding recognizing her as an accomplished novelist, essayist, and anthropologist, few critics (with the notable exceptions of Hill, Kraut, Lowe, and Richards) make much of the fact that Hurston was, also, an accomplished stage master. At several historically black southern colleges she worked as a performer, director, choreographer, playwright, and drama teacher. Her commitment to theatre is revealed in her ideas about everyday experiences in the black community. By emphasizing the significance of performance we can best view the impact of her theories on one representative play, *Color Struck*.

Zora Neale Hurston's important 1934 essay, "Characteristics of Negro Expression," describes the collective experiences of people of the African Diaspora. The essay, published in *Negro: An Anthology*, explores a manifestation of cultural expression and the details of African American religion and nightlife, while emphasizing public performance in identifying "characteristics" of racial "expression." Hurston provides a nuanced account of blackness in the rural South in terms resonating with performance art and the folklore she sought to systemize. Influenced by Franz Boas and the Columbia School of Anthropology (where she attended in the late 1920s and early 1930s), she emulated Boas's demand for fieldwork and objectivity. Under his tutelage Hurston made use of the "spy-glass of Anthropology" in order to reveal southern African American culture (1979: 82). For Hurston the "real Negro theatre," a phrase she repeats often, "is in the Jooks and the cabarets" (1934: 31). The "real Negro theatre," she says, might be "lacking in wealth, so it is not seen in the high places" (1934: 31). However, it is in the "Jook"—what she describes as "a pleasure house in the class of gut-bucket," originating in "the lumber, turpentine and railroad camps of Florida ... common all over the south,"—where "the cradle of the Blues" is experienced ("Harlem Slanguage"). She adds that "in the [Jook's] smelly, shoddy, confines has been born the secular music known as the blues, and on blues has been found jazz" (1934: 29). In a letter to her sponsor Charlotte Osgood Mason (January 6 1933), Hurston outlined her goals: "You said so often that you had planned an auditorium in connection with it so that *real* [double underlined] Negro folk music could be heard in the midst of it all. ... If we can give *real* [single underline] creative urge a push forward here, the world will see a New Negro and justify our efforts" (2002: 277). For Hurston music and theatre are mediated through a performance aesthetic. Throughout her work she underscores the inseparability of performance and the everyday within the context of the "black experience."

Hurston criticized the elitist view of theatre and art as necessarily detached from everyday life. According to Carla Kaplan, she believed that the "so-called black drama available to the public was inauthentic, watered down, and washed out" (2002: 172). Hurston sought a "real Negro theatre" in place of the artificial one found on Broadway. In the words of Lynda Marion Hill, she examined "the social rituals and the verbal art" of African American southern folklore in order "to capture the depth of experience implicit in ordinary expression" (32). Her published and unpublished plays, as well as her work as an actress and director, stressed this "depth of experience" in folkloric humor and pastoral life. Hurston, in particular, viewed the southern rural black community as grossly undervalued and misconstrued. In her unpublished 1934 essay, "You Don't Know Us Negroes," she claimed that "most white people have seen our shows but not our lives. If they have not seen a Negro show they have seen a minstrel or at least a black-face comedian and that is considered enough. They know all about us" (1934a: 2). "Negro life" for whites came only through the lens of Broadway musical theatre (*Shuffle Along*, among others), film (the popular 1927 *The Jazz Singer*, for example), and radio (*Amos 'n' Andy* in the late 1920s and 1930s). These misrepresentations popularized "primitivism" and the resurgence of "blackface." Even Depression-era sociological novels and plays by black authors presented dubious representations, what Hurston sardonically refers to as "a prolonged wail on the tragedy of being a Negro," yielding "a catalog of incidents intended to show starkly the pity of it all." This, she said, is an "insincere picture." She also criticized "Northern Negroes," who, "unless they have spent years in residence and study, know no more about Negro life in the South than Northern white folks do" (1934a: 5, 6). The southern vernacular and folk idioms that Hurston had assembled in the course of her ethnography provided, according to Anthea Kraut, "a corrective to contemporaneous presentations of African American culture" (440). Distressed by misconceptions, Hurston wrote "Characteristics of Negro Expression" to set the record straight.

"Characteristics of Negro Expression" begins with the idea that "the Negro's universal mimicry is not so much a thing in itself as an evidence of something that permeates his entire self. And that thing is drama" (1934: 24). Hurston adds: "Every phase of Negro life is highly dramatised. No matter how joyful or how sad the case there is sufficient poise for drama. Everything is acted out ... No little moment passes unadorned" (1934: 24). She spoke of black culture in terms of theatricality; indeed, theatre permeated her life. In 1934, she was invited to establish a school of dramatic arts based on "Negro expression" at Bethune–Cookman College. She described her goals for this job in a letter (January 22 1934) to Carl van Vechten: "I wish to work out some good nigger themes and show what can be done with our magnificent imagery instead of fooling around with bastard drama that can't be white and is too lacking in self respect to be gorgeously Negro" (2002: 288). She used terms such as "nigger themes," "magnificent imagery," and "gorgeously Negro" to jolt her assimilationist colleagues from their complacency and examine differences rather than similarities among the races. On one occasion Hurston went so far as to insist on "laws" describing black performance. In a letter to Langston Hughes (April 12 1928)—an important letter anticipating "Characteristics of Negro Expression"—she enumerated several such laws: "The Negro's outstanding characteristic is drama. That is why he appears so imitative. Drama is mimicry." She added that for African Americans, "*Angularity* is everything, sculpture, dancing, abrupt story telling." Hurston hoped to produce "the new, the *real* Negro theatre," which will "act out the folk tales ... with abrupt angularity and naiveté" (2002: 115, 116). She repeatedly stressed that the Deep South represents the real theatre experience uncontaminated by urban life and untrammeled by northern influences.

Hurston views mimicry as essential to African American theatre because it ensures the passing of traditions from generation to generation. In a culture barred from education, deprived of heritage, and denied identity, mimicry became an instrument of self-preservation and one of the few mechanisms for enacting social transmission, educating the young, and preserving cultural memory. Hurston emphasizes mimetic experience because it provides a basis for understanding life and culture. For her, experience is a transaction between humans and the world. She privileges the experiential and participatory over the textual and conceptual, with drama serving as the crucial way by which experience leads to knowledge. In her unpublished essay, "Folklore," Hurston writes that folklore is "the boiled down juice of human living and when one phase of it passes another

begins which shall in turn give way before a successor" (n.p.). Folk
performance, as Hurston defines it, is an interaction of ideas and
experiences, yielding an intelligibly connected system of communication
and transformation. Sandra L. Richards contends that "the critical tradition
within African American literature locates 'authentic' cultural expression
on the terrain of the folk, but the folk have articulated their presence most
brilliantly in those realms with which literature is uncomfortable, namely in
arenas centered in performance" (65). Performance provides the sensual
cum tactile experience lacking in formalist abstract analysis. For Hurston
the maintenance of performance "experiences," which are always public,
communicative, and subject to change, is the essential ingredient for
"authenticity." In a 1934 interview with the *ChicagoDaily News* she
remarks on the importance of folklore, saying that "It would be a tremendous
loss to the Negro race and to America if we should lose the folklore and folk
music, for the unlettered Negro has given the Negro's best contribution to
America's culture" (1934c: 27). Folk preservation through performance
was Hurston's objective. Her emphasis on mimetic performance is best
understood as not only aesthetic but political as well. Mimetic experience is
a cultural survival tactic from the Middle Passage, through slavery, and into
the present. Addressing the folklorist Alan Lomax regarding the ways in
which she learns folk songs, she says in "Florida Folklore":

> I just get in a crowd with the people and if they're singing I listen as best
> I can and I start to joining in with a phrase or two. And then, finally, I
> get so I can sing a verse. And then I keep on until I learn all the songs,
> all the verses, and then I sing them back to the people until they tell me
> that I can sing them just like them. And then I take part, and I try it out
> on different people who already know the song until they are quite
> satisfied that I know it. And then I carry it in my memory (1935).

Like the Pragmatists of her time, Hurston defines experience as interactive,
continuous, and transformative. In the year of Hurston's "Characteristics,"
the Pragmatist John Dewey writes in his influential book *Art as Experience*
that "art, in its form, unites the very same relation of doing and underdoing,
outgoing and incoming energy that makes an experience to be an experience
… In an emphatic artistic–aesthetic experience, the relation is so close that
it controls simultaneously both the doing and the perception" (48, 50).
Hurston stresses doing and perception, and likewise Dewey forcefully
opposed the academic–Cartesian fallacy of privileging abstraction and form
over experience and content. She cites as an example of experience the
"black bottom," a rollicking dance with roots in jooks and taverns of the
South, which is verified for its authenticity against the intent of those who
invented it. Hurston reports that when "the Negroes who knew the Black
Bottom in its cradle saw the Broadway version they asked each other, 'Is
you learnt dat new Black Bottom yet?'" This question serves as "proof that

it was not *their* dance" (1934: 31). The dance had been "proven" in "its cradle," whereas the Broadway version had become so formalized and abstracted as to be rendered unrecognizable to the very people who originated it. Hurston, as did the American Pragmatists, regards experience and verification as providing the ultimate litmus test of how a performance—in this case the *ur*-Black Bottom dance—functions as a benchmark for "authenticity." The performance is "authentic" only if the community recognizes it as such and acknowledges its evolving nature. In Hurston's words, "Negro folklore is not a thing of the past. It is still in the making. Its great variety shows the adaptability of the black man: nothing is too old or too new, domestic or foreign, high or low, for his use" (1934: 27). Hurston shares the values of American Pragmatism in which meaning is flexible and satisfies an interest. Flexibility, interpretation, evolution, and the theatrically of "rehearsal"—the process of learning through repetition—is fundamental to her performance theory. The experience of storytelling can, therefore, be both universal and local; a version of a story, for instance, can remain fundamentally the same, though altered subtly at different locales by different storytellers. The "will to adorn" and "angularity" are merely two of Hurston's significant departures from the view of representation as fixed. Static conceptions eviscerate performance, stripping it of its experiential vitality. Performance incorporates a shared understanding of experience but it also involves imagination. The African American, Hurston asserts, "mimics for the love of it, and not because he wishes to be like the one imitated" (1934: 28). Mimicry is not an occlusion of creativity, but rather an undisguised celebration of theatricality. Geneviéve Fabre and Michael Feith contend that in Hurston's "Characteristics of Negro Expression," the "specifically performative dimension of African-American identity" yields "several levels, from a use of language favoring action words and metaphor, to a certain theatricality pervading every situation of communication and communal intercourse" (17).

Theatricality is inextricably linked to what is in all likelihood Hurston's first play, *Color Struck: A Play in Four Scenes. Color Struck*, written in the early 1920s and published in the 1926 one-issue journal, *Fire!*, examines the experiences of a dark-skinned African American woman, Emmaline Beazeby (called Emma throughout the play) who competes for her lover, John, with a lighter-skinned woman. The publication in *Fire!* is important for several reasons, not the least of which is Hurston's association with the journal's radical editors. Although it cannot be ascertained with certainty what audience the authors of *Fire!* aimed to reach, the subtitle of the journal, "A Quarterly Devoted to Young Negro Artists," suggests that its editor Wallace Thurman and its editorial staff, consisting of Langston Hughes, the artist Aaron Douglas, and Hurston, intended it primarily for African Americans. Aaron Douglas maintains in an unpublished open letter on *Fire!* stationery that "the Negro is fundamentally, essentially different from their Nordic neighbors. We are proud of that difference … We believe Negro art should be trained and developed rather than capitalized and exploited. We believe finally that Negro art without Negro patronage is an impossibility" (n.p.). Certainly whites were allowed to patronize it; but the radical nature of its content and the advocacy of its contributors suggest Garvey-like militancy and independence rather than accommodation and supplication. Langston Hughes affirms this sentiment in *The Nation* just prior to the publication of *Fire!*, saying, "We younger Negro artists who create now intend to express our individual dark-skinned selves without fear or shame. If white people are pleased we are glad. If they are not, it doesn't matter" (694). In *Fire!*, Thurman, Hughes, Douglas, and Hurston produced a unique black voice tailored for a black audience in an essentially *heuristic* way: to make progress in black aesthetic expression and, more precisely, to have control over key elements of that expression. Hurston and others often had to curry white patronage in order to survive; *Fire!*, however, was one rare exception expressive of a distinctive black voice. Diligently and self-consciously they were perfecting a style that catered to blacks—something "concerning" a black public. That *Fire!* survived for only one issue indicates the nobility, if naivety, of this endeavor.

Color Struck vividly conveys theatricality, heightened emotions, and picturesque setting. The period is "Twenty years ago and present," and the locale is "A Southern City." The importance of locating the play in a specific southern place stresses what Hazel Carby calls Hurston's artistic representation that marks "not only a discursive displacement of the historical and cultural transportation of migration, but also is a creation of a folk who are outside history" (77). Rather than celebrating northern migration, the play challenges migration as a positive connotation of the Harlem Renaissance. Elsewhere I have suggested that in *Color Struck* Hurston "creates a world made up of those 'outside history,' having fallen through the interstices of social recognition" (114). Emma, the play's protagonist, "is black, poor, disenfranchised, and rural" (114); she therefore epitomizes the outsider in every way: "She is not the 'New Negro' fashioned by the doyens of the Harlem Renaissance. Rather, she defies commodification as a cultural artifact made for the amusement of whites and the progressive faction of the black elite." Hurston "was in revolt against a black northern elite culture that rejected the values of the black South as well as its people, and she was embarking on a creative process of reclaiming southern, poor, black women from the dustbin of history" (114).

The first scene opens on a segregated railway car, where passengers are en route to a cakewalking contest in Jacksonville, Florida. Emma arrives late because she had been inveighing against her partner John. John had apparently been flirting with light-skinned African American women, although he vehemently denies it. Reading the play evokes a sense of John's integrity; his denials are firm and convincing. But performing is another matter. In performance John's affection and duplicity are evident. After John and Emma dance before the denizens of the railway car, one of the characters,

Wesley, beckons Effie, "a mulatto girl," to dance. Effie is partnerless, and Wesley cries "Come on out, Effie! Sam aint heah so you got to hold up his side too" (8). Effie dances *"a modified Hoochy Koochy, and finishes up with an ecstatic yell."* John, *"applauds loudly,"* and says, "If dat Effie can't step nobody can" (8). When Emma confronts John over his enthusiasm, he appears nonchalant, even sitting down with his arms around her. He accuses her of needless jealousy. Emma explains the reasons for her emotion:

> Emma (*sadly*). Then you don't want my love, John, cause I can't help mahself from being jealous. I loves you so hard, John, and jealous love is the only kind I got.
> (*John kisses her very feelingly.*)
> Emma. Just for myself alone is the only way I knows how to love (9).

Emma's emphasis on her loneliness and pain is accentuated in performance. Her isolation is conveyed by actors—what they look at and where they direct their flirtatious behavior.

In scene two, the train has arrived. People, the stage directions note, *"come in by twos and three, laughing, joking, horse-play, gauchely flowered dresses, small waists, bulging hips and busts, hats worn far back on the head, etc"* (9). Hurston evokes a specifically southern and theatrical ambience. Her vivacious suggestions come to life when actors strut and preen in this robust setting. Only the highly emotional and painfully withdrawn Emma remains reticent and suspicious. John tries to set her at ease:

> John (*squeezing Emma's hand*). You certainly is an ever loving mamma—when you aint mad.
> Emma (*smiles sheepishly*). You oughtn't to make me mad then.
> John. Ah don't make you! You makes yo'self mad, den blame it on me. Ah keep tellin' you Ah don't love nobody but you. Ah knows heaps uh half-white girls Ah could git ef Ah wanted to. But (*he squeezes her hard again*) Ah jus' wants *you!* You know what they say! De darker de berry, de sweeter the taste! (10)

John, however, abandons Emma for the "half-white" Effie the moment Emma balks at entering the dance hall. Despite his entreaties of love to Emma, he takes up with Effie, wins the contest with her, and likely leaves with Effie for parts North at the conclusion of scene three.

Scene three, the Dance Hall, is perhaps the play's most theatrical moment. The text describes briefly the cakewalking dance and Emma's abandonment. Hurston's stage descriptions are highly theatricalized:

> Emma springs to her feet and flings the curtains wide open. She stands staring at the gay scene for a moment defiantly, then creeps over

to a seat along the wall and shrinks into the Spanish Moss, motionless (11).

Spanish Moss (*tillandsia setacea*) grows abundantly from South Carolina to South America. Its branches often extend to the ground. Depending on the director, Emma can "shrink into the Spanish Moss" either on her seat or even fall to the ground. During this time Emma watches as "*Effie takes the arm that John offers her and they parade to the other end of the hall*" (11). The visual effect of Emma watching as John betrays her is meant to evoke powerful emotions. Hurston is very clear that the dancing occurs "*Seven to nine minutes*" (11). As a director who enjoys actors, Hurston is allowing time for performers to dance and for the actress playing Emma to portray considerable and varied reactions. The form of the play gives way to its content, the style of the dancing, and the psychological nuance of the actress's performance as she observes her lover dancing with another. After the dance a Man sees Emma and says:

> You from Jacksonville, ain't you? (*He whirls her around and around.*) Ain't you happy? Whoopee! (*He releases her and she drops upon a seat. She buries her face in the moss*) (12).

Emma is anything but happy, and Hurston makes this evident by the exuberance of the Man, the other dancers, and John and Effie enjoying their newfound partnership. The background of joyous cakewalking contrasts against the foreground of Emma having been "released," either on a seat, or, perhaps even more dramatically, thrown to the ground. Like the dancing in *A Raisin in the Sun*, Hurston establishes an African American theatre that is driven by improvisation. Rather than bound by the formalities of text, Hurston stresses dancing and acting. Performance, rather than structure, is what Hurston adds to the theatre.

John returns to Emma in scene four unannounced after twenty years. At the curtain's rise Emma has given birth to a half-white child who is now extremely ill. Like Charity in *Plumes*, Emma rejects the doctor's advice to bring the child to a hospital because she is poor and, more importantly, distrustful. Suspicion of the medical profession in African American culture has a long history, largely justified when one considers the Tuskegee medical experiments on blacks during the 1930s and 1940s. Blacks were denied penicillin for syphilis, even though the cure had already been discovered. This incident of mistrust was one of many dating back to slavery. In reading the play John's sudden appearance seems earnest, and many have interpreted John, not Emma, as victim. Tiffany Ruby Paterson, for example, argues that Emma's "self-hatred and anguish is so deep that she destroys the love she so desperately yearns for" (92). In performance, however, we can observe John's double-dealing and surface charm affecting Emma's (and our) doubt. John claims to have returned from Philadelphia because his wife died.

Emma: Bet you' wife wuz some high-yaller duckty-doo.
John: Naw she wasn't neither. She was jus' as much like you as Ah
could get her (13).

John's remark suggests that he did not run off with the "high-yaller" Effie.
But why should Emma believe him? Already he has lied, promising to love
Emma and dance solely with her when in fact we (and Emma) observe him
dance with Effie—for seven to nine minutes! Why, then, should Emma, or the
audience, take him at his word? In reading the play his deceit is not manifest
because his words carry weight. But in performance, where audiences observe
his relationship with Effie for what is in stage time considerable, his dishonesty is empirically evident. Emma is not without fault; her love has blinded
her to his deception much as Walter Lee Younger's desire for a liquor store
blinds him to the eventual scam. However, Walter Lee's and Emma's hubris is
understandable: the hope of black characters in *Color Struck* and *Raisin* for
a meaningful life is illuminated in Langston Hughes's poem "Harlem." In that
poem, which Hansberry uses for her title, Hughes reminds us that when a
dream is deferred it dries up like a raisin in the sun. Emma, likewise Walter
Lee, is driven to illogicality upon seeing her opportunities wither on the vine.

Hurston's portrayal of southern African American life is, like Johnson's
Plumes, a folk play emphasizing the concerns of black women. Emma is the
fulcrum of what Sandra Richards astutely calls the "absent potential." "For
the reader," Richards asserts, "Emma's intensely hostile reactions to light-
skinned Negroes seem unwarranted because her partner continually seeks
to reassure her of his affections, and no one makes disparaging remarks
about her skin color. But because the body onstage, through its carriage,
gestures, and spatial relationships to other bodies, resonates with social
history, the viewing experience is considerably different" (77). In speech–act
terms, Hurston favors the performative over the constative, rejecting the
formalism of 1930s–1940s New Criticism. According to Marc Manganaro,
Hurston's performance theory is a "New Critical nightmare, pure gaudiness
without reference to the architectonics of functional spareness" (188).
Hurston's extravagance is "an implicit critique of American formalist criticism of the period, a defense of her own methodology and style, a feminist
redefinition of modernist aesthetics and an assertion of Boasian cultural
relativism" (188). Performance as emphasized by Hurston is antithetical to
the mainstream conformity of her day, a *sui generis* of black expression, and
an affirmation of theatricality.

Because few of her plays were produced during her lifetime, it is particularly tragic that Hurston never fully realized her love of the theatre—with
all its improvisatory, spontaneous, and visceral immediacy. Directing her
production of *All De Live Long Day* at Rollins College, the program notes
that "Zora Hurston and her group of Negro Canters reveal, as has never
been done before, the native instinct of the negro for art expression ...
Anyone wishing to get a glimpse of negro life in Florida should not miss this

performance" (Rollins College). Her plays were meant to be staged, bringing out realities unavailable on the mere page. Her emphasis on the improvisatory nature of black folk life would become central to the twentieth century African American theatre. The folk traditions of "colorism" established in *Color Struck* (see Classon) would play a significant role in Adrienne Kennedy's work, and Hurston's radical adherence to theatricality would add significantly to Hansberry's *A Raisin in the Sun*.

Bonner and the avant-garde

In her essay, "On Being Young—A Woman—and Colored," Marita Bonner (1899–1971) writes that "You long to explode and hurt everything white; friendly; unfriendly. But you know you cannot live with a chip on your shoulder even if you can manage a smile around your eyes—without getting steely and brittle and losing the softness that makes you a woman"(1987: 6). Suppressed rage thus underscores Bonner's three plays, *The Pot Maker: A Play to Be Read* (1927), *The Purple Flower* (1927), and *Exit, an Illusion* (1928). Her works include allegorical figures who defy psychological portrayals. In realist drama, narrative proceeds linearly in time. *Plumes* and *Color Struck*, for example, move parallel with real time. *Color Struck*'s last scene takes place twenty years after the first three. But this is no different from Chekhov's typical four act structure, with his plays traversing considerable time. Nor is it contrary to Ibsen's change of locals. Bonner's *The Purple Flower*, however, dismantles any stability of time and place. The opening stage directions say "Time: *The Middle-of-Things-as-They-are (Which means the End-of-Things for some of the characters and the Beginning-of-Things for others).*" Place is defined as "*Might be here, there or anywhere—or even nowhere*" (30). *Purple Flower* pits the "Us's" versus the "White Devils," and challenges Booker T. Washington's accommodationism. For Bonner concepts are more important than any fidelity to verisimilitude. As an expressionist, she questions the interlocking of subject and object through mimesis. She also takes to task the very idea of an objective reality that can be observed and recreated as an isolated phenomenon. August Strindberg's prefatory remarks for his 1901 *Dream Play* can suffice for Bonner's *Purple Flower*. Characters in his play, Strindberg says, "split, double, multiply, evaporate, condense, disperse, assemble" (175). Bonner's characters split, double, and expose the arbitrariness of the "real," raising the specter of uncertainty, ambiguity, and new ways of seeing. Terry Eagleton put it best when he said that for "drama to break with these [old] ways of seeing, it would need to move beyond naturalism altogether into some more experimental mode—as indeed did the later Ibsen and Strindberg. Such transfigured forms might jolt the audience out of the reassurance of recognition—the self-security which springs from contemplating a world which is familiar" (187). Bonner, like Adrienne Kennedy, Suzan-Lori Parks and even Bertolt Brecht, operates in the unfamiliar, attempting to disrupt comfortable relationships between events onstage and the world.

Bonner's modernism emulates Strindbergian dream-like Expressionist drama. In lieu of realism's confidence that the world can be represented if the author can only get the details right, Bonner, who studied German Expressionism in its original language, offers provisional meanings accentuating ambiguity. This style sets her apart from her contemporaries. Her plays fulfill the criteria of avant-garde drama set forth by Richard Murphy: first, "rather than presenting an integrating and unified perspective on reality, such expressionist texts offer a 'monoperspective,' a skewed and idiosyncratic view, in which the spectator is unlikely to find either an accommodating 'subject-position' or any other source of compensation within a unified imaginary." Second, "the reduction of plot to a series of shifting scenes without a vital and dramatic relation to a central conflict reinforces the idea that any sense of harmonious world has also vanished, along with the conventional orienting notions of time, space and causality" (20). Unlike Charity in *Plumes* or Emma in *Color Struck*, Bonner's plays defy a central character and subject position or certainty of time, place, and causality.

Annemarie Bean remarks that Adrienne Kennedy, Anna Deavere Smith, and Suzan-Lori Parks "consider freely playing with the historical as integral to their work—personal histories, local histories, and American history" (4). This line of thinking begins with Bonner. Bonner, Kennedy, Smith, and Parks create figures of history but use them imaginatively. When in this anthology Philip Kolin writes that Adrienne Kennedy's "traumatized heroines speak to the cruelties of white institutionalized history determined to erase African Americans," or of the way Kennedy "portrays her characters as mad and diseased, surrealistically reflecting their tormented, guilty minds because they are not white," he is likewise describing Bonner's work. Bonner, perhaps the most underrated dramatist of any race or gender, wrote three plays. Her influence, however, ought not to be underestimated. Her expressionist rage reappears in the anguish of Hansberry's Walter Lee Younger and the longings of his sister, Beneatha.

Hansberry and social realism

Situated between the Civil Rights movement's 1954 Brown v. Board of Education Supreme Court decision and the 1965 Voting Rights Act Legislation, Lorraine Hansberry's 1959 *A Raisin in the Sun* established a socially conscious African American theatre. Her timing played no small part in the Civil Rights era. "Never before in the entire history of American theater," James Baldwin confirms, "has so much of the truth of black people's lives been seen on the stage" (1969: xii). In Hansberry's play, "black people recognized the house and all the people in it—the mother, the son, the daughter, and the daughter-in-law, and supplied the play with an interpretative element which could not be present in the minds of white people: a kind of claustrophobic terror, created not only by their knowledge of the house but by their knowledge of the streets" ("Introduction," *To Be Young* 1969: xii).

Hansberry's drama emerges from the influence of mid-twentieth-century American social realism. Like other social realists her work was rooted in the spirit of justice. Hansberry's play extols the virtues of equality and exhorts a radicalism that unmasks American culture across racial and economic lines. In other words, Hansberry's play is not only about race but also class. When Walter Lee's mother inquires why he wants to run his own business, she asks:

> Mama: Son—how come you talk so much 'bout money?
> Walter: (*With immense passion.*) Because it is life, Mama!
> Mama: (*Quietly.*) Oh—(*Very quietly.*) So now it's life. Money is life. Once upon a time freedom used to be life—now it's money. I guess the world really do change ...
> Walter: No—it was always money, Mama. We just didn't know about it (345–6).

The dialogue above illustrates Hansberry's commitment to economic as well as social change. In *Rethinking Social Realism*, Stacy I. Morgan writes that while social realism among white artists and writers began to evaporate during the 1950s, "African American cultural workers were too intimately involved with the institutions and informal networks of the American left not to know which way the prevailing winds of the nation were blowing during World War II and the early cold war era" (34). The rise of conservatism, formalism, and abstract art did not deter African American cultural workers from using their "respective media to articulate interlocking but distinctive aspects of a broader social realist agenda and sensibility" (37). African American social realists tend to portray a fractured American dream based on racial and economic conditions. As a "cultural worker," Hansberry's specific location of Chicago during the early 1950s displays a concern for increasing segregation and impoverishment of black neighborhoods. According to Nikhil Pal Singh, tensions arose when "Chicago's South Deering Improvement Association (SDIA) helped to dump progressive, New Deal Mayor Edward Kelly in 1947 because he was 'too good to the niggers.' Their *South Deering Bulletin* routinely tarred the director of the Chicago Housing Authority, Elizabeth Wood, with 'communistic connections' for her efforts to further desegregate public housing." Furthermore, between 1953 and 1955, "blacks moving into Chicago's predominantly white ethnic Trumbull Park neighborhood were victims of repeated fire-bombings ... For the remainder of the decade, charges of communism and subversion of the racial status quo would be the basis for the FBI's intensifying scrutiny of the emerging civil rights movement and blind eye to resurgence of white supremacist terror" (165). Hansberry's play addresses the reality of Chicago politics and its impact on ordinary people.

Diana Adesola Mafe remarks that Hansberry's *Raisin* is often misread as either "universal" or "particular," rendering the universal and the particular as "mutually exclusive." Instead Mafe argues that the combination of universal and particular "was crucial" (31). This combination is also the core thinking of the Hungarian Marxist critic Georg Lukács. Lukács, writing three years before the opening of *Raisin*, says that the "typical is not to be confused with the *average* (though there are cases where this holds true), nor with the *eccentric* (though the typical does as a rule go beyond normal). A character is typical, in this technical sense, when his innermost being is determined by objective forces at work in society" (122). The same can be said of Hansberry's characters: they are "typical" in their innermost being for desiring economic justice against objective forces of society.

The formal aspects of modernism—montage, documentary material, fragmentation, and multiple perspectives—were attacked by Lukács for technical sleight of hand. Such pyrotechnics undercut the purpose of drama and literature. The author, for Lukács, is held accountable for a coherent world view. When modernist techniques encroach upon the art object, the scientific coherency of Marxist social reality is obscured. For Lukács the work of art should demonstrate the internal dialectics of society, the Hegelian conflicts manifest in character versus social forces. He also rejected Naturalism as conveying "basically a static approach to reality" (34).

Naturalist reportage is simply a one-to-one reproduction of reality without artistic intervention—without the artist's world view encouraging social change. Hansberry defends realism against naturalism in the same fashion. Naturalism, she writes, "Tends to take the world as it is and say: this is what it is, this is how it happens, it is 'true' because we see it every day in life that way—you know, you simply photograph the garbage can." But in realism, she says, the artist "imposes on it [the art work] not only what *is* but what is *possible* ... because that is part of reality too. So that you get a much larger potential of what man can do. And it requires a much greater selectivity—you don't just put everything that *seems*—you put what you believe *is*" (1969: 236). For Hansberry, likewise Lukács, reality and the performance reflecting it are not related merely in a dyadic manner, but rather a third element—the artist's worldview—must enter, incorporating an interpretative selectivity. *A Raisin in the Sun* attains this interpretative illumination of social struggle and is the antithesis of the subjectivism and formalism of later plays such as *for colored girls* (1975) or *Fires in the Mirror* (1992). Like other realists á la Lukács, Hansberry adheres to objectivity yet manipulates the narrative for maximum ideological value.

Hansberry deserves recognition as one of the foremost dramatists of the twentieth century. And yet she did not spring fully formed, nor does *A Raisin in the Sun* commence the history of African American theatre. Her play's "concern" for black people had many antecedents, three of which have been discussed here. Johnson, Hurston, and Bonner deserve credit for establishing traditions that have since been refined and perfected.

Each contributes to the formation of a black theatrical aesthetic. The following essays in this collection analyze dramatists Kennedy, Shange, Smith, Parks, Sonia Sanchez, Pearl Cleage, Glenda Dickerson, Lynn Nuttage, Aishah Rahman, and Alice Childress. (Kia Corthron, Cheryl West, and Rita Dove are also part of the tradition being examined here.) Each playwright is indebted to the four authors briefly discussed here, while each simultaneously pushed the boundaries of dramatic possibilities further.

Works cited

Amos 'n' Andy radio show, originally produced as *Sam 'n' Henry* radio show (1926, Chicago WGN radio), changed to *Amos 'n' Andy* in 1928 (Chicago WMAQ radio).

Bean, Annemarie, ed. "Introduction." *A Sourcebook of African-American Performance: Plays, People, Movements*. London: Routledge, 1999. 1–5.

Bennett, Gwendolyn B. "The Ebony Flute." *Opportunity* 5 (1927): 212.

Bonner, Marita. *Frye Street and Environs: The Collected Works of Marita Bonner*, Joyce Flynn and Occomy Stricklin, eds. Boston: Beacon Press, 1987.

——*The Pot Maker: A Play to Be Read* 1927.

——*The Purple Flower* 1927.

——*Exit, an Illusion* 1928.

Carby, Hazel. "The Politics of Fiction, Anthropology, and the Folk: Zora Neale Hurston." *New Essays on Their Eyes Were Watching God*. Michael Awkward, ed. Cambridge: Cambridge University Press, 1990. 71–93.

Classon, H. Lin. "Re-evaluating *Color Struck*: Zora Neale Hurston and the Issue of Colorism." *Theatre Studies* 42 (1997): 5–18.

Dewey, John. *Art as Experience*. New York: Capricorn, 1934.

Douglas, Aaron, handwritten "open letter" on *Fire!* Stationery. No. 88–52, Box 1, Folder 9, Douglas Papers, Schomburg Center for Research in Black Culture, Sc MG 308. (c. 1926).

Du Bois, W. E. B. "Krigwa Players Little Theatre." *Crisis* 32.2 (1926): 134–36.

Eagleton, Terry. *Literary Theory: An Introduction*. Minnesota: University of Minnesota Press, 1983.

Fabre, Geneviéve and Michael Feith. "Introduction." *Temples of Tomorrow: Looking Back at the Harlem Renaissance*, Fabre and Feith, eds. Bloomington: Indiana University Press, 2001. 1–30.

Grimké, Angelina Weld. Grimké Papers, Box 37–13, Moorland Spingarn Research Center, Howard University. (n. d.)

——*Rachel* 1916

Hansberry, Lorraine. *To Be Young, Gifted and Black*. New York: Signet, 1969.

——*A Raisin in the Sun*. In: *Six American Plays for Today*. New York: Modern Library, 1961.

Hill, Lynda Marion. *Social Rituals and the Verbal Art of Zora Neale Hurston*. Washington, D.C.: Howard University Press, 1996.

Hughes, Langston. "The Negro Artist and the Racial Mountain." *The Nation* 122.318 (1926): 692–94.

Hughes, Langston. "Harlem." *Montage of a Dream Deferred*. New York: Henry Holt, 1951.

Hurston, Zora Neale. *A Life in Letters*. Carla Kaplan, ed. New York: Doubleday, 2002.

——"Mules and Men" (1935). In: *I Love Myself When I Am Laughing: A Zora Neale Hurston Reader*. Alice Walker, ed. New York: Feminist Press, 1979.

——"Characteristics of Negro Expression."(1934) *Negro: An Anthology*. Nancy Cunard, ed. London; reprinted (abridged), Hugh Ford, ed. New York: Continuum, 1996. 24–31.

——"You Don't Know Us Negroes." Lawrence E. Spevik file, Box 37, MSS Division, Library of Congress, 1934a. 1–6.

——"Campaign Here for Negro Art in Natural State." *Chicago Daily News* (16 November 1934c): 27.

——*Color Struck: A Play in Four Scenes*. In: *Fire!: A Quarterly Devoted to Young Negro Artists* 1.1 (1926): 7–14.

——"Florida Folklore." Recording at the Library of Congress by Alan Lomax, c. 1935, from the WPA Collection, http://memory. loc. gov.

——"Folklore." Special Collection, University of South Florida, Florida's Federal Writers Project, Negro Unit, n. d.

——"Harlem Slanguage." Reference number 50 describing "Jook," unpublished manuscript, Zora Neale Hurston Collection, JWJ, MSS 9, Box 1, folder 16, Beinecke Library, Yale University, n. d.

Johnson, Georgia Douglas. *The Plays of Georgia Douglas Johnson: From New Negro Renaissance to the Civil Rights Movement*. Judith Stephens, ed. Urbana: University of Illinois Press, 2006.

The Jazz Singer, based on a 1925 play by Samson Raphaelson, dir. Alan Crosland. Prod. Warner Brothers, 1927.

Krasner, David. *A Beautiful Pageant: African American Theatre, Drama, and Performance in the Harlem Renaissance, 1910–1927*. New York: Palgrave, 2002.

Kraut, Anthea. "Between Primitivism and Diaspora: The Dance Performances of Josephine Baker, Zora Neale Hurston, and Katherine Dunham." *Theatre Journal* 55.3 (2003): 433–50.

Locke, Alain. *The New Negro* 1925.

——"The Drama of Negro Life." *Theatre Arts Monthly* 10.10 (1926): 701–06.

——"Notes on Drama." Locke Papers, Box 164–139, folder 29–30, Moorland Spingarn Research Center, Howard University, n. d.

Lowe, John. "From Mule Bones to Funny Bones: The Plays of Zora Neale Hurston." *Southern Quarterly* 33. 2–3 (1995): 65–78.

Lukács, Georg. *Realism in Our Time: Literature and the Class Struggle*, John and Necke Mander, tr. New York: Harper, 1971.

Mafe, Diana Adesola. "Black Women on Broadway: The Duality of Lorraine Hansberry's *A Raisin in the Sun* and Ntozake Shange's *for colored girls*." *American Drama* 15. 2 (2006): 30–47.

Manganaro, Marc. *Culture, 1922: The Emergence of a Concept*. Princeton: Princeton University Press, 2002.

Morgan, Stacy I. *Rethinking Social Realism: African American Art and Literature, 1930–1953*. Athens: University of Georgia Press, 2004.

Murphy, Richard. *Theorizing the Avant-Garde: Modernism, Expressionism, and the Problem of Postmodernity*. Cambridge: Cambridge University Press, 1999.

Patterson, Tiffany Ruby. *Zora Neale Hurston and the History of Southern Life*. Philadelphia: Temple University Press, 2005.

Richards, Lloyd. "Woodie King, Jr. and Lloyd Richards Celebrate New Federal's 30th Anniversary." *TDF-Sightlines* 16; 2 (2002) 1–3.

Richards, Sandra L. "Writing the Absent Potential: Drama, Performance, and the Canon of African-American Literature." *Performance and Performativity*, Andrew Parker and Eve Kosofsky Sedgwick, eds. New York: Routledge, 1995. 64–88.

Rollins College. Remarks made by Edwin Osgood Grover and R. W. France (Professor of Economics), on the Playbill for the Dramatic Art Departments production of Hurston's "All-Negro Production of Afro-American Folklore," *All De Live Long Day*, subtitled "An unique and authentic representation of real negro folk life by talented native artists. " 5 January 1934. Department of Archives and Special Collections, Rollins College, Winter Park, Florida. (Thank you to Wenxian Zhang, librarian for retrieving and sending copies of this material.)

Shange, Ntozake. *for colored girls who have considered suicide/ when the rainbow is enuf*. Toronto: Bantam, 1977.

Singh, Nikhil Pal. *Black is a Country: Race and the Unfinished Struggle for Democracy*. Cambridge: Harvard University Press, 2004.

Smith, Anna Deavere. *Fires in the Mirror*. New York: Anchor Books, 1993.

Stephens, Judith. "Introduction." *The Plays of Georgia Douglas Johnson*.

Stewart, Jeffery C. "Alain Locke and Georgia Douglas Johnson: Washington Patrons of Afro-American Modernism." *George Washington University: Washington Studies* 12 (1986): 37–44.

Strindberg, August. *Strindberg: Plays Two*. Michael Meyers, tr. London: Methuen, 1991.

Synge, J. M. *Riders to the Sea* (1904).

3 Dialectical dialogues

Performing blackness in the drama of Alice Childress

Soyica Diggs

There is a sense of being in anger. A reality and presence. An awareness of worth.

Toni Morrison, *The Bluest Eye* (50)

In the rancorous encounter that ends the first scene of the second act of Alice Childress's *Wedding Band* (1966), the enraged and determined African American heroine, Julia Augustine, confronts her white lover's mother, Frieda, in the yard that Julia shares with her neighbors. Marked by prejudice and familiarity, betrayal and loyalty, commitment and neglect, the confrontation between Julia and Herman's mother dramatizes a battle for social legibility. The conjunction of the landscape of the play, set in the shared backyard of three houses in Charleston, South Carolina in 1918, and the players, Fanny, Julia's intrusive landlady, Lula and Nelson Green, Julia's neighbors, Annabelle, Herman's sister, and Frieda, creates the interstices within which Julia and Frieda appear before each others' eyes. After ten years of courting, *Wedding Band* depicts a female heroine anxious about growing old and tired of waiting for her lover to move north with her so that they can escape the legal limitations of the Jim Crow South and marry. By the middle of the first act, frustrated, Julia decides to attend a worship service in the yard that the houses share. At the end of the first act Herman stumbles into the yard and faints. Realizing that her lover suffers from influenza, which reached epidemic proportions in 1918, Julia must decide if she will call a doctor and risk exposing the fact that she has violated anti-miscegenation laws, or try to save Herman's life. Finding a middle ground, Fanny insists that Julia send for Herman's family. By attempting to prevent judgment by the state, Julia invites profoundly personal criticism into her domestic space.

Up until the end of the second act of the play, Julia casts a shadow that haunts Frieda's provincial home, marking Herman's, the provider's, absent presence. Similarly, Frieda's influence on her son limits the progression of his ten-year relationship with Julia. Annabelle arrives first and shows disdain for Julia and contempt for her relationship, since Annabelle thinks it has prevented her from being able to move out of her mother's house. Herman's inability to marry has prevented him from providing a wife to assume Annabelle's role as caretaker of their mother. Annabelle insists Julia give her and Herman some privacy. Displaced onto the porch, Julia responds to Nelson and Franny's scornful accusations that she has betrayed black people and their community by dating Herman. Before Frieda enters the yard the social stakes of Herman and Julia's relationship have been set. Therefore, when the women see each other each appears, or comes "forward into view," by way of a preestablished discursive landscape (Silverman 3). The confrontation interweaves anger and embittered speech into the process of racial construction. At one point Frieda calls Julia a "Black, sassy nigger" and Julia counters designating Frieda "White trash." As the women battle to be heard and seen, they enunciate latent linguistic histories that render themselves and each other invisible, inaudible.

Childress's unsentimental provocative heroines often participate in discursive struggles filtered through racial categories that mark the climax of her plays. "Master of the well-made play form," Childress utilized the knowledge of the theater that she gained as a member of American Negro Theater (ANT) in creating her eighteen plays and developing her signature theatrical form (Hill and Hatch 361). Childress's four decades of work in the theatre placed her at the forefront of many African American dramatic movements. While a member of ANT, she was nominated for a Tony Award in 1944 for her portrayal of Blanche in a revival of *Anna Lucasta*. She was the first black female playwright to have a play, *Gold Through the Trees* (1952), produced professionally and the first to win an Obie Award for *Trouble in Mind* (1955). In *Trouble in Mind* and a collection of short-stories, *Like One of the Family ... Conversations from a Domestic's Life* (1956), Childress explores the occupational roles black women play. Throughout the 1950s and 1960s, she continued to write, and by the end of the decade, in part due to her appointment as a playwright to the Radcliffe Institute, she finished *Wedding Band, String* (1969), and *Wine in the Wilderness* (1969). All three plays consider performances of blackness as intersectional activities that are constantly leveraged against modes of identification. For example in *String* and *Wine in the Wilderness*, Childress investigates intraracial policing of behavior, and the ways it functions to create an idealized category of blackness. *Wine in the Wilderness* also explores black artists' investment in a blackness that reflects the influence of African culture. Similar to a play Childress writes at the beginning of the next decade, *Mojo* (1970), *Wine in the Wilderness* demonstrates how class and social affiliations inform African Americans' desire to incorporate a partially imagined, historically unmediated, and, for the most part, ideal-ized African culture into their lives.[1]

Critics have asserted that Childress's dynamic heroines distinguish her writ-ing and address the need for more powerful lead female characters in African American drama.[2] Theorists, however, have not examined these heroines' performances in terms of the construction of blackness. The introduction to La Vinia Delois Jennings *Alice Childress* evaluates Childress's ability to *review shd contain a few essays* [handwritten annotation in top margin]

create autonomous black female characters and the effect Childress's choices have had on the canonization of her work. *Alice Childress* contains a chapter, "'Ain't You Mad?': Women, Anger, and Interracial Conflict," which builds on Jennings's character analysis through an exploration of the theme of anger in Childress's drama. She contends Childress's first phase of writing (1949–1968) contains "dramas of revolution, protest, or accusation, generally centering on violent verbal confrontations between blacks and whites" (18). Moreover in *Their Place on Stage: Black Women Playwrights in America*, Elizabeth Brown-Guillory asserts Childess's plays "are an outgrowth of the militant tradition in that [her] black characters are atypically assertive, brutally caustic, and unyielding to the demands of whites" (27). I extend Jennings' and Brown-Guillory's analysis by considering how performances of protest, accusation, or violent verbal confrontation create identities and identifications. Childress's heroines participate in creating performative categories (i.e. whiteness, blackness, and femaleness) that serve to name identities and call attention to the function of particular discursive, social, and political histories. [left margin handwritten: *thesis*]

Childress's drama shows black females in angry verbal confrontations, which rearrange what qualifies as normative behavior for black women and expose the social and civil laws that call for certain modes of action. For example, Childress's heroines often resist or question the conventions of motherhood, the implicit racial hierarchies within professional relationships, and the social protocols limiting the content of public conversations. In *Wedding Band*, after Julia reads a letter to her neighbor Mattie, the heroine reveals to Mattie and Lula, "without shame" that she has been "keepin' company" with Herman for ten years (90). Childress's direction, "without shame," indicates that in staging this scene Ruby Dee, the actress that created Julia, might assume the confession to be imbued with shame. The direction indicates a particular rendering of the lines. In Childress's plays the heroines engage other characters in conversations that demonstrate the ways whiteness bestows certain subjects with power and denies others. From their socially situated positions, these women talk back to the cultural mandates of shame and fear that support and maintain the materialization of race. The heroines' speech acts and embodied performances challenge racial hierarchies. In the aforementioned scene, Julia's lack of shame specifies her status as a black woman secretly dating a white man. The repudiation of shame defies the implicit affective quality attached to Julia's act of hiding her relationship, while it questions South Carolina's anti-miscegenation laws.

Childress's plays expose the permeability of power relations that create perceptions of blackness and whiteness as static categories. Her drama insists that blackness and whiteness signify, in part, linguistic categories that are materialized through performance. The process of materialization, especially when it rubs up against what has historically been recognized as blackness, creates friction and is often expressed in Childress's drama as anger. In her work, the anger that emerges through performances of race creates a dialectic which "never arrives at abstract truth but tries to uncover or recover the truth of the particular" (Diamond 209). The dialectical dialogues function as formal devices that demonstrate the productive power of anger. As the epigraph to this essay suggests, anger is a useful emotion that allows the creation of presence and "an awareness of worth." In "The Uses of Anger: Women Responding to Racism," Audre Lorde delineates how anger can function as a curative force that enacts "corrective surgery, not guilt" (124). She explains that women must mobilize the anger produced in response to racism by articulating the pain and hurt caused by "exclusion," "unquestioned privilege," "racial distortions," "stereotyping," "defensiveness," "misnaming," "betrayal," and "co-optation" (124). Building upon Lorde, this essay considers "anger" to be a "grief of distortions between peers, and its object is change" (129). Morrison and Lorde's trajectories, from anger to worth or from anger to change, distinguish the affective dynamic utilized in Childress's drama.

Childress's early plays depict situations that theorize performances of blackness in terms of affective dynamics that anticipate portrayals produced during the Black Arts Movement (1965–1975). Her black heroines, who participate in the formal strategy of confrontational dialogue, supplement performances of blackness usually associated with the Black Arts Movement. Mama Whitney of *Florence* (1949), Wiletta Mayer of *Trouble in Mind* (1955), Julia Augustine of *Wedding Band* (1966), and Tomorrow Marie Fields of *Wine in the Wilderness* (1969) contribute to conversations that demonstrate the construction of blackness as a part of a discursive network of signification. In Childress's work, blackness is historically and culturally specific, always in tension and development. Just as Childress's heroines demonstrate how confrontations can create productive conflict that comments on the construction of blackness, reading Childress's plays alongside her contemporaries provides a dialectical dialogue that extends the dramatic history of the Black Arts Movement.

Florence shifts the African American theatrical terrain at mid-century from the predominance of musicals and vaudeville to a conflict driven drama. Written for the Committee for the Negro in the Arts (CAN), an offshoot of ANT, *Florence* was first staged on 18 September 1950 alongside two other one-acts, Les Pine's *Grocery Store* and Childress's adaptation, *Just a Little Simple*, of Langston Hughes's *Simple Speaks His Mind*. *Florence* depicts a mother who embarks on a trip to New York to convince her daughter to concede to her failing acting career and return home. While waiting in a Jim Crow train station, Mama Whitney has a conversation with a white woman that convinces her that she should support her daughter's aspirations; evidently no one else, particularly white liberals, will.

Childress's first play stages a gender inflected performance of blackness that demonstrates how professional identifications participate in policing racial identities, in regulating what black and white mean in terms of an

mot - all questions respond to reading

individual's occupation. In this one act play, identifying as an actress trig-
gers the materialization of racial categories. Mama Whitney resists the
causal relationship, between being an actress and being white, her antagonist, Mrs. Carter, attempts to assert. At first the women share the reasons
for their trips. Once Mama and Mrs. Carter realize they both have investments in the theatre, Mama asks Mrs. Carter to help advance Florence's
acting career. In response, Mrs. Carter says she can certainly convince a
friend to hire Florence as a maid. Mrs. Carter explains, "I'll just tell her ...
no heavy washing or ironing ... just light cleaning and a little cooking ...
does she cook?" Stunned, Mama "slowly backs away from MRS. CARTER
and sits down on bench" (119). Mrs. Carter's refusal to engage Mama's
request reflects her inability to imagine Florence as anything other than a
maid, even after Mama tells her explicitly that her daughter is an actress.
The idea of Florence as an actress transgresses the parameters Mrs. Carter
has established for women like Florence. Mrs. Carter has never met
Florence; therefore, the immediate discursive action of repositioning
Mama's daughter suggests that Florence embodies a social threat that must
be contained. The ellipses in Mrs. Carter's first lines, which would signal a
break or hesitation, denote her coming to terms with what she perceives as
the danger to her position posed by the thought of a young black female as
a professional actress.

Furthermore, the choreography of bodies emphasizes the impact of
Mama's request on Mrs. Carter. Mama's action of retreat illuminates the
aggressive quality of Mrs. Carter's statement; Mrs. Carter's hostile response
seems unwarranted unless she aims to use her words to reclaim a position
that has been put at risk. Seeing Mama withdraw, Mrs. Carter reinforces
her authority by transgressing the civil law that situates her on one side of
the rail. Mrs. Carter asserts, "Don't worry, that won't matter to Melba" as
she "(moves around the rail to "Colored" side, leans over MAMA) I'd take
your daughter myself, but I've got Bennie. She's been with me for years, and
I just can't let her go ... can I" (119–20)? She hovers over Mama as she
offers condescending words of consolation. Mrs. Carter's aggressive action
qualifies as a performance of whiteness because it consists of her leveraging
her social privilege to deny and rewrite a social narrative. To quote Judith
Butler, "In this sense, a dominant 'race' is constructed (in the sense of *materialized*) through reiteration and exclusion" (275, emphasis in original).
Mrs. Carter repeats and revises Mama's narrative in order to exclude
Florence from participating in the discursive fields that designate certain
professional arenas. Within Mrs. Carter's framing, Florence would
have all her needs met if she had "her own room and bath, and above
all ... security" (120).

Childress's stage directions place Mama on one side of the rail and
Mrs. Carter on the other, which creates a spatial dynamic that mimics the
power relationships, generated in the scene. The exchange of power
between the women results, in part, from static designations, black and

white, that enable Jim Crow laws to demand each woman stay on her side of the railing. Physically pitted against each other, Mama's anger emerges by way of Mrs. Carter's arrogance. Even though Mrs. Carter assumes a physical position over Mama, this white woman does not anticipate that Mama will challenge the spatial and symbolic reordering of things. Mama "reaches out, clutches MRS. CARTER's wrist almost pulling her off balance" and her antagonist responds "(frightened) You're hurting my wrist" (120). The dialectical relationship between Childress's black female protagonist and her interlocutor offers insight into how performances marked by social, professional, personal, and familial investments produce encounters ripe with opportunities to negotiate power. Mrs. Carter's domineering hunched position allows Mama to pull her off balance, symbolically reestablishing her daughter's identification as an actress and, at the same time, asserting the variable nature of Mrs. Carter's posture. Mrs. Carter assumed that she could assert certain roles, and they would emerge instantaneously. But, Mama reminds her that she too must authorize the materialization of whiteness.

The rhetorical questions that accompany Mama's physical response to Mrs. Carter's assertion of whiteness further inscribe this heroine's agency and elucidate that all racial performances require multiple actors to consent. After Mama grabs Mrs. Carter's arm she questions, "I mustn't hurt you, must I" (120). Her questions serve to deconstruct the way social situations utilize discursive fields to call for certain performances of whiteness and blackness. Mama makes a conscious decision to not enact violence. Further, she instructs her interlocutor to "get over on the other side of the rail," "I don't want to break the law," inferring that Mrs. Carter must abide by some of the same laws which demand and police Mama's performances (120). Mrs. Carter attempts to interpellate Mama within a social matrix, of her own fashioning, but Mrs. Carter's actions do not anticipate how she must too answer to certain codes.[3]

Florence demonstrates how Childress's work participates in crafting performances of blackness, an aesthetic most often associated with the Black Arts Movement. Although not usually categorized as an artist of the Black Arts Movement, Childress's ability to create heroines who appear to be black and that gain a more acute self-definition by confronting the sources of their anger calls to mind black aestheticians' theories concerning the performance of blackness.[4] In *Performing Blackness: Enactments of African-American Modernism*, Kimberly Benston examines Clay's final speech in Baraka's *Dutchman* (1964), a classic text of the Black Arts Movement, and explains, "Baraka's interpellation of a longed-for end envisions play as either a prerevolutionary diversion or, more radically, a postemancipatory sacrament in which the coded meaning of historical black expression would become 'very straight and plain'" (12). The either/or dynamic that Benston describes underpins the movement toward revolution that *Dutchman* exemplifies. In this case, unlike Baraka's Clay, Childress's heroines occupy a space that engages but does not fully embrace the radical rhetoric of the black aestheticians. Her protagonists often reside somewhere between "a prerevolutionary diversion" and "a postemancipatory sacrament." Childress's drama draws attention to the implications of the black aesthetic for female centered plays, questioning black aestheticians' choice to advocate revolutionary performances and repudiate more nuanced modes of resistance. In that way, Childress's plays exist along a continuum described by Jennings as prefiguring, and, I would argue, contributing to "the revolutionary drama of Sonia Sanchez, Barbara Molette, Martie Charles, Ntozake Shange, Leroi Jones (Imamu Amiri Baraka), and Ed Bullins in the mid-1960s and 1970s" (18).

Childress's drama extends the aesthetic of the Black Arts Movement, consistently presenting her characters as situated by discourses that define the performance of blackness as the materialization of affective, social, historical, and cultural discursive networks. *Florence*, which predates what most scholars consider the beginning of the Black Arts Movement by sixteen years, complicates the binary of whiteness and blackness, presenting women who simultaneously must consider how their class and gender inform their occupations, mobility, and safety. In 1955, with the production of *Trouble in Mind*, Childress continued her analysis of the relationship between the theatre as professional space and racial performance; however, in this play she added the well established formal device of a play within a play to situate the performances of blackness within a specific historical continuum. *Trouble in Mind* depicts a group of white and black actors rehearsing an anti-lynching drama, "Chaos in Belleville," in a Broadway theatre. The inner play, "Chaos in Belleville," enacts a formal signification that reads a violent social history back onto the performances of blackness in the outer play. Each invocation of a performance inflected by blackness, including how the play opens with Wiletta, a veteran actress, instructing John, who is performing in his first professional production, to "cater to these fools," exists within a historical context established through the reference to lynching (297).

While informed by a violent racial history, Wiletta's instruction to John to "cater to these fools" also draws attention to a dialectic that secures Wiletta's job and the director's, Al Manners's, ego. The active nature of her command highlights the need to constantly reinforce the "fools" positions by undercutting her own. At the beginning of the first rehearsal, Manners throws a piece of paper on the floor and then asks Wiletta to pick it up. Shocked, she does not react immediately and Sheldon, another black cast member, begins to retrieve the paper. Manners chastises Sheldon and insists that Wiletta picks up the paper. "Shocked into a quick flare of temper" she responds with indignation, saying "Well, hell! I ain't the damn janitor!" Immediately, however, she tempers her display of anger by stuttering, "I ... well, I ... shucks ... I ... damn" (307). Wiletta's response to Manners's request demonstrates how double-consciousness informs her performance of blackness. W. E. B. Du Bois describes double consciousness as "the sense of always looking at one's self through the eyes of others, of measuring one's soul by the tape of a world that looks on in amused contempt and pity" (9). Du Bois introduces language to describe the vexed affect that emerges by way of the contradiction between how the black subject sees herself and how she perceives she is being seen. Her initial response (a quick flare of temper) ruptures her obedient performance, and renders a judgment of it as she registers anger with Manners and with herself. Both parts of the response, her "quick flare of temper" and the apologetic stammering, highlight the gap between identity and identification. Even though Wiletta does not identify as a janitor, her identification as actress corresponds to Manners's role as director and his need to subordinate her so that his self-conception remains intact.

The hesitation and uncertainty that follows Wiletta's quick flare of temper foreshadows the alienation she will feel when she refuses to play her part in "Chaos in Bellville." The feeling of alienation further explicates a quality of the performance of blackness and presents certain risks for the racialized subject. "Chaos in Belleville" scripts the character Wiletta plays to surrender her son, Job, to a lynch mob. The character's willingness to satisfy the yearnings of the mob correlates with Wiletta's early investment in being a "yes woman" in impetus but not in degree. While Wiletta does not recognize the irony, she resists the vilification of her character. Again, Manners attempts to discipline Wiletta, insisting, "I will not allow you to interrupt in this disorganized manner" (340). However, Wiletta pinpoints the instability of his assertion that he must authorize her "disruption." Wiletta responds, "You been askin' me what I think and where things come from and how come I thought it and all that ... (*company murmuring in the background*) ... I'm his mother and I'm sendin' him to his death. This is a lie" (340). Wiletta's defiance ushers in a moment of self-realization. Totally disregarding Manners's claim that he will not allow her interruption, Wiletta's aggressive reflection highlights how she consistently mediates Manners's authority. At the same time, her self-empowering disruption signals the beginning of her alienation as the company murmurs in the background.

The complicated interweaving of alienation and liberation categorize this performance of blackness. Wiletta's combative assertion, "You been askin' me what I think," reestablishes the psychic condition of double conscious-ness while it also intersects with what José Esteban Muñoz calls "feeling brown." In "Feeling Brown: Ethnicity and Affect in Ricardo Brancho's *The Sweetest Hangover (and Other STDs)*," Muñoz describes the feeling of being Latino/a in "a world painted white, organized by cultural mandates to 'feel white'" (68). Even though "Feeling Brown" focuses on the implications of the Latino/a subject position as an affective dynamic, the author's analysis provides a critical framework to analyze Wiletta's interaction with Manners. Wiletta's role in "Chaos in Belleville" causes her to examine her position in the theatre and question Manners's insistent command to keep John as Job on his knees. Her analysis of the direction creates a sense of "feeling brown" even as it liberates her.

Yet, Wiletta and Manners's dialogue brings to light the way the ideal of whiteness remains unavailable to everyone, including people who identify as white. Therefore, the director must reinstantiate his whiteness through performances. In the final exchange between Wiletta and Manners she repeatedly asks him "would you send your son out to ... " Each time Wiletta questions Manners's hypothetical choice she implicitly questions his authority. As a result, each of his responses must more explicitly instate his privileged position. Finally, as Manners's anger escalates, he declares, "(*So wound up, he answers without thinking.*) Don't compare yourself to me! What goes for my son doesn't necessarily go for yours! Don't compare him (*points to John*) ... with three strikes against him, don't compare him with my son, they've got nothing in common ... not a Goddamn thing!" (342). Manners issues his bold reply without realizing Wiletta has decided that she will no longer supplement his performance of whiteness. Her repeated question unnerves Manners by asking him to empathize with the social position of her character. The repetition of Wiletta's question also points to the insufficiency of Manners's answers. The lack structured into the dialogue signifies the performance of whiteness in this scene. Although Wiletta begrudgingly supported Manners's assertions of his white privilege in the first act of the play, by the second act her unwillingness to play her part exposes their interdependence. Manners refuses to assume the role Wiletta requests and, simultaneously, desires to maintain the division between her son and his. He attempts to solidify his whiteness when he disassociates himself from John's character, but he needs Wiletta to authorize his racial performance by identifying his response as sufficient. Therefore, each time Manners answers Wiletta his explanation serves as euphemism for his assertion "What goes for my son doesn't necessarily go for yours." His disclosure reads like a confession of white privilege that shifts the dynamic among Wiletta, John, and Sheldon from individual to collective preservation.

Wiletta's determination to only play certain roles in the theatre, even at the risk of sacrificing her Broadway debut, is reminiscent of Childress's position in relationship to the production of *Trouble in Mind* and *Wedding Band*. In 1957 talks that *Trouble in Mind* would be revived in a Broadway production never came to fruition.[5] Similarly, Rosemary Curb and Childress charge that the thwarted production history of *Wedding Band*, Childress's most popular play, reflects the playwright's refusal to compromise her aesthetic. Ruby Dee, Abbey Lincoln, and Moses Gunn starred in the first production of *Wedding Band* at the University of Michigan in December 1966. On November 26, 1972, New York Shakespeare Festival, The Public Theater presented the play, directed by Joseph Papp and Alice Childress. In 1973, ABC aired the Public Theater's production, "but because of its taboo interracial theme, eight affiliates refused to broadcast it. Others aired it only after midnight" (Jennings 10). Loften Mitchell wrote of *Wedding Band*, "Miss Childress writes with a sharp satiric touch ... Characterizations are piercing, her observations devastating" (104). Although generally more critical than Mitchell, in the *New York Times* Clive Barnes critiqued, "Indeed its strength lies very much in the poignancy of its star-cross'd lovers, but whereas Shakespeare's lovers always had a fighting chance, there is no way that Julia and Herman are going to be able to beat the system. Niggers and crackers are more irreconcilable than Montagues and Capulets" (30). With these relatively positive reviews Curb explains the six year gap in production history reflects Childress's determination to portray "an authentic portrait of American racism in a rarely dramatized historical period with credible characters" (67). For Childress it was important to maintain the integrity of *Wedding Band*, even if the theme and the structure of the play impeded its commercial viability. In an interview with Roberta Maguire, Childress recalls, "Joe told me, 'You know we'd be on Broadway, Alice, if it wasn't Julia's play—if it became more of Herman's play'" (55). Papp's comment reinforces the way the performances Childress imagined redefined political and artistic conventions concerning black women's roles.

Julia, the heroine in *Wedding Band*, confronts the ways performances of race gain social legibility through contemporary and extant discursive fields. Therefore, as she tries to reposition herself, she recognizes the tension between the histories that give her actions meaning and her ability to reshape her identification as a black woman. From its inception, Childress's work presents heroines; however, this work engages the possibility generated by the development of the women's rights movement to explore the particular implications of performing black femaleness.[6] As the play opens, Julia guards herself and displays physically how uncomfortable she is with her living arrangements; Childress describes her as embarrassed and weary in the first scene of the play. By the end of act one scene one, Julia begins to create bonds with the other women when she reads a letter to Mattie from her husband, October. Soon, Julia tells her neighbors, Mattie and Lula, that she has a white lover. Despite her neighbors' negative judgment of Herman, Julia still yearns to be part of their community. As Julia begins to forge bonds with the women, what remains of her relationship with Herman begins to crumble.

The strain produced by Julia's multiple affiliations subsides quickly when Herman's mother, Frieda, and sister, Annabelle, arrive. Before Frieda and Annabelle take Herman away, Julia confronts his mother's accusations, which cast her as the sickness that invades him. Later, Julia's mocking turns to fury when Herman's mother suggestively asserts, "And you, you oughta be locked up ... workhouse ... jail! Who you think you are!?" (119). While common parlance, Herman's mother's question demarcates an attempt to limit Julia's being. Frieda's question, "who you think you are?" suggests Julia, in fact, is not who she thinks she is. Julia's response challenges

Herman's mother's bigoted scopic position. Julia attempts to clarify Frieda's view by charging, "I'm your damn daughter-in-law, you old bitch" (119)! The rage Julia expresses towards Frieda, but which really stems from her frustration with Herman, allows her to recognize the limits of her romantic relationship. Even though Julia responds with fury, Herman's mother's refusal to recognize Julia as more than a criminal impedes Julia's ability to see herself as Herman's wife. Frieda's comment forces Julia to recognize how she has participated in producing her unhappiness. The heroine's assertion that she is Frieda's daughter-in-law does not automatically produce that relationship; instead, her pronouncement signifies a futile attempt to shift her social and legal status.

Julia and Frieda's argument reaffirms the hegemony of whiteness and maleness as it subordinates both of their positions as females. The confrontation between the two women follows Herman's somewhat incoherent recitation of a racist speech by John Calhoun that his mother taught him as a child. Julia and Frieda battle to be heard through a cacophonous din of white male privilege alluded to by Herman's speech and Julia's need to be "the mistress of Frieda's house." The argument escalates as Julia continues to try to codify her status with a list of her actions. She details, "The black thing who bought a hot water bottle to put on your sick, white self when rheumatism threw you flat on your back ... who bought flannel gowns to warm your pale, mean body. He never ran up and down King Street shoppin' for you ... I bought what he took home to you" (119). Julia's exchange with Frieda reflects the heroine's desire to dismantle what has kept her acting like a mistress for the past ten years. However, because Julia sees Frieda as her adversary and refuses to recognize the commonality of their positions, the argument concretizes Julia's lack of power. Frieda and Julia's comments establish Herman as the referent: "*He's* better off dead", "*He* never ran up and down King Street," "*he* took home to you." Each woman demands the other recognize her relationship with Herman and the authority it grants, but neither woman will assume a perspective that does not position Herman as the intermediary. Frieda and Julia see each other through Herman; he acts as a prism that skews their ability to form new identifications.

Julia's inability to assume the status of wife does not reflect only Herman and his mother's refusal. It also demonstrates how all of the actors in the play exist within a social matrix marked by "all-a Carolina" (119). Set in 1918, *Wedding Band* possesses the anticipating quality of Childress's other work. Just one year after the University of Michigan production, the Supreme Court (1967) found in the case of Loving vs. Virginia that prohibiting interracial marriage was unconstitutional. The setting of the play references American's historical and ongoing negotiation of interracial relationships. By bringing Frieda a hot water bottle, shopping for her and Herman, and moving from town to town, Julia attempts to perform as Herman's wife. As Rosemary Curb points out in "An Unfashionable

Tragedy of American Realism: Alice Childress's *Wedding Band*"; "Herman does not even know his own size in socks or where to buy them because Julia has been taking care of his clothes for years" (61). *Wedding Band* depicts civil law as a force that prohibits certain relationships, even when the individual's actions seem to necessitate certain associations. No matter how expertly Julia acts as Herman's wife and Frieda's daughter-in-law, her social legibility as a black woman will always supersede her ability to be identified as Herman's wife. Although Herman shares Julia's desire to see her as his mate, the predetermined civil order requires that her blackness interrupt her familial association with him. It is not just that Julia has "all-a Carolina 'gainst" her, but significantly, that she is "black with all-a Carolina 'gainst" her (119).

Julia's argument with Herman's mother does not serve its seeming purpose, to dismantle the logic that underpins Frieda's categorizations; however, it does demonstrate the utility in a performance of blackness that is irreverent to whiteness. Julia confronts Frieda and begins to realize how she participates in her own subordination. The argument draws Julia's attention to the agency she has sacrificed, and convinces her that she is unwilling to continue to play that part. Similar to the confrontation in *Florence*, Julia's verbal sparring with Frieda highlights the intersection of social and civil law and its contribution to the formation of blackness. The heroine of *Wedding Band*'s willingness to couple her ongoing violations of civil law with a breach of social law places her "on the road to clarity" (Lorde 132). Julia recognizes that her socially appropriate performances (i.e. hiding her relationship with Herman, fixing him dinner, and helping him care for his mother) facilitated the slippage caused by mimicry. Harry Elam explains Homi Bhabha's foundational definition of mimicry and extends its application to American performances of blackness.

Bhabha argues that the ambivalence inherent in the colonial project of *mimicry*—an attempt by the colonizer to remake the colonial subject as "almost the same, but not quite"—produces "an uncertainty which fixes the colonial subject as a 'partial' presence. By 'partial' I [Bhabha] mean 'incomplete' and 'virtual.'" Expanding Bhabha's critique of the partiality of colonial mimicry, the partiality that results from the ambivalence of performance is productive ... This "incomplete," or virtual, status is critical to the performer's ability to transcend and even subvert the socially patrolled boundaries of race and gender." (289)

Julia finds the authority to "subvert the socially patrolled boundaries of race and gender" precisely in the slippage between her identification as Herman's wife and how others identify her as his concubine. In yelling back at Frieda, Julia finds space to mourn losing an unattainable position that she fixated on for ten years and establishes the limits of performing as wife and daughter-in-law.

Florence, Trouble in Mind, and *Wedding Band* present the ways the heroines' interlocutors could benefit from the clarity found by these leading women, but the plays do not stage that communion. *Wine in the Wilderness* picks up where Childress's other plays end by staging a discursive battle between a black female protagonist and a group of individuals that results in the group coming to some greater sense of understanding. Building on the function of performances of blackness, *Wine in the Wilderness* presents an audience learning from a performance and, therefore, stages a meta-commentary on the function of the theatre. The play takes place in Harlem during a riot on a summer night in 1964. In the play the violence on the streets and the resulting police barricades displace Tommy, the heroine, from her home. Cynthia and Sonny-Man meet Tommy in a bar and bring her to their friend's, Bill's, apartment so that he can paint her. The environmentally mediated chance meeting creates an insider/outsider dynamic marked by Tommy's status as displaced and the other characters' belief that they reside solidly in a place. The dynamic between Tommy and the other characters highlights some of the ideology that informs other black women writing in the last decades of the twentieth century, Childress's female characters "speak form a multiple and complex, social, historical, and cultural positionality which, in effect, constitutes black female subjectivity" (Henderson 35).

Eventually, within the confines of Bill's apartment (a space that marks Tommy as Other), Tommy calls attention to Bill, Cynthia, and Sonny-Man's illogical conflation of physical and social place. The entire play takes place in Bill's one room apartment, which is filled with African and African American inspired art as well as artifacts from Mexico, Japan, and the West Indies. Bill, who imagines himself as acutely attuned to the needs of *the* black community, expresses to Cynthia and Sonny-Man the type of woman he needs to model for the third panel of his triptych on black womanhood entitled "Wine in the Wilderness." Before the start of the play Bill has already finished painting the panels called "Black Girlhood" and "Mother Africa." He now needs a model for the "Lost Woman" panel. Sitting in his apartment with a neighbor, Oldtimer, he describes the ideal figure for this panel; she is "ignorant, unfeminine, coarse, rude ... vulgar ... a poor, dumb chick that's had her behind kicked until it's numb ... and the sad part is ... there's no hope for her" (126). Oldtimer jokes that Bill has described his first wife. Bill increases the stakes of his representation and his distance from it and Oldtimer by authorizing his neighbor to "stomp her to death ... after I [Bill] paint her" (126). The violent imagery positions Tommy as an embodied threat that Bill first must displace and then destroy. Tommy comes to the apartment and thinks she is being presented as a romantic interest for Bill. Once he tells her he wants to paint and not date her, she assumes she will pose for the "Mother Africa" panel. Eventually, Cynthia, Sonny-Man, and Oldtimer leave Bill's apartment. As Bill prepares to paint Tommy they begin to discuss the figures that he has placed on his walls and her personal history. Eventually, she removes her wig, and changes into an African wrap; in this new attire Tommy appears different to Bill, attractive, less threatening. Instead of painting and posing, Bill and Tommy spend a romantic night together. The intimacy the couple develops acts as a preface to Bill's transformation.

Tommy's physical reappearance does not supplant her displacement or the social status that Bill, Cynthia, and Sonny-Man fold into it. The next morning, Oldtimer returns to Bill's apartment to retrieve some goods he looted during the riot and stashed there. At first, he does not recognize Tommy, but, once he does, he asks about the painting and reveals that her portrait will represent "the worst gal in town. A messed-up chick" that must fill the blank canvas he unveils (145). Oldtimer accepts Bill's arrogant assertion that his artistic interpretation of "the Lost Woman" does not create a slippage; it fills a gap in the black community created by this imagined figure's lived experience. By positioning his interpretation of Tommy between "Mother Africa" and "Black Girlhood," Bill fashions a prototype of community predicated on the other images' ability to fill Tommy's lack with their innate surplus. Oldtimer's confession sets in motion the confrontation among Tommy, Bill, Sonny-Man, and Cynthia that leads to the trio's self-analysis. Tommy's confrontation with Bill and his friends creates a new lens for them to see themselves and to view her.

Bill, Cynthia, and Sonny-Man each fashion a sense of self in relationship to an idealized blackness that invokes Africa, supports a black male to female hierarchy, and demonizes African Americans living in the south, experiencing poverty, and lacking formal education. Cynthia and Sonny-Man see Tommy as a victim and therefore think she is perfect for Bill's picture; she is poor, not formally educated, boisterous and opinionated, and she wears mismatched clothes and a wig that covers her natural hair. Alternatively, Tommy contends that they attempt to victimize her by assuming that they have a vision of blackness and black community that she cannot imagine or access. Offended by Bill, Cynthia, and Sonny-Man's perceptions, when Cynthia and Sonny-Man enter the apartment Tommy insists that they stay. Mockingly calling them "Brother" and "Sister" she tells Oldtimer to explain the triptych (145). The trio freely uses the terms "*the* black people" and "*the* Afro-American" suggesting a singularity of identity. Yet, the friends seize every opportunity to distinguish themselves from Tommy and Oldtimer. Tommy identifies how the trio uses language to perform solidarity, yet they also attempt to police the boundaries of what qualifies as acceptable performances of blackness through the idea of the "messed-up chick." At one point Tommy tells Bill, "Ain't no we-ness in your talk" (147). As the heroine notices Cynthia's embarrassment, she sarcastically reassures her, "You and Sonny-man gave me comfort, you cheered me up and took me in ... took me in" (145)! The repetition of "took me in" helps communicate Tommy's belief that Cynthia, Sonny-Man, and Bill participate in policing of blackness without considering how their behavior establishes a normative hierarchy of behavior. Furthermore, Tommy's biblical reference saying, "I was lost but now I'm found! Yeah, the blind can see," questions the trio's assumed access to a liberated or salvific position (145). The trio thinks its membership in the middle-class grants the authority to judge, police, and direct Tommy's behavior. The intraracial hierarchy reinforces the pre-existing difference between blackness and whiteness while it reproduces the logic that certain types of performances are normal and therefore superior.

Similar to *Trouble in Mind*, *Wine in the Wilderness* situates performances of blackness within a historical trajectory. *Trouble in Mind* uses the imagery of lynching; alternatively, *Wine in the Wilderness* utilizes the setting of a Harlem riot and the discourse that emerges about a derogatory racialized term. As a method to mark Tommy's ability to signify community through language, and to demonstrate how it can serve to fracture affiliations, she repeats the word "nigger" throughout the confrontation. Bill, in an attempt to quiet Tommy, concedes "Okay, you called it, baby, I did act like a low degraded person" (146). At first, Bill recognizes the word as an insult removed from historical specificity. Bill's admission, "I did act like a low degraded person," does not acknowledge the racial history of the word or the ways Tommy signifies on that history by invoking it in the context of their argument. Bill does not make an epistemological shift until he consults a dictionary, a reliable authoritative source, only to find "(reads from the book) Nigger, N-i-g-g-e-r, ... A Negro ... A member of any dark-skinned people" (147). By calling Bill a "nigger," Tommy stresses his participation in a system of classification that shifts the power dynamics between him and her, but simultaneously reasserts the power that underpins the hurtful nature of this word. Bill's attempt to imagine the world in a de-racialized historical context points to his desire to sustain his localized privilege.

Tommy continues to take Bill to school by situating his actions within an even broader historical context. She questions his fidelity to the black community and accuses, "Ain't a-one-a us you like that's alive and walkin' by you on the street ... you don't like flesh and blood niggers" (146). She clarifies, "If a black somebody is in a history book, or printed on pitcher ... and can't talk back, then you dig'em and full-a so much-a damn admiration and talk 'bout "our" history. But when you run into us livin' and breathin' ones ... then you comin' on 'bout we ain' never together. You hate us, that's what! You hate black me" (146)! Tommy contends Bill categorizes her and the members of the working class generations before him as "niggers" through his celebration of certain types of blackness and his repudiation of others. She represents a cultural memory that threatens him and fills him with hate. Tommy's language signals the historical interconnectedness of "the Ma and Pa that worked in the post office" and the Nubian Queen Bill imagines as the subject of his painting. Even though he projects that hate onto her, the process of projection serves as a temporary remedy to the incongruity between "a black somebody in a history book" and "us livin' and breathin' ones." Tommy's discourse enables Bill to see his disdain for "flesh and blood" working-class African Americans acts to temporarily allay his own sense of insufficiency.

Love acts as the catalyst that facilitates the trio's epistemological reordering of things. At the end of Tommy's tirade she admits to Bill, "I love you," then quickly retreats with the comedic assertion, "(y)ou must be runnin' a fever, nigger, I ain' said nothin' 'bout lovin' you" (148). In order for Bill to receive Tommy's love he must consider himself worthy of love. The acceptance she shows him enables him to reimagine his triptych. In this new version the "the real beautiful people," Oldtimer, Sonny-Man, and Cynthia, will flank the central painting, which will be of Tommy. Bill's description ushers in Cynthia and Sonny-Man's revelation that they are, in fact, beautiful people when seen in relationship to and not above Tommy. The play ends with Bill participating in the imaginative process of reforming the triptych, suggesting the instability of the category of blackness and the potential that can be imagined within a new frame.

The performances of blackness depicted in Alice Childress's drama point to the way race comes to stand in for a myriad of power relations, including professional, familial, and communal. In presenting her subversive representations of blackness, Childress challenged the American commercial theatre to accept more diverse depictions of black women. Yet, as Ruby Dee notes in a discussion about Childress, "We may salute and savor the glory of the black theatrical pioneer, but in a land where materialism is all-important, the real salutes take longer" (Mitchell 222). In terms of a commercial theatre, Childress's dialectical dialogues act as a call that the Lady in Brown responds to in the opening monologue of Ntozake Shange's *for colored girls who have considered suicide/ when the rainbow is enuf* (1975), which had its Broadway premiere in 1976 and successfully staged 747 performances. The Lady in Brown urges, "somebody/ anybody sing a black girl's song." Shange's character highlights the dearth of complicated female characters on the America stage, marking the groundbreaking nature of Childress's dynamic heroines. Childress's drama creates space on stage for the flawed, innovative, and dynamic characters in Shange, Adrienne Kennedy, Anna Deavere Smith, and Suzan-Lori Parks's work. The dialectical dialogues in Childress's plays create a tension that disrupts American theatre and makes room for other black female writers interested in knowing, hearing, and staging the sound of their own voices. Childress's heroines act as leaders during historical periods when they were often asked to play supporting roles.

Notes

1 Similar to the plays central to this essay, *Mojo: A Black Love Story* presents a dialogue that participates in and comments on an ongoing cultural issue. The play considers how the rhetoric of black nationalisms serves a healing function for a divorced couple who reunites when the heroine, Irene, visits her former husband, Teddy after discovering she has cancer. Irene finds comfort in the idea that blackness has a legacy in Africa. The formation of blackness that they explore and critique allows the wounded characters to access some dignity and pride.

44   Soyica Diggs

2 In " 'I Wish I was a Poet': The Character as Artist in Alice Childress's Like One of the Family," Trudier Harris discusses Mildred Johnson's assertive narrative position in Childress's collection *Like one of the Family: Conversations from a Domestic's Life* (1956). Although not one of Childress's plays, Harris notes the dramatic nature of *Like one of the Family*, commenting on its use of the structure of monologue. Also see John O. Killens's "The Literary Genius of Alice Childress" and Margaret B. Wilkerson's "Introduction" to *9 Plays by Black Women*.

3 My reading of the interaction between Mama and Mrs. Carter is informed by Louis Althusser's description, in "Ideology and Ideological State Apparatuses (Notes towards an Investigation)," of how ideology hails individuals (174).

4 Houston Baker's *Blues, Ideology, and Afro-American Literature* makes an important critique of the Black Arts Movement. *Blues, Ideology, and Afro-American Literature* examines, in part, the implications of Stephen Henderson's *Understanding the New Black Poetry*. Baker's investigation of Henderson's book provides fertile ground for ongoing scholarship about the period.

5 Even though Childress won an Obie for the 1955 Greenwich Mews Theatre production of the *Trouble in Mind*, after two years of negotiation the play never made it to Broadway because Childress refused to approve the requested script changes. The play "was abandoned as a poor commercial risk" (Jennings 7). Also see Zolotow, Sam, " 'Trouble in Mind' Will be Revived," *New York Times* 8 Feb, 1957: 17.

6 Margaret B. Wilkerson elaborates, "As the Civil Rights and Women's Movements changed the face of the country, these writers [Hansberry, Childress, Kennedy and Shange] opened the theatre to new dramatic realities" (xxiii). Considering the increase in black women's writing in the late twentieth century, Cheryl Wall elucidates, "[a] confluence of social and historical events enabled the creation of 'the community of black women writing' that Hortense Spillers designated a 'vivid new fact of national life.' Chief among these were the civil rights movement and the women's movement" (7). Wilkerson and Wall present the communal nature that supported black women writing in the 1960s and 1970s. Nevertheless, throughout her career, Childress confronted several impasses regarding the production of her work.

7 The Harlem riot of 1964 was one urban uprising among many that occurred throughout the decade, including the Watts Riot of 1965, the Newark Riot of 1967 and the Detroit Riot of 1967. The Harlem riot of 1964 erupted in response to a white police officer shooting James Powell, a 15-year-old African American young man.

Works cited

Althusser, Louis. *Lenin and Philosophy, and Other Essays*. Ben Brewster, tr. New York: Monthly Review Press, 1971.

Baker, Houston. *Blues, Ideology, and Afro-American Literature: A Vernacular Theory*. Chicago: University of Chicago Press, 1984.

Baraka, Imamu Amiri. *Dutchman and the Slave, two plays*. New York: Morrow, 1964.

Barnes, Clive. "Stage: *Wedding Band*." *New York Times* 27 October, 1972: 30.

Benston, Kimberly W. *Performing Blackness: Enactments of African-American Modernism*. London: Routledge, 2000.

Brown-Guillory, Elizabeth. "Black Women Playwrights: Exorcising Myths." *Phylon* 48 (1987): 229–39.

Brown-Guillory, Elizabeth. *Their Place on Stage: Black Women Playwrights in America*. New York: Greenwood Press, 1988.

Butler, Judith. *Bodies that Matter: On the Discursive Limits of "Sex."* New York: Routledge, 1993.

Childress, Alice. *Just a Little Simple* 1950.

——*Gold Through the Trees* 1952.

——*Like One of the Family … Conversations from a Domestic's Life*. Brooklyn, NY: Independence Publishers, 1956.

——*Florence. Wines in the Wilderness: Plays by African American Women from the Harlem Renaissance to the Present*. Elizabeth Brown-Guillory, ed. New York: Greenwood Press, 1990. 110–21.

——*Mojo: A Black Love Story. Black World* (April 1971): 54–82.

——*Mojo and Sting*. New York: Dramatists Play Service Incorporated, 1971.

——*Trouble in Mind. Black Drama in America: An Anthology*. Darwin T. Turner, ed. Washington D.C.: Howard University Press, 1971. 291–346.

——*Wedding Band. 9 Plays by Black Women*. Margaret B. Wilkerson, ed. New York: New American Library, 1986. 75–133.

——*Wine in the Wilderness. Wines in the Wilderness: Plays by African American Women from the Harlem Renaissance to the Present*. Elizabeth Brown-Guillory, ed. New York: Greenwood Press, 1990. 122–155.

Curb, Rosemary. "An Unfashionable Tragedy of American Realism: Alice Childress's *Wedding Band*." *MELUS* 7.4 (1980): 57–68.

Diamond, Elin. *Unmaking Mimesis: Essays on Feminism and Theater*. London: Routledge, 1997.

Du Bois, W. E. B. *The Souls of Black Folk*. New York: Barnes and Noble Classics, 2003.

Elam Jr., Harry J. "The Black Performer and the Performance of Blackness: *The Escape; or, A Leap to Freedom* by William Wells Brown and *No Place To Be Somebody* by Charles Gordone." *African American Performance and Theater History: A Critical Reader*. Harry J. Elam, Jr. and David Krasner, eds. Oxford: Oxford University Press, 2001. 288–305.

Harris, Trudier. "'I Wish I was a Poet': The Character as Artist in Alice Childress's *Like One of the Family*." *Black American Literature Forum* 14.1 (1980): 24–30.

Henderson, Stephen. *Understanding the New Black Poetry: Black Speech and Black Music as Poetic References*. New York: William Marrow, 1973.

Hill, Errol G. and James V. Hatch. *A History of African American Theatre*. New York: Cambridge University Press, 2003.

Hughes, Langston. *Simple Speaks His Mind*. New York: Simon and Schuster, 1950.

Jennings, La Vinia Delois. *Alice Childress*. New York: Twayne Publishers, 1995.

Killens, John O. "The Literary Genius of Alice Childress." *Black Women Writers, 1950–1980: A Critical Evaluation*. Mari Evans, ed. New York: Doubleday, 1984. 129–33.

Lorde, Audre. "The Uses of Anger: Women Responding to Racism." *Sister Outsider: Essays and Speeches by Audre Lorde*. Freedom, CA: Crossing, 1984. 124–133.

Maguire, Roberta. "Alice Childress." *The Playwright's Art: Conversations with Contemporary American Dramatists*. Jackson R. Bryer, ed. New Brunswick, NJ: Rutgers University Press, 1995. 48–69.

Mitchell, Loften. "The Words of Ruby Dee." *Voices of the Black Theatre*. Clifton, New Jersey: James T. White & Company, 1975. 211–22.

Morrison, Toni. *The Bluest Eye*, originally published 1970. New York: Plume, 1994.

Mūnoz, José Esteban. "Feeling Brown: Ethnicity and Affect in Ricardo Brancho's *The Sweetest Hangover (and Other STDs)*." *Theatre Journal* 52 (2000): 67–79.

Pine, Les *Grocery Store* 1950.

Shange, Ntozake *for colored girls who have considered suicide/ when the rainbow is enuf,* originally published 1975. New York: Simon and Schuster, 1997.

Silverman, Kaja. *World Spectators*. Stanford, CA: Stanford University Press, 2000.

Yordan, Philip. *Anna Lucasta*. New York: Random House, 1945.

Wilkerson, Margaret B. Introduction. *Nine Plays by Black Women*. Margaret B. Wilkerson, ed. New York: New American Library, 1986. xiii–xxv.

4 "Shaking loose"
Sonia Sanchez's militant drama

Jacqueline Wood

rel to blk male voices in theater
gon't during black power

Sonia Sanchez's dramatic works occupy a select space in the development of African American theatre. Particularly during the militant period, she demonstrated a distinctive courage in producing work that threatened the dynamics of black male militant discourse, while she still remained a recognized literary force within that domain. Over time, in her plays she developed purposefully shocking language, often fraught with ritual and aimed toward shattering the complacency of Eurocentric and black audiences. Her ability to raise difficult questions from within the black community, to challenge boundaries in terms of dramatic structure and language, and to offer new terrain in the effort to understand and ameliorate the struggles of black women has resulted in a rich foundation for the several contemporary, successful, young black female playwrights garnering acclaim today. Sanchez thus must be acknowledged as an important figure in the development in general of African American literary tradition and as a key force in the development of African American women's dramatic literature.

Sanchez has impacted black militant drama in numerous ways, including her contributions to the radicalization of its language, her privileging of women's questions in the movement, and, perhaps most significantly, her audacious challenges to form. Her early innovations were contemporary with the unique early work of Adrienne Kennedy and much in anticipation of the innovative contributions of black female playwrights like Ntozake Shange and, most recently, Suzan-Lori Parks, winner of the 2001 Pulitzer prize. In her approaches to dramatic structure, for example, Sanchez's use in *Sister Son/ji* (1969) of cumulative memory visions and on-stage shifts in scene is in keeping with Kennedy's unusual "dream landscapes" in *Funnyhouse of a Negro* (1964) or *The Owl Answers* (1965). Sanchez's memory visions also anticipate Ntozake Shange's "dream-memories" in such plays as *boogie woogie landscapes* (1979). Additional experimental efforts by Sanchez anticipate Shange's and Suzan-Lori Parks's radicalized reconfigurations of black drama. For example, Sanchez's development of groups paired with choral dancers, rather than scenes or acts, in her play *Uh Huh, But How Do It Free Us?* (1974), provides an alternative dramatic structure where the layering of meaning occurs via implication, repetition, synecdoche and metonymy. Her efforts here foreshadow Parks's "drama of accumulation" (*"from* Elements of Style" 1995) evident in, for example, *Mutabilities of the Third Kingdom* (1986), *The Death of the Last Black Man in the Whole Entire World* (1989), or *Topdog,Underdog* (2000). Also in *Uh Huh,* Sanchez's use of choral dancers to provide communal and moral commentary upon the action within each grouping anticipates Shange, in this case Shange's use of the specialized dramatic "choreopoem" (Shange 16), as in *for colored girls who have considered suicide/ when the rainbow is enuf* (1976). Furthermore, in *I'm Black When I'm Singing, I'm Blue When I Ain't,* choruses also illustrate Sanchez's consistent interest in nontraditional choral figures as devices of community voice, anticipating performative communal interaction evident in experimental plays like Robbie McCauley's *Sally's Rape* (1992).

Sanchez's plays, however, have not been critically acknowledged or examined as they deserve. There are numerous possible reasons for this paucity of attention toward her dramatic works. Most of her plays were written and produced during the Black Arts Movement, from the early 1960s to roughly the end of the 1970s (Williams 80–81). This period of African American literary productivity is in itself one of the most understudied periods of black literary history. Sanchez also has written fewer plays than poetic works—currently she has published over 16 books of poetry. Her plays number only half a dozen. Yet these works reflect the historicity of Sanchez's community work, relating directly to her development as a postcolonial consciousness and predicting a consistency in Sanchez's development into a world-renowned writer and human rights figure. Her dramatic works represent a key period in her development as a writer and activist. They reveal her authorial endeavor during the Black Power Movement, and her direct involvement in the development of the Black Arts Theatre and the black arts aesthetic. More specifically, her plays offer insight into the militant as well as feminist stances that Sanchez evinces with increasing conviction and skill in her writing over the second half of the twentieth century and into the twenty-first. Sanchez has written five plays that have actually seen publication and/or production—*The Bronx Is Next* (1968); *Sister Son/ji* (1969), *Dirty Hearts* (1971); *Malcolm Man Don't Live Here No Mo* (1972); and *Uh Huh, But How Do It Free Us* (1974).

To understand the place of Sanchez's drama within her oeuvre, it is necessary to examine the development of her poetic voice, one that has been immensely successful since she has received numerous awards for her poetry, including the Robert Frost Medal, the Patricia Lucretia Mott Award, and the American Book Award. From the earliest periods of her creativity, Sanchez saw the purpose of writing as both functional and political, reflecting the perspective of black revolutionary art that was informed by adoption and adaptation of African art precepts in the works of the period. A committed, engaged audience is critical to the African concept of artistic expression.

This view of engaged art inspired and informed many black revolutionary playwrights and dramatic theorists, including Sanchez. Envisioning writing as a vehicle for attaining her political goals, Sanchez states her political purpose: "until Black people's social reality is free of oppression and exploitation, I will not be free to write as one who's not oppressed or exploited" (417). For Sanchez, black writing must work in two ways; it must establish ethos and function. In her essay on artistic responsibility, "The Poet as a Creator of Social Values," Sanchez identifies for revolutionary writing six necessary characteristics: it must be "functional," "inspirational," "educational," "instructional," "ideological," and "political" (14). Any liberatory author who subscribes to these principles becomes both a poet and a priest; s/he stands as an example of "men/women who had the power to interpret life for their society" (14). Devoting him/herself to "developing symbols of collective experience in teaching tools that inculcat[e] the social values and wisdom of the culture" (3), the poet demonstrates the "wisdom" of such poetics through privileging two perspectives, political and personal integrity in African American life. Sanchez, like her militant counterparts, here envisions an African American context for African aesthetic traditions and identifies the central focus of her work as an artist committed to expressing the "collective experience" of the black community.

Sanchez's plays, like her poetry, both embraced and transformed the political and social issues of the Black Power movement and the Black Arts movement ("To Wash My Ego," Wood 3). Her work engaged the conventional protest rhetoric and the militant ideologies of the period and attempted artistic manifestation of black activists' politico/cultural consciousness-raising in the black community. Her dramatic rhetoric included black modes of discourse—wordplay, signification, irony, tonal meaning, repetition, and cumulative narration—and three key rhetorical approaches of militant activism, agitational language, socio-political unity as a goal, and emphasis on ritualized performance and dialogue. As various pieces in the 1968 *The Drama Review* (*TDR*), a special issue that articulated the crucial role of drama in the Black Arts movement, declare, drama was considered a crucial venue in informing, politicizing, and actuating black audiences and had far reaching effects on the aesthetic development of the Black Arts movement in general.

Working with key contributors to the *TDR* such as Larry Neal, Ed Bullins, and LeRoi Jones/Amiri Baraka (Hill and Hatch 393), Sanchez was the only black female revolutionary playwright published in the *TDR* 1968 Summer Issue. Her presence is significant because, while not the only black woman of the period writing oppositional poetry and plays, Sanchez comfortably crossed genres and centered both her poetic and her dramatic artistry of this period in decidedly militant black rhetoric and ideology. However, while she was clearly an active and recognized Black Arts dramatist, Sanchez's political sensibility as a black woman demanded that her works both embrace and challenge black militant discourse. Black male militants shared with Sanchez the political rhetoric of the times and the awareness of the potency of drama as a political venue, but Sanchez felt it necessary to challenge them in terms of the questions of women's roles and the larger centrality of communal health in the movement. In this strategy she singled herself out as a unique voice, both a member of the black revolutionary dramatic cadre and one of its most vocal womanist/humanist critics. In both her poetry and her drama, Sanchez, as she describes it, "shakes loose" (quoted in *Power Plays*, Wood n.p.) from the familiar environs of what was clearly a male-dominated black arts aesthetics by broadening the communal perspective beyond the parameters envisioned by her male counterparts. She looks also to, as Samuel Hay observes, "assess the impact that historical events, personal decisions, and rite of passage had on a woman's life" (101) and how these in turn impacted the life of the community. Her stauncher privileging of community becomes the crucible for the development of her most sustained thematic: the struggle of African American women to gain equality as both blacks and as women, a view that broadens the domain of black militant views of oppression. Sanchez accomplishes the radicalization of dramatic form (fractured characterizations, transgressions of traditional structure, and innovative use of language) by challenging the text through expressions of the personal and displacing militant views of black politics and community. Sanchez thus adds dimension to black perceptions of American oppression, complicating polarities through the necessities of African American female and familial communal experience. This less polarized view of black community predicts her eventual incorporation of post-colonial stances in her poetry and her drama.

From her very first play forward, Sanchez explores questions of militancy in conjunction with an ever-increasing examination of the value and rights of black women in the black community. *The Bronx is Next*, Sanchez's first play, is quintessentially a black militant play, focusing on the impact of American racism and the radical response of the black community to that oppression. The central focus of this play is an examination of the frustrated anger brewing in isolated and impoverished black communities and the militant vision that recognizes these communities as prime places for fostering revolutionary change. The play is bold in tenor. As one-dimensional characters, the militants perform radical actions in the play (enhanced by ritual images of fire as a source of cleansing) that are more significant than character development. The characters' grass roots response to the debilitating effects of exploitative slum-lords and unlivable conditions in the Harlem ghettoes culminates in the young militant characters' plans to burn all of the tenements down. After convincing or forcing their neighbors to move into the streets or be burned, three black revolutionaries, Roland, Charles, and Jimmy (the only characters with specific proper names), begin to set fire to the slum apartments in their neighborhood. Theirs is a violent and triumphant street-informed "strategy" (819), a response to the vicious conditions of racial poverty in the black New York boroughs.

Sanchez employs elements of black revolutionary dramatic rhetoric most directly in this play, presenting black vernacular as agitational language and using ritualized symbolic action with socio-political education and unification of the audience as the ultimate goal. Yet, even at this earliest moment in her playwriting career, Sanchez also demonstrates an effort to address latent complications within the militant agenda—primarily sexism. This courageous effort culminates in what Mike Sell deftly describes as "the most acutely self-critical, resolutely revolutionary plays of the Black Arts era" (71–2). In this first play, Sanchez initiates a burgeoning self-reflexive interrogation of the black militant community through the characters Old Sister and Black Bitch, whose experiences illustrate a central criticism concerning generational and sexist bigotry evident in male militant discourse and activism.

These two characters, the only females figures in the play, experience head-on the fierce disrespect of male militants. Early in the play, Old Sister refuses to cooperate with the young men's demands that she leave her home. When Charles points out to her that she cannot take anything but "jest the important things," Old Sister replies, "Yes son, I knows what you say is true. But you see them things is me. I jest can't leave them" (812). Charles recognizes in this moment that the woman's resistance could hold up the progress of his plan. Without a second of remorse, knowing full well that he will shortly be engulfing that tenement in flames, he sends the woman back to her apartment with the comforting remarks, "You don't have to come tonight. You can come some other night when we have room for your stuff." The old woman ironically responds, "Thank the lord there is young men like you who still care about old people" (812). Charles's thoughtless dismissal and actual eventual murder of Old Sister demonstrate a cruel callousness of the young male militants toward the aged in the community. While this act certainly evidences the focused thinking of the militants that will not allow individuals to undermine the larger purposes of the movement, it also points to Sanchez's awareness of ambiguity concerning the negative impact of militant events on the community.

The fact that Old Sister may be so easily discarded for being female as well is corroborated by the ensuing similar abusive behavior of the young militants toward the only other female character in the play, referred to simply as Black Bitch. A young mother of two boys who is struggling to survive in poverty, Black Bitch is known to have had an ongoing paid affair with White Cop. Larry complains that he could not get her to cooperate until he slapped her. Charles in a confrontation, after first flirting with her, knocks her to the ground repeatedly and gives her a black eye. These images of devaluation and disrespect for this second woman character elucidate Sanchez's sensitivity concerning the complexities of grass roots militant activism—its purpose, its ideology, and its violent and harsh realities. She is clearly intent upon exposing the way in which these strategies, while aimed toward the larger empowerment and liberation of the black community, at the same time clearly could and would complicate, harm, splinter, even undermine communal health and welfare.

Sister Son/ji, Sanchez's second published play, offers a more distilled study of women in the militant community and was her most substantially produced and reviewed play.[1] Son/ji is an aged female character whose memories are representative experiences of black female militants. An early activist, she exhibits an idealism for the movement that is not daunted by the sexist attitudes of her fellow activists. She exclaims "this morning I heard a sister talking abt blk/women supporting their blk/men ... having warriors and young sisters" (159). However, this supporting role soon becomes less attractive. She begins to discern a breakdown in the relationships between black male and female militants within the community fostered by the men's self-centered pursuit of multiple outside love relationships. Son/ji laments her own love interest's lack of attention, warning him that "blk people ... [will] fall into the same traps their mothers and fathers fell into ... one called it retaining their manhood while the other called it just plain/don't/care/about/family/hood" (159). As Son/ji works through her dream memories and eventually comes back to her present day old age, we glimpse the struggles she endures as a woman growing strong in the movement. She succumbs to a mental breakdown but finally comes into her own. As a battered but not beaten old woman warrior, she claims her strength and that of the community: "these mississippi hills will not give up our dead/and neither will i" (162). She ultimately provides a model of activism for her people and a final call to action, "we dared to pick up the day and shake its tail until it became evening ... Anybody can grab the day and make it stop. can u my friends? or may it's better if I ask:/will you?" (162). In this play we see Sanchez more directly addressing, among the issues of militant activism, a search for black female dignity.

In the play *Dirty Hearts*, Sanchez's explorations of oppression take on wider dimensions as a metaphorical exegesis of variant oppressions and the stances of power that work within conquest and domination. The play on the simplest level is the gathering of four individuals intent upon playing cards. One loses the game Dirty Hearts through acquisition of points and it is the first indication of a more complexly working dynamic in this simple gathering. The Dirty Queen of Spades (implications of the term *spade* as dirty or unwanted and its racialized use in reference to a black person should not be lost on the audience here) carries most of these bad points. The metaphor of being dealt a bad hand is ironically pursued, as the race and gender of the characters are central to who deals and receives winning or losing game cards. The play begins with two white male players, First Man and Second Man, and their lack of naming as well as their description as being "neither young nor old" signals the generic nature of their representation. They are in a sense representative of white America, a generalized, "natural" presentation of the norm, of a dominant ontological presence.

Two other main characters, Shigeko and Carl, on the other hand, are distinguished by their specific names and the groups they represent. Shigeko is a Hiroshima Maiden, a young woman emigrated from Japan after World War II. She is described as "wearing a beach hat that covers most of her face … heavily made-up—but from the nose down the face is disfigured" (249–50). The first two characters in the play see Shigeko as human "refuse" of the Atomic bomb and as a kind of inconvenience, a thorn in the self-satisfied consciousness of these white men of power. For example, First Man has employed her as his estranged wife's maid. However, his concern for her is merely ostensible; at the end of the play he seeks to ease her anguish by offering her a different job. But he is much more interested in his appointment with "a beautiful lady" than with Shigeko's riveting emotions, which she expresses so frighteningly: "i have been under bleached skies that drop silver/ … i have been fed residual death in a bottle" (250). Oppression in this instance is characterized through the power of imperialism, military domination, racial difference, and gender bias.

The character Carl fares little better in this gathering. He is a black businessman bent upon convincing himself of his success and value in a white dominated world. He not surprisingly measures these in terms of material goods and power, neither of which he truly possesses. He describes himself early in the play, " i am a blk/capitalist … i am the american dream" (251). However, First Man consistently deals the Dirty Queen to Carl so that in each game he is the loser. Carl is angered at this ongoing strategy and responds, "why me again, today? i received the queen of spades yesterday. i don't deserve it" (251). What Carl knows, but chooses not to admit, is that he consents to play the game despite the kind of cards he will receive. His participation in the quest for material wealth and power in a white capitalist society leaves him no choice. The men know that his response is mere posturing. He will return to the game again and again because he defines himself by it. He finally admits this inconsistency later in the play when he exclaims " listen u dirty crackers … and laugh … i own … a goddamn ordinary furniture store and nothing else" (255). Carl exits this scene shrieking into the streets, but the implication is that he will be back tomorrow to play again.

Sanchez characterizes a commonality of victimization in the two figures Carl and Shigeko. They both are objects wedged within the workings of systemic oppression. Shigeko seems to recognize this commonality when she seeks to sooth Carl's anguish by suggesting a partnership and the possibility of another kind of game, "please Carl … we'll play bridge and beat them unmercifully" (254). But Carl ignores her and avoids his own truth by lashing out against and running from the white men who control the game. The representation of oppression as multi-dimensional through the two disempowered figures of Carl and Shigeko leads the audience to recognize the ideological expanse of white hegemony. We are encouraged to see the breadth of white power and influence in the recognizable dimensions of the black/white conflict Carl's experiences present, but also in the new formations of cross-cultural and gendered bigotry and violence embodied in Shigeko's words and actions. Thus Sanchez moves to new levels of complexity in her examination of dominance and oppression and communal response to them. She enhances the effect of this complexity by complicating the seeming straightforward realistic structure of the play with disruptive poetic moments of litany (repetitive lines uttered for ritualistic effect or alteration of consciousness). In these moments of intense feeling, the peripheral characters in the play refuse moments of reality and lyrically reveal the anguish of their struggles.

Both Shigeko and Carl turn to litany in more than one instance to express the complexity of their struggles. Another character also on the periphery, Poet, uses litany, however, as a way to expose his loss of integrity and authenticity. Poet is resigned to his emotional and creative bankruptcy and prophecies his own demise. He once believed in his creative imagination but as an older man has given into his weakness and abandoned his poetic vision. Now he only sees that "the nites reveal the tears of disillusioned old men who have lost themselves among unseeing sights" (254). The bankruptcy of Poet's litany is in stark contrast to the raw honesty of those litanies of Shigeko and Carl. Perhaps in these contrasting images of disfranchisement Sanchez attempts to distinguish the implications of levels of choice in succumbing to the workings of the dominant discourse as opposed to involuntary victimization. Sanchez does seem to present here a view of possible personal responsibility within a victim's own destabilized position.

This idea of personal responsibility is further demonstrated in her next major play, *Uh, Huh, But How Do It Free Us?* , which acknowledges that a victim's response can have significant impact on the effectiveness of his/her confrontations with oppression. This notion is effectively demonstrated in *Uh, Huh* when we encounter three groupings (in themselves strategies counter to traditional structures of drama) as scenes in the play. Group I is an examination of the negative impact of polygamy as a social experiment informed by African traditions within the militant community. In this first section of the play, the characters reveal an increasing tension among two wives, Waleesha and Neferteria, and their husband, Malik. Sanchez's commentary here is clear. Polygamy, touted as a new way to strengthen the black militant community, in effect, is a great detractor of unity in family and community. Sanchez characterizes in this section the lack of sincerity of some young black male militants who seemed more interested in their libidos than in furthering the revolutionary cause. The dance interlude that follows Group I (Sanchez injects dance sequences as a kind of chorus or commentary at the end of each of the three groupings) interprets her intent here for the audience. In this first dance sequence, the dancers demonstrate without question that Waleek is intentionally playing his wives for fools.

Group II in *Uh, Huh* is a stinging critique that presents with shocking frankness the impact of hedonism and violence upon certain black communities during the 1960s and 1970s. Through five male characters (First, Second, and Third Brothers, White Dude and Brother Man), and two female prostitutes (Black Whore and White Whore), Sanchez examines the degrading effects of drug addiction, sexual excess and perversion, and violent sexism on self-identified "heroes" successfully working for black empowerment. Their definitions of success are troubling, however; the men are narrowly focused on their own personal gains of influence and money; they see themselves as "new black m[e]n raging in the land" (173). But, rather than supporting and developing the possibilities of the black community through activism, these so-called celebrators of blackness in effect prefer to control the community through drug dealing, robbery, pimping, and violence. They represent a very real aspect of "serving the community as in rip-off" that operated within the black community, which obviously caused great contempt on Sanchez's part.

The characters in Group II are some of the ugliest and most absurdly presented figures that Sanchez has created in all of her dramatic works. The horrible dimensions of these characters are augmented by the props and action. All five men ride hobbyhorses throughout the grouping, which are striking visuals for the ludicrous yet gripping influence of cocaine upon the behavior and consciousness of these addicts. Furthermore, the men participate in debasing behaviors of perversion, demanding that the prostitutes humiliate them through sado-masochistic sexual acts. The men ingest cocaine and order the whores to satisfy their physical and emotional whims. At one point, Brother Man insists that Black Whore get down on her hands and knees. He puts a collar on her and rides her like a horse, demanding that she echo his ridiculous interpretations of the weather and time of day. His generalized references to all black women as whores raises in a very direct way Sanchez's ongoing concern with the strained relations between black men and women and their negative effects upon the black woman's psyche. This damage is evident as Black Whore so eloquently describes her own anguish when asked "What yo name, girl?" (177); "Lost my name when I was eleven years old ... All ya need to know is on my face and body. If you can read a map you can read me" (177).

The lack of respect, violent attitudes, and willingness of the men to abuse women in this play provide serious scrutiny of the growing chasm between black men's perceptions of black women in the militant community and the identity and needs of black women themselves. This inference is supported by an interpretive dance chorus that again reiterates and reveals the intent of the action. As the men "ride their horses. Quietly staring out at the audience, each one involved in his own orgiastic dreams" (186), the dancers perform a dance that illustrates the loss of innocence of a young girl dancer who is stalked, raped, and sold into prostitution. She is then portrayed in the dance as one who "goes mad and becomes a woman." The sequence ends with the homosexual interaction of several male and female dancers while "discordant music is heard" (186). As this play demonstrates, the afflicted role of black women as members of the community introduced from her very first play, *The Bronx is Next,* becomes for Sanchez a central motif of her oeuvre; her works develop a trajectory that does not waver in attempting to answer the struggles of black women.

Group III of *Uh, Huh* also examines degrading positions foisted upon black women in the movement. A re-examination of black male militants who lose direction in their activism, looking rather toward buttressing their sagging sense of worth, Group III again exposes the male militants' inordinate attention to their sexual conquests. However, this time Sanchez injects the loaded question of race loyalty by staging a love triangle among three characters, Brother, Sister, and White Woman. Brother is a divided figure. His loyalties lie on both sides of the proverbial fence or, more accurately, the "color line." This split is metaphorically manifested in his costume. As the stage directions explain, he "has on a two/toned suit, one side is brown suede ... One side is an orange dashiki" (166). As the character moves about the stage, he is constantly aware that "he must stand or sit always with the dashiki side showing and never show the other side while visiting Sister" (187). Brother is a popular activist in the militant movement. Out of necessity for his image, he has a black woman (Sister) as his live-in companion, whom he describes as "My Black woman ... My choice for the world to see" (192). However, while presenting himself as Sister's faithful, loving companion, Brother, since he does not work, bankrolls his life style with the support of a secret liberal white woman/lover, reiterating situations Sanchez herself had observed.

White Woman is Sanchez's characterization of hypocritical white liberalism. This character declares early in the play that her intentions are for the welfare of the black community and for Brother's personal comfort: "I mean the money is rightfully yours ... [I]t's the money that my father got by underpaying Black people for years ... I can share you any time as long as you turn up here" (192). However, when it eventually becomes evident that Sister is pregnant, White Woman's motivations are suddenly more starkly revealed: "She's tied to you forever ... You just need ... want ... me for my money" (198). When White Woman ultimately insists that Brother participate with her in a humiliating ceremony where they "marry one another to each other" (203), Brother is manipulated into doggedly repeating ceremonials vows of commitment that White Woman composes during the makeshift ceremony. White Woman's political generosity has in fact very demanding conditions that Brother must satisfy, expectations that are clearly personal in nature. Eventually, Brother, still compelled to demonstrate a sense of loyalty to his black woman, leaves White Woman's apartment and returns to Sister a shaken man.

When Sister confronts him with her suspicions concerning his absences, Brother finally exposes his misogynist nature. He begins to abuse Sister. Slapping her repeatedly, he declares: "You a Black woman bitch ... same as every Black woman ... born to cry in the night." He then kisses her "long and hard" (210). Brother ultimately determines to find a way to continue to manipulate both women to his advantage. While fingering the onyx gift from White Woman and in the presence of Sister, he cogitates, "I'll see if I can work it out … Yes, Maybe it can be done" (210). As with the first two groups, a dance sequence follows this final scene. The questionable intent of the central male dancer in this visual interpretation is demonstrated when he approaches two female dancers in white and black masks, "turns and looks at both of them, tosses a coin to see which one he'll visit." He then is described as visiting them both with a "hip/walk" (214).

Group III eloquently concludes Sanchez's biting commentary concerning the dangers threatening the growth and welfare of the black community. In the whole of the play, Sanchez focuses on revealing the distressing attitudes of many black men, attitudes effectively extirpating the dignity of women, whether black or white. Sanchez identifies here the necessity of the militant community to become self-aware, purge itself of the negative, and gain ground in the footrace toward social equality.

Sanchez's most recent play, *I'm Black When I'm Singing, I'm Blue When I Ain't*, was written over ten years after *Uh, Huh*. And, although last produced over twenty-five years ago in 1982, the play amazingly still offers a relevant approach to issues in the black community. This examination of the direct psychological implications of racist oppression sets Sanchez within the parameters of current post-colonial discourse, resonating in particular with the theories of Franz Fanon. Fanon's work as a psychoanalyst, philosopher, and socio-political theorist on the French–Algerian conflict revolutionized thought at a global level concerning the debilitating effects of colonization and similar forms of oppression. He emphasized in particular a Freudian analysis of the pathological behaviors and sufferings that manifest in oppressed peoples. Mental breakdown, paranoia, and obsessive behaviors are some outcomes that occur, he concludes, primarily within the white colonizer/black colonized power paradigm. In fact, race is a central operative in the psychological complications resulting from oppression, according to Fanon. His major works, such as *Black Skin, White Masks* and *The Wretched of the Earth*, were embraced by militant writers during the Black Arts movement and informed new ways for militant playwrights to look at the African American experience in the USA as a kind of colonization.

Many of Fanon's conclusions illuminate Sanchez's *I'm Black When I'm Singing, I'm Blue When I Ain't*. This play confronts urban life in terms of racist, economic, and social oppressions and their debilitating consequences on the mental health of a young black woman, Reena. She suffers from multiple personality disorder, the consequence of numerous traumas in her life precipitated primarily through familial rejection. Her light mother treats her harshly and ridicules her because of her dark skin; her husband is overbearing and abusive. Reena has retreated from her conflicted reality into the relative safety of an insane asylum, where her different selves emerge. Like Reena, a talented young singer/musician from Philadelphia, her selves, who are patterned after actual famed black American blues/jazz singers, are gifted in music and have experienced sexually and racially motivated traumas (Ward 5).

In the asylum, Reena is confronted by a curious doctor and attendants who evoke responses from her and her other selves. The slow revelation of her fragmentation can in some ways be seen as a historical mapping of evolving black female consciousness. Mama B., the first personality to reveal herself in Reena, provides a glimpse of some of the most blatant and aggressive manifestations of white racism on black female lives. Mama B. comes out of the raucous 1920s and 1930s. She is an untamed, indecorous, and immensely popular blues circuit singer, whose monetary success (although severely limited by dishonest white agents and producers) enables her to feel a rebellious sense of empowerment. She acts out her notion of personal authority through coarse public behavior and by frequenting illicit venues called "buffet flats," areas known for selling illegal bathtub gin and offering prostitution and homosexual encounters. Challenging Reena's control over her consciousness, Mama shouts at her, "I don't share my stage with no other blues singer … So you just shut your northern Philadelphia mouth up" (18, manuscript).

Mama's demeanor is in direct conflict with the expectations of the black middle class, a milieu black women like Reena's mother were encouraged to emulate and/or enter if possible. Mama's refusal of the white informed and controlled middle class values sought after and prized by most blacks offers an early image of independence for Reena, a way to confront the limiting aspects of her mother's world. However, Mama's success and values are confined to the "low" world of popular music. Her ultimate demise reiterates that money and fame cannot insulate her from the vicious outcomes of white racism and classicism in America. Involved in a terrible car crash in Alabama, reminiscent of Bessie Smith's crash and subsequent death when refused treatment by a white hospital, Mama dies alone with Reena's consciousness present and commentating. This portrayal of the unequal treatment of blacks and of Mama's inability to break free of her social and educational limitations suggests Mama as an abortive representation of empowered black womanhood, isolated and ultimately defeated by an incomplete, misdirected independence.

In Act II, Toni reveals herself as the second personality challenging Reena's control. Accused at ten years old of tempting the man who raped her, she is placed in a Catholic home for wayward girls. There Toni suffers varied forms of psychological abuse at the hands of the self-righteous nuns. They are intent upon reforming her supposed corruption. In one instance, as punishment for her sullenness and defiance, she is forced to remain all night in a room with the corpse of another little girl from the home. She bangs on the door to be released until her knuckles are bloody. At the end of this scene, she morphs into a troubled young woman who walks the streets and is eventually given a chance to sing in a nightclub.

Reminiscent of 1940s and 1950s and the experiences of Billie Holliday, Toni ultimately acquires great notoriety as a blues/jazz club singer. However, her fame cannot overcome her feelings of worthlessness. She eventually attempts to escape her anguish through an addiction to heroin. Toni's damaged sense of womanhood is shaped by her victimization as an object of cruelty and relentless exploitation. She signals the weakened stature of black women who lack personal resources in facing the challenges of sexual and psychological abuse from members of their own communities. As Reena exclaims, "look at me ... set me free from the pain of years of hating myself" (60), Toni exacerbates her weakened state with a final drug overdose. Reena, ultimately, regains control, commenting that Toni, " was short termed ... dead. She didn't know how to hold herself" (45).

In response to Toni's inability to "hold herself," at the end of Act II Sanchez seems to finally offer Reena some hope, through Reena's last personality, Malika. Malika is Sanchez's solution to the incomplete and harassed black female personalities in the play. Malika is a well-adjusted, confident, and culturally centered young black woman whose strength comes out of her clear connection to her African heritage and her under-standing of the essential nature of self-worth and self-love. She offers Reena a comforting solution through a culturally rooted identity, a way to resolve her divisions: "I'm not trying to replace you. I just want to continue you in a newer form ... I will rock you in your blackness so you will grow to love yourself" (54–6). But Reena does not give up her discreteness without a fight. As a symbolic black woman, she cannot see through her own struggles and weaknesses what holds her back. She fights the very insights that can help her attain personal freedom: the importance of sisterhood, communal cohesion, personal strength, and a cultural integrity that comes with a confidence in the relations of heritage and family. This confidence encourages an emphasis on internal connections, an avoidance of colorism, a refusal of internal division, jealousy, and the bankruptcy of dominant social and personal values. Malika, representing these elements of cultural strength, ultimately convinces Reena that she can be part of what can work toward a synthesis of all toward a better self.

Shining through the character Malika are the qualities that Sanchez envisions as necessary for a healthier black female soul and spirit. In this last play, Sanchez provides a new way of translating well-being and happiness for black women and more broadly for the black community. Her approach emphasizes a conscious awareness of personal value and strength and eschews dominant insistences on fame, individuality, and material goods. This vision evolves throughout her dramatic oeuvre, increasingly privileging the essential role of the healthy black woman in the welfare of the community and in the well-being of African American psychology. Although Sanchez has expressed a continued interest in writing more plays ("This Thing," Wood 124), *I'm Black When I'm Singing* ... certainly serves as a kind of capstone for her career as a playwright. This dramatic piece effectively presents Sanchez's lifelong efforts as an activist and a writer: to feature the issues of black women, to gain positive communal self-awareness, and to initiate a redemptive acknowledgement of the possibilities of the African American community.

Notes

1   Numerous reviews of *Sister Son/ji* appeared during and immediately after the premiere of the play in sources such as *The New York Post*, *The Nation*, *The New York Times*, *Women's Wear Daily*, *Newsweek*, and *The New Yorker*. See, for example, Clive Barnes's review of "Black Visions" in *The New York Times* April 5 1972, 37:1; Richard Watts's "Four Plays by Black Authors," *The New York Post* April 5 1972, 67; or T. E. Kalem's "Black on Black," *Time* May 1972, 53.

Works cited

The Drama Review 12.4 (1968).

Fanon, Frantz. *Black Skin, White Masks.* Charles Lam Markmann, tr. New York: Grove Weidenfield Press, 1967.

——*The Wretched of the Earth.* Constance Farrington, tr. New York: Grove Press, 1963.

Hay, Samuel A. *African American Theatre: An Historical and Critical Analysis.* New York: Cambridge University Press, 1994.

Hill, Errol G. and Hatch, James V. (eds) *A History of African American Theatre.* Cambridge, UK: Cambridge University Press, 2003.

Kennedy, Adrienne. *Funnyhouse of a Negro. In One Act.* Minneapolis: UP of Minnesota, 1991.

——*The Owl Answers. In One Act.* Minneapolis: UP of Minnesota, 1991.

McCauley, Robbie. *Sally's Rape. Black Theatre U.S.A. Plays by African Americans—The Recent Period 1935–Today.* New York: The Free Press, 1996.

Parks, Suzan-Lori. *Mutabilities of the Third Kingdom. The America Play and Other Works.* New York: Theatre Communications Group, 1995. 23-71.

——*The Death of the Last Black Man in the Whole Entire World. The America Play and Other Works.* New York: Theatre Communications Group, 1995. 99-131.

——*Topdog,Underdog.* New York: Theatre Communications Group, Inc., 1999.

——*"from* Elements of Style." *The America Play and Other Works.* New York: Theatre Communications Group, 1995. 6–18.

Sanchez, Sonia. *The Bronx is Next. Cavalcade.* Arthur P. Davis and J. Saunders Redding, eds. New York: Houghton Mifflin Company, 1971. 811–19.

——*Dirty Hearts. Breakout: In Search of New Theatrical Environments.* James Shevill, ed. Chicago: Swallow Press, 1973. 248–56.

——*I'm Black When I'm Singing, I'm Blue When I Ain't.* Unpublished manuscript. 1982.

——*Malcolm Man Don't Live Here No Mo. Black Theatre* 6 (1972): 24–27.

——"The Poet as a Creator of Social Values." *Crisis in Culture: Two Speeches by Sanchez.* New York: Black Liberation Press, 1983.

——"Ruminations/Reflections." *Black Women Writers (1950–1980): A Critical Evaluation.* Mari Evans, ed. New York: Doubleday, 1984. 415–18.

——*Sister Son/ji*. *Wines in the Wilderness: Plays by African American Women from the Harlem Renaissance to the Present*. Elizabeth Brown-Guillory, ed. Westport, CT: Greenwood Press, 1990. 156–62.

——*Uh Huh, But How Do It Free Us? The New Lafayette Theatre Presents*. Ed Bullins, ed. Garden City, NY: Anchor Press, 1974. 165–215.

Sell, Mike. "The Black Arts Movement: Performance, Neo-Orality, and the Destruction of the 'White Thing.'" *African American Performance and Theater History: A Critical Reader*. Harry J. Elam and David Krasner. New York: Oxford University Press, 2001. 56–80.

Shange, Ntozake. *for colored girls who have considered suicide/ when the rainbow is enuf*. New York: Samuel French, 1981.

——*boogie woogie landscapes*. *Three Pieces*. New York: Penguin Books, 1992. 53–108.

——"A History: for colored girls who have considered suicide when the rainbow is enuf." *See No Evil: Prefaces, Essays & Accounts* 1976–1983. San Francisco: Momo's Press, 1984.

Ward, Karen Turner. "Creating Four Distinct Characters by Using Historical Models in a Production of Sonia Sanchez's *I'm Black When I'm Singing, I'm Blue When I Ain't.*" M.A. Thesis, Virginia Commonwealth University, 1985.

Williams, Dana. *Contemporary African American Female Playwrights: An Annotated Bibliography*. Westport, CT: Greenwood Press, 1998.

Wood, Jacqueline. "This Thing Called Playwriting: An Interview with Sonia Sanchez on the Art of Her Drama." *African American Review* 39.1–2 (2005): 119–32.

——"'To Wash My Ego in the Needs ... of My People': Militant Womanist Rhetoric in the Drama of Sonia Sanchez." *CLAJ* 48.1 (2004): 1–33.

——*Power Plays: The Dramatic Works of Sonia Sanchez*. Durham, N.C.: Duke University Press. Forthcoming.

5 American history/African nightmare

Adrienne Kennedy and civil rights

Philip C. Kolin

Adrienne Kennedy is one of the most influential black avant-garde playwrights of the twentieth century. Inescapably, her plays led to a revolutionary style in African American theatre. According to Billie Allen, who starred in (1964) and later directed (2006) *Funnyhouse of a Negro*, Kennedy created "a major legacy" for dramatists like Ntozake Shange and Suzan-Lori Parks through her "surrealistic effects and characters who deliver haunting interior monologues" (Kolin, "Revisiting *Funnyhouse*" 175). An intensely confessional author, Kennedy has created "the most personal plays of any playwright in America" (Cummings 7) and readily admits that some of her works grew out of her dreams, such as *A Rat's Mass*, performed in 1966 (Bryant-Jackson and Overbeck 7). While many of Kennedy's works occur in the world of the subconscious, the harrowing territory of nightmares, we enter that hallucinatory world through her young black and mulatta characters who search for their identity in a prejudiced, Eurocentric society that brands them as transgressive and grotesque. The psychic instability of Kennedy's protagonists reflects their desire to be white, but being black or yellow, they are forced to bear the "curse of blood" (Brown) and, tragically, are destroyed by the fictions of their projected white selves.

Though we encounter Kennedy's characters in surrealistic dreamscapes, the voice of history is strong in almost all of her works. Yet, as Robert Vorlicky maintains, "history refuses to acknowledge them, to 'place' them" (47) because they are black. There can be no denying, however, that Kennedy's tormented, nightmarish heroines are victims of as well as witnesses to the history in which they are embroiled. Like Anna Deavere Smith or Suzan-Lori Parks, Kennedy "freely play[s] with the historical as integral to [her] work—personal histories, local history, American history" (Bean 4). As Craig Werner claims, Kennedy has written a "revisionist history" (45) in *Funnyhouse*, her signature play. There is an implacable political radicalism in her work, rooted in the psychic and physical terrors that have plagued black Americans. "We were underdogs, and underdogs must fight in life," she claimed in her 1987 autobiography *People Who Led to My Plays* (11). Her traumatized heroines are caught in the cruelties of a white institutionalized history determined to erase African Americans, "the underdogs," from full citizenship. Dramatizing their cultural memory, black characters in Kennedy's plays live white history as nightmare. In *The Face of Emmett Till*, Mamie Till-Mobley, his mother, hears her martyred son scream "Mama? Help me!" and confesses "The nightmare always comes back" (56), referring to his being savagely murdered by white racists in 1955 Mississippi. Blending American history and African nightmares, one spilling over into the other, Kennedy portrays her characters as mad and diseased, reflecting their tormented, guilty minds because they are not white. Yet in their madness she also indicts a decadent white culture that wants to punish black identity, encoding African Americans as the dangerous, polluted Other. More than individual nightmares, then, Kennedy's plays mirror the collective African American memory of racism and violence. Personal tragedies become public/cultural horrors in her canon.

Kennedy's background prepared her well to create politically-charged plays. *People Who Led to My Plays* is essential to understanding the political events that serve as catalysts for her works. A psychic scrapbook of Kennedy's journey through childhood and early adulthood (the early 1930s to the early 1960s), *People* records in word and image a black woman's cultural memories, hopes, and fears. Kennedy grew up in a family dedicated to racial justice. Her father was secretary of the Cleveland YMCA and was active in the National Association for the Advancement of Colored People (NAACP) in the 1930s and 1940s, delivering speeches and fighting for racial equality as Assistant Head for Race Relations for city hall. When she traveled south from Cleveland to Montezuma, Georgia to visit relatives each summer, including her maternal white grandfather, a wealthy planter, Kennedy painfully recalls having to switch to Jim Crow cars in Cincinnati.

In 1952, she married Joseph Kennedy, and after he completed his Ph.D. in social psychology at Columbia University in 1960, she accompanied him to Ghana where she saw the struggle for independence and the resulting bloodshed, all of which had a profound impact on her work (Kolin, *Understanding* 116). Her husband was a friend of Algerian psychiatrist Frantz Fanon, whose highly influential study *Black Skin, White Masks* (1967) exposed the pernicious effects of colonization in a postcolonial world. Imprinted on Kennedy's conscience, Fanon is featured in *She Talks to Beethoven*, where he reads his work on the radio (1992), and in *The Film Club* (1992) and *Dramatic Circle* (1992). Kennedy has also written political parables such as *Sun: A Play for Malcolm X Inspired by His Murder* (1968); *An Evening with Deod Essex* (1973) about a black Vietnam veteran gunned down after shooting at people from atop the Howard Johnson's in New Orleans; and *Sleep Deprivation Chamber* (1996),[1] coauthored with her son Adam and based upon his being falsely arrested and prosecuted by the Arlington, Virginia police. For her works combating racism Kennedy won the Lifetime Achievement Award from the Anisfield–Wolf Foundation in 2003.

Given this strong political dynamic in Kennedy's works, her plays should be read as part of a theatre of racial resistance. While her surrealistic techniques and incantatory lyrical refrains were far different from the polemical dialogues of Amiri Baraka, Ed Bullins, Sonia Sanchez, or other writers who criticized Kennedy's representation of blackness, she nonetheless confronted the same racial prejudices. Like the black soldier in Yusef Komunyakaa's Vietnam War poem, "Tu Do Street," her characters carry "a nation inside" (268). Their demonized bodies agonizingly testify to the pain of black America's battle for civil rights. Far more aggressively activist than has been suggested before, Kennedy's canon unpacks many of the tragic incidents that energized the struggle for civil rights in the 1950s and 1960s as well as those that continue today. Her earlier plays (*Funnyhouse, The Owl Answers* [1965]), *A Rat's Mass, A Lesson in Dead Language* (1964) were written at the height of the civil rights era (1961–1969)—the years of church bombings, the assassination of Dr. Martin Luther King, Jr., the beatings and murders, the riots, the bloody protests and valiant sit-ins. In fact, the workshop production of *Funnyhouse of a Negro* (1962) occurred only three years after the Broadway premiere of Lorraine Hansberry's impassioned *Raisin in the Sun* (1959) and opened Off Broadway the year Baraka's revolutionary *Dutchman* (1964) stormed New York stages.

For over forty years, then, Kennedy has dramatized the politics of racial identity, allegorizing America as a "funny house," "a crazy house for minorities" (Tapley), where bigotry is always drawn along blood lines. Violations of civil rights consistently underpin her hallucinatory tragedies of identity. But Kennedy's dramas against racial injustices are not confined to events from the 1960s. The trajectory of her canon reflects the evolving context of civil rights in which she has worked, from discrimination against black students majoring in English in the 1940s in *Ohio State Murders* (1984) to the colonizing oppression that damns Sarah in *Funnyhouse* to the contemporary horrors of racial profiling in *Sleep Deprivation* (1996). This essay will foreground the ways in which incidents in an ongoing struggle for civil rights are embedded in and help to contextualize Kennedy's works. Such an approach will, I hope, bring a renewed immediacy to her canon while at the same time profitably expand how it might be evaluated.

1

Lynching, its ideology and metaphors, provides a key civil rights context for *Funnyhouse of a Negro*. As Jacqueline Goldsby has argued, lynching is not just a cruel punishment from the nineteenth and early twentieth centuries. It functions as an important and complex symbol of race relations, and much of the violence of prejudice today (*Spectacular Secret*). A 1999 production of *Sleep Deprivation Chamber* at De Paul University's Reskin Theatre in Chicago appropriately troped lynching by having Kennedy's fictionalized son Teddy Alexander look up at a suspended noose over the witness stand at his trial. Read against and within the lynching code, Sarah's tragedy of identity is condemningly rooted in America's racial violence, past and present, North and South. According to the politics of racism, lynching was necessary to protect white feminine innocence and purity (Matthews "Southern Rite"), and to terrorize the black community into submission. Black men were inevitably and unjustly cast in the role of sexual predators endangering the safety of white women, and could be executed for the slightest infraction, as the vigilante justice behind the Scottsboro Boys case in the 1930s, the Willie McGee trial in the 1950s, and the bludgeoning of 14-year old Emmett Till in 1955 prove. Till's body, with a 70-pound cotton gin fan tied around his neck, was found in the Tallahatchie River in the Mississippi Delta, and the crime was rightly labeled a lynching (Metress). Noting that a "seething sexual tension" helped explain lynching, Matthews concluded with an observation relevant for a study of Kennedy's plays: "Psychologists who were arrested by the 'sexual alibi' of protecting white women, nonetheless found that ... the mechanism of projecting one's own forbidden thoughts onto black men was the source of white man's lust" ("Southern Rite" 20). Also reflecting white lusts, is Tennessee Williams's early short story, "Big Black: A Mississippi Idyll" (1931), which begins by confirming a stereotypical portrait of the sexualized black man but then, more daringly, thwarts a white audience's expectations for a cruel racial expiation (Kolin, "Tennessee Williams" 11).

Exploring and exploding the racial ideology behind this quintessential civil rights violation, Kennedy incorporated, and problematized, lynching stereotypes that lurk in the subtext of *Funnyhouse*. Evoking the African American cultural memory of lynching, she shapes events in Sarah's schizophrenic world to condemn the white man's image of the black man, thereby contextualizing the suffering of the black experience in America. While Sarah is yellow, her father is black, the "blackest of them all," and "Black is evil," she declares. Hating her own blackness and wanting to be white, Sarah attacks with lynch-like fury her father who raped her "mother who looked like a white woman" (*Funnyhouse* 15). Portrayed as a victim of a black rape, Sarah's mother exclaims at the beginning of the play, "Black man, black man. I never should have let a black man put his hands on me. The wild beast raped me and now my skull is shinning" (13). But ambiguity often surrounds Kennedy's presentation of race. White men also rape black women. In *The Owl Answers*, Clara Passmore is conceived after her mother is raped in an outhouse by her father, the Richest White Man in Town who is also the Dead White Father, a heinous case of the institutional white rape of black women. In *Funnyhouse*, Sarah is the unhappy issue of a forced racial union, and through her white and black selves—Queen Victoria and the Duchess of Hapburg—claims that her black father "haunted my conception, diseased my birth" (24). Racialized by Sarah's white selves, the black man is again victimized for violating the purity of a woman who looks white and for diseasing his daughter's birth, a doubly treacherous crime for the white-identity seeking Sarah.

Appropriately, too, the black father–rapist is associated with the jungle, the landscape of unbridled African lust that lynching was designed to eradicate. Sarah's Duchess of Hapsburg self declares, "He is the wilderness. He speaks niggerly groveling about wanting to touch me with his black hand" (17). When he comes to her apartment begging her forgiveness, she rejects him with contempt. Ironically recalling the lynching code, her father "tries to hang himself" in remorse for what he did to Sarah's mother (20) and later, in Kennedy's pulsating refrain, we learn, "He came to see her once before he tried to hang himself, appearing in the corridor of my apartment" (22). The allusion to hanging this "black ugly thing ... sitting in [the] hallway ... surrounded by the blackness of in himself" calls to mind the historical inevitability of lynching as a weapon of white retribution in the African American memory.

Lynching was also justified according to the canons of a white Christianity, another racial tenet that *Funnyhouse* interrogates and resists. A black man who sexually transgressed white female purity unqualifyingly merited execution as a sacrifice to white Christian justice. "Because the myth of God's just vengeance permitted whites' obsession with punishment to rule their relations with blacks there was no restriction within the myth to the racism that clouded their vision" (Matthews 42). Through Sarah's schizophrenia, Kennedy represents the grotesque ways white Christianity sanctified lynching. Linking his own failure as a missionary with raping Sarah's mother, the father exclaims, "I wanted to be a Christian. Now I am a Judas. I betrayed my mother [who wanted him to save the black race]. I sent your mother to the asylum. I created a yellow child who hates me" (21). Then the Man who has first spoken these lines adds, "And he tried to hang himself in a Harlem hotel." The rope around the father's neck is an emblem of both his secular and spiritual crimes.

Further demonizing a white religion's endorsement of lynching, Kennedy introduces a yellow Jesus, dwarfish and lustful, to revenge the crimes of the Black Man. Combining the voice of the Black Man with the zeal of an African revolutionary, Jesus justifies white revenge against blacks: "I am going to Africa and kill this black man named Patrice Lumumba. Why? Because all my life I believed my Holy Father to be God, but now I know that my father is a black man. I have no fear for whatever I will do in the name of God, I will do in the name of Albert Saxe Coburg, in the name of Victoria, Queen Victoria Regina, the monarch of England" (23). But, as Jesus's own confused racial heritage indicates, things are not just black or white in Kennedy's nuanced world. Jesus's/The Man's father is black yet he seeks revenge in the names of a consanguineous God and the most colonial of white queens, Victoria, and her prince-consort. White becomes dangerously problematic in Kennedy's world; it does not simply equate with good and black with bad. Endorsing the colonial subjugation of black people, a yellow savior figure represents a disfiguring Christianity, the dominance of a decaying white religion on the African American soul. Through such characterizations, Kennedy hauntingly collapses a ruling Anglo-Saxon church's punishment for apostasy into the politics of lynching.

References to lynching, verbally and visually, also ironically affix to and indict Sarah. Hating herself for being a "thing of darkness," to quote Prospero, Sarah likewise suffers lynching-style for her and her father's crimes. When Sarah first appears on Kennedy's surrealistic set, "*She is a faceless, dark character with a hangman's rope around her neck and red blood on the part that would be her face*" (13). With the rope around her neck, she embodies the fate of many black Americans lynched for trumped-up crimes, slaughtered as scapegoats for white hate. Billie Holiday, one of Kennedy's heroes whose picture she includes in *People*, was famous for her 1939 anti-lynching ballad, the "first musical assault against racial lynching," entitled "Strange Fruit," and written by Abe Meeropol under the pseudonym of Lewis Allen:

> Southern trees bear a strange fruit
> Blood on the leaves and blood at the root
> Black body swinging into the southern breeze
> Strange fruit hanging from the poplar trees.
>   (quoted in Margolick)

Holiday's song of terror helps to gloss Sarah's lynched body and bloody face in terms of the history of racial crimes. Studying the iconography of lynching, Matthew Wynn Sivils aptly concludes with a point relevant to Sarah's suspended figure: "Southern trees are inextricably linked to and spring from a literature preoccupied with time, place, race and warped grotesque bodies" (89). A young Lorraine Hansberry, who also wrote about this scourge of African Americans in her early poem "Lynchsong" (1951), provides a further political context for Sarah's tragedy.

> I can hear Rosalee
> See the eyes of Willie McGee
> My mother told me about
> Lynchings
> My mother told me about
> The dark nights
> And dirt roads
> And torch lights
> And lynch robes
> The faces of men
> Laughing white
> Faces of men
> Dead in the night
> sorrow night
> and a
> sorrow night.
>   ("Lynching")

In the "dark night" of her psyche, Sarah could intimately relate to "My mother told me about/Lynchings," as the opening of *Funnyhouse* with its allusions to her mother's tragic plight and the rope around her own neck demonstrate. Sarah will also see the "Faces of men/Dead in the night," as Clara Passmore does in *Owl*.

The lynching motif found in "Strange Fruit" and "Lynchsong," as well as in the works of numerous other nineteenth- and twentieth-century African American writers (e.g., Ida B. Wells's *Southern Horrors* [1892], Angelina Weld Grimké's *Rachel: A Play in Three Acts* [1920], or Alice Childress's *Trouble in Mind* [1955]), is compellingly evoked again at the end of *Funnyhouse*. Graphically pointing to the means of Sarah's death, the white Funnyhouse Lady mocks: "The poor bitch has hung herself" (25). Kennedy's accompanying stage direction then links the father's incessant knocking with Sarah's tragic undoing:

> The Negro Sarah is standing perfectly still, we hear the knocking.
> The Lights come on quickly, her father's black figure with bludgeoned hands rushes upon her, the Light Goes Black, and we see her hanging in her room. (25)

In her first appearance and in her last tableau, Sarah wears a rope, a historically-charged symbol of lynching (in 1964 as it had been for many decades before), a torture awaiting any black person guilty of defying racial codes. Claiming to have a white boyfriend, Raymond, a Jewish poet who is the Funnyhouse Man, Sarah discovers herself that black sex with a white person can be branded a lynching sin. Again, a victim of white history and her own schizophrenic guilt, Sarah receives the same punishment allotted to the condemned sexualized black man, the lynching noose. Like her father, she can be culturally assimilated into Willie McGee, the black man executed in Mississippi accused of having relations with a white woman. A crucial piece of civil rights legislation puts Sarah's guilt into a political context. Shockingly, it was not until 1967, three years after the premiere of *Funnyhouse*, that the Supreme Court, in Loving v. Virginia, declared as unconstitutional the laws in sixteen states that forbade interracial marriages, miscegenation (Robinson, *Dangerous Liaisons* 138). For attempting to couple with Raymond in 1964, Sarah would have been found guilty not only in her nightmare world but also in the courts of law in those states that upheld such racial prohibitions.

But lynching becomes a polyphonic signifier in *Funnyhouse*. Kennedy subverts its very ideology as she alludes to the cruel traditions behind lynching. She uses the rope to document that race is not unequivocally dichotomous, but, rather, a shifting signifier of hybridity destabilizing a white hegemony. Pretending to be a regal figure from the white world, Sarah tragically projects herself as Queen Victoria and the Duchess of Hapsburg. Yet wearing the lynching noose in her hallucinatory state, she undercuts her desire to be white and to be accepted by white culture. This is seeing self as empowered Other. Moreover, in ghoulishly imitating the white world they want to join, Sarah's selves are *"made up to appear a whitish yellow"* (12) with their *"kinky hair spring*[ing] *out from under"* (21) tawdry tiaras. Their cake-like masks deconstruct these selves' painful dreams of being white, as does Sarah's lynching rope. This racial tension/anxiety/contradiction is at the center of Kennedy's plays. As Clive Barnes recognized early in Kennedy's career: "Of all our black writers, Kennedy is most concerned with white, with white relationships, with white blood. She thinks white but remembers black" (24). Applying Barnes's insights to Kennedy's characters, we see that Sarah thinks and projects herself as white but is punished for being, and remembering, black. *Funnyhouse* thus provocatively challenges the historical certitudes about race and politics audiences may bring with them into Kennedy's theatre. Ultimately, in Sarah's nightmare world, the symbolic rope destabilizes an either/or white historiography.

Ironically, too, because Sarah thinks she does not deserve to be white, she assumes the transformative role of white executioner, impelling appropriate lynching punishment on herself. Analogous to the ambiguities of minstrelsy that Jacqueline Wood has uncovered in *Funnyhouse*, where the white makeup does not conceal but reveals black skin beneath, a lynching rope engenders Sarah's self hatred. Her warring racial identities distort and blur what Tru Leverette has termed the "boundaries and frontiers of self" (80). Reflecting the African nightmare (inside) in American history (outside), Sarah is double-voiced. By impersonating someone in a subject (white) position, she is ignominiously erased from the white world as an object of contempt by Raymond and the Landlady who mock her "hanging figure" and then smirk, "She was a funny liar" (25). Sarah's earlier words can serve as the epitaph for her lynched body at the end of *Funnyhouse*— "I want not to be." Ironically, she is cast as both victim and criminal, the devastating legacy of the black man in America, a sacrificial offering to white violence as well as an offender against its racial/sexual codes enforced by lynching justice.

In a major revival of *Funnyhouse* for the Classical Theatre of Harlem in January–February 2006, director Billie Allen had a rope descend over Sarah's large bed (which also functioned as a huge coffin) situated at center stage so audiences could see her hanging body above the very space where she had earlier writhed in desire while watching the sexual foreplay between her lusty, white Duchess self and Raymond (Kolin, "Revisiting *Funnyhouse*"). Suggesting a lynch mob, all the characters in Allen's production "came together and [immediately before her hanging] converged on Sarah, yelling and pushing," as Lisa Armstrong noted in her review. In Allen's revival, Sarah's crime was unforgettably emblematized in sexual, racial, and political terms, all tied in a lynching noose. The scene "scared audiences to death" (Kolin, "Revisiting *Funnyhouse*" 168).

Raising a central question about the ending of *Funnyhouse*, Allen asked whether Sarah's calamitous fate was indeed real or a part of her schizophrenic dream ("Revisiting *Funnyhouse*" 174–5). Has she become a suicide, or is she a black spectacle of ridicule only in the mad theatre of her mind? Either way Allen's question is answered, the conclusion of Kennedy's play indicts a white lynching mentality and what it has done culturally to the minds and bodies of African Americans. In her theatre of alienation, Kennedy chronicles the traumatized memory of lynching events from white history as they enter and shape Sarah's African American experience. An ambiguous ending about Sarah's fate is consistent with the conflicting interpretations about her father. When the Landlady affirms that "her father hung himself in a Harlem hotel when Patrice Lumumba died," Raymond contradicts her: "Her father never hung himself in a Harlem hotel ... I know the man. He is a doctor, married to a white whore. He lives in the city in rooms with European antiques ... Her father is a nigger who eats his meals on a white glass table" (25–6). Whether in reality or in her hallucinations, then, Sarah, like her father, is renounced by a white hegemony that imposes its punishment on any black person daring to cross the color line. The lynched Sarah is trapped on either side of that line.

2

Mirroring the turbulent times in which her early plays were written and first produced, Kennedy's theatre also evokes the hate crimes against black children as a result of segregation, exploitation, and white brutality. For example, a white English professor in *Ohio State Murders*, Robert Hampshire, kidnaps and murders the twin black daughters he has fathered, and *Sleep Deprivation Chamber* ominously opens with a reference to Emmett Till, whose face was magled and whose skull was crushed after being pierced by a white-hate bullet in Mississippi in 1955. But two of Kennedy's early works in particular—*A Rat's Mass* (written in 1963; first staged in 1966 by the Theater Company of Boston) and *A Lesson in Dead Language* (1964)— concentrate unrelentingly on the nightmares black children suffer in white America. Dramatizing their wounds, physically and psychically, these plays reverberate with terrifying imagery, nightmarish settings, and grotesque characters and punishments, reminiscent of the civil rights atrocities that stained America's conscience in the 1950s and 1960s. Black children in these as well as in later Kennedy plays are tortured by a surrealistic Clybourne Park, the segregated white neighborhood that wants to keep the Younger family out in *A Raisin in the Sun*.

In *A Rat's Mass*, Kennedy historicizes the white supremacy movement in America, analogizing its attacks on black children with the racist tactics of the Nazis. Incorporating Kennedy's memories of her World War II childhood in a racially mixed Cleveland neighborhood (*People*), this one-act play dramatizes a surrealistic horror story about two black children, Brother

Blake and Sister Kay, transformed into rats by an avenging white community accusing them of committing incest on a playground slide. The first line of the play contains explosive historical signifiers that detonate Kennedy's political allegory. Brother Rat, Blake, tells Sister Rat, Kay, "Within our room I see our dying baby, Nazis, screaming girls and cursing boys, empty swings, a dark sun" (47). With true Gestapo spite, a bigoted white community poisons the children's minds into thinking they are rodents, filthy, rejected, fit for execution, the propaganda agenda of American racists as well as the Nazis, led by Joseph Goebbels, who personified the Jews as rats (Kolin, *Understanding* 82). Kennedy's stage direction tragically allegorizes the children's degradation in this Nazi-like America: "*Brother Rat has a rat's head, a human belly, a tail. Sister Rat has a rat's body, a human head, a tail*" (47). Reinforcing this outrageous racial stigma imposed on Kay and Blake are the sounds of gnawing rats in the rafters and rat feet scurrying over the rooftop. Mercilessly, these two rat-personified black children are hunted down because of their race. "Nazis have invaded our house," Brother and Sister cry. Later, Sister screams, "Now the Germans and Caesar's army are after us" (53). Numerous incidents from contemporary violations of civil rights help to contextualize American Nazi racists in *Rat's Mass*. George Lincoln Rockwell, founder of the American Nazi Party, used a Volkswagen van painted with swastikas to preach white supremacy. And Black demonstrators attempting to integrate all-white neighborhoods, such as Marquette Park in Chicago in the 1960s, for instance, were verbally and physically threatened by Neo-Nazis in Fascist dress—swastikas and black shirts. Preparing to deliver a speech at the Civil Rights Museum in Montgomery on November 5, 1989, the day it was dedicated, Mamie Till-Mobley was assaulted by angry "outside voices" shouting "*Zeig Heil*! White Power! White Power!!!!!!!" (*Face of Emmett Till* 12).

The children's Nazi-acting enemy in *Rat's Mass* is Rosemary, an Italian girl wearing a "Holy Communion dress" and with worms in her head like Medusa. She informs them that blacks cannot be Catholic, nor are they entitled to claim her ancestors (the Roman guardians of Eurocentric purity), and declares that her "greatest grief was [their] life together" (53). Even though Rosemary had once befriended them, leading Blake to think they would be married, and had the children swear on her Holy Communion book, she now pronounces them outcasts, excommunicating them for being black and dehumanizing them as rats. In Kennedy's racist America, black children are denied souls as well as human bodies. Punishing the children racially and spiritually, a procession of "*Jesus, Mary, and Joseph, Two Wise Men and a Shepherd*" turns into a firing squad "bearing shotguns" to execute them. In Kennedy's stinging indictment of religious bigotry, Rosemary refers to the arrival of these creche figures as "The Nazis have come" (53). The children's once pristine home is metamorphosized into a rodent-ridden ghetto where dead rats hang from the ceiling and where Brother and Sister petition, "God we ask you to stop throwing rat babies" (52). Although Blake admits, "I am damned," he later deceives himself: "When I grow up I will swing again in white trees because beyond this dark rat run and gnawed petals there will remain a Capitol" (52). But there is no resurrection into a "white tree" paradise for these black children. Their sun will forever remain "dark." The "Capitol" to which Brother Rat refers can ambiguously represent the classical location where Caesar was assassinated as well as a metonymy for the ineffectual federal government that failed to protect black children in the 1950s and 1960s.

In carrying out their racial blitzkrieg, Rosemary and her Nazi-inspired culture indict Blake for a trumped up crime of incest and send Sister Rat to an asylum, a "State Hospital," where she loses her baby. Sister goes to the hospital to have a state-mandated abortion in Kennedy's prejudiced America of the 1960s. The recurrent images of dying baby rats never let audiences forget the enormity of this hate crime against black children. As Brother exclaims, "I am alone in our old house with an attic full of dead rat babies" (52). There are "dying baby voices" coming from the "beams" as well (53). Together Brother and Sister Rat lament, "Now every time we will go outside we will step over the grave of our dead baby" (53), further visualizing Kennedy's landscape of death. Sister tells Brother, "Blake, now that I am home from the hospital we must rid our minds of my rat's belly" (53). But Brother can only reply, "Everywhere I go I step in your blood." The image here is made flesh and the flesh made image in Kennedy's frightening transformations. Far reaching in its political outrage, *A Rat's Mass* might well represent what has been called the "Black Holocaust," an umbrella term for the suffering and torment extending from slavery to lynching to black global genocide (Hawthorne; Jones). The holocaust in Kennedy's drama points to a merciless policy of eugenics aimed at reducing the number of black children to make America more white.

Undeniably, *Rat's Mass* compellingly voices the agony of the African American community over the murder of their children, one generation at a time, victims of a white society that Kennedy attacks through her political allegory. Her political metaphors recall the horrors of civil rights atrocities of the 1950s and 1960s. Dehumanizing black babies as rats, Rosemary's white world promotes racial categories of identity that neo-Nazis and other white hate groups vigorously applied to ensure Aryan racial purity and continuity. As Boss Finley, the epitome of a racist demagogue, swears in his "Voice of God" speech upholding white purity in Tennessee Williams's *Sweet Bird of Youth* (1959): "I got a mission that I hold sacred to perform … To shield from pollution a blood that is not only sacred to me but to Him [God]. I cannot and will not accept, tolerate, or condone the threat of a blood pollution" (107). The Boss's Christian justification for racial purity and intolerance sounds exactly like those reasons advanced by white segregationists that Rosemary typifies. Chronologically, the Boss's speech falls between the events at Little Rock and Selma, landmark civil rights battles to end white oppression against blacks.

Affording another civil rights context for *Rat's Mass* is the process by which some states completed birth certificates to define and to defend racial identities/categories, thus privileging an all-white caste system. To determine and sustain racial classifications, Louisiana, for instance, practiced "race flagging," or "pulling out a birth certificate that lists a baby as white but bears a name common to blacks. Such certificates [were] checked against a 'race list' maintained by the Vital Records Office" (Powell). Anyone who had the slightest amount of African blood was automatically issued a birth certificate identifying the person as "colored." For many decades, Louisiana "state law allowed anyone with more than one thirty-second black blood to be defined as 'black'" (Omni and Winnant). A famous case brought by Susie Guillory Phipps in New Orleans in 1977 helps to foreground the racial/identity politics underlying *Rat's Mass*. "Believing all her life that she was white," Phipps learned that because her great grandmother, four or five generations removed, was a slave, the New Orleans Bureau of Vital Records designated her as "colored" (Omni and Winnant). Correspondingly, Kay and Blake thought they were accepted into Rosemary's white world, including being the beneficiaries of her history, religion, and love. But like Brother and Sister Rat, Phipps lost her claim to be considered "white" in Louisiana, and even the U.S. Supreme Court refused to review her case in 1986. Further exemplifying the dystopian world of racial categorization and marginalization in *A Rat's Mass*, many health care systems throughout America up until 1989 continued to assign a baby's race according to the racial heritage of the non-white parent (Jones).

In decrying the large-scale murder of innocent black children, *A Rat's Mass* hauntingly evokes—in its date, setting, characters, and imagery—one of the most brutal crimes of the civil rights era. In September of 1963, racists planted 15 sticks of dynamite in a bathroom at the Sixteenth Street Baptist Church in Birmingham, Alabama on "Young Day," killing four black girls, ages 11–14, while they were in Sunday school. Birmingham became Bombingham. The blast also injured "dozens of survivors, their faces dripping with blood from the glass that flew out of the stained glass windows, staggered around the building in a cloud of white dust raised by the explosion." Dr. Martin Luther King, Jr. accused Gov. George Wallace of having "the blood of four little children ... upon your hands" ("Six Dead") and preached at their funeral that "the precious blood of these innocent children replaced caution with courage" (King, *Words That Changed a Nation*). This tragic event became the turning point in the war against black children and mobilized even greater support for civil rights legislation and protection. This church bombing has major cultural significance for studying Kennedy's play against the violent backdrop of the 1960s. I am not arguing that the bombing of the Sixteenth Street Church is a direct source for *Rat's Mass* (written, coincidentally, the same year), but the tragic event does provide an inescapable civil rights context. Through such a terrifying historical lens, *Rat's Mass* can be read as a contemporary nightmare about how a white culture created and consumed racial myths about black identity.

The imagery and setting of *A Rat's Mass* also, surrealistically, replicate the horrors witnessed at the Sixteenth Street Church. The children murdered in Birmingham were victims of a white hatred that turned their identity and innocence into a racist sin. The same prejudice also targeted Kay and Blake for execution. Just as it spilled over the Sixteenth Street Church, the blood of black children (perversely transformed into rats) saturates *A Rat's Mass*. "Now there is blood on the aisle of our church," cries Brother (50). Contextually, Dr. King's condemnation of Gov. Wallace could be directed to Rosemary and other white supremacists. By setting her play in a "chapel," moreover, Kennedy commodifies one of the most vulnerable sites for white hatred during the civil rights struggle. Some of the most gruesome crimes against the African American community were committed against black churches, resulting in their being burned, bombed, erased from the landscape of hope. For instance, the three famous civil rights workers— Andrew Goodman, James E. Cheney, and Michael Schwerner—were responding to calls for help in finding the bigots who burned a black church when these three young men were murdered by the Ku Klux Klan in Philadelphia, Mississippi in 1964. The violence Kennedy personifies in *Rat's Mass* thus evokes the racial *zeitgeist* that turned the holy ground of the Sixteenth Street Church into an execution chamber—its windows blown out, its insides gutted, its innocent children savagely turned into blood and tears. Like the Sixteenth Street Church, Kay and Blake's idealized church/chapel home is desecrated by Rosemary and her Nazi-like religious figures. In a racist parody of its original sacramental identity, they demonize the children's pristine chapel, transforming it into a loathsome ghetto, a concentration camp.

Like *A Rat's Mass*, *A Lesson in Dead Language*, which premiered in 1964 and was subsequently staged in London in 1968, concentrates on the degradation of black children. In one of Kennedy's most symbolically political scripts, seven black girls wearing "*organdy dresses, white socks, black shoes*" (43) are tortured by their grotesque teacher, the "great and stiff" White Dog, really a woman "*costumed like a dog from the waist up.*" A hallmark of Kennedy's style, the girls incessantly refer to bleeding—"I am bleeding mother," "we all bleed," "blood came out of me"; and a "great circle of blood" appears on the backs of their organdy dresses to reinforce Kennedy's verbal imagery. As in *Funnyhouse*, Kennedy dresses black bodies in white costumes, symbolizing the racial tension fueling her canon, the depressive disparity between desire and reality. Though clad in white, like Sarah's European selves, the seven students are condemned for their blackness. The crimes, for which these girls must suffer, can be traced to menarche—"it started when I became a woman." As in *Funnyhouse*, *Owl*, and *Ohio State Murders*, a biological event is chained to a historical one. Caesar's death and the onset of the girls' menstrual cycle commingle.

The girls are branded conspirators who must perish because they threaten the Greco-Roman (and American) world of white supremacy symbolized by Caesar. As in *Rat's Mass*, the crèche figures, agents of a distorted, white Christianity, join in the condemnation of these black children. "The bleeding started when Jesus and Joseph and Mary, the two wise men, and my shepherd died, and now Caesar" (50). Sharing Kay's fate, these seven students are attacked physically and spiritually because of their black womanhood, another example of the Black Holocaust. Rosemary Curb has tellingly argued that in *Lesson*, a white society, fearful of black fertility, condemns these girls for their capability of bringing more black children into the world.

Such a reading is consistent with seeing *Lesson* in light of the civil rights attack on discrimination based on race as well as gender. Two monumental pieces of civil rights legislation inform *Lesson*. The Supreme Court decision in Brown v. Board of Education (1954) outlawed segregation while the Civil Rights Act of 1964, passed the year *Lesson* debuted, prohibited segregation in public places and further empowered the federal government to enforce this law. But contrary to Brown v. Board of Education and the Civil Rights Act, black students were still forcibly discriminated against. Civil rights legislation guaranteeing equal education was resisted and renounced, most notably by Govs. Orval Faubus in Arkansas, Ross Barnett in Mississippi, and George C. Wallace in Alabama. In 1957, the Little Rock Nine, the first black students to integrate Central High School, were blocked from attending this all-white institution. Wallace, on June 11, 1963 arrogantly stood in front of Foster Auditorium at the University of Alabama to prevent two black students, Vivian Malone and James Hood, from enrolling. In the 1950s and 1960s, the Sovereignty Commission in Mississippi was officially designated as the "segregation watchdog agency" to combat integration, including Lt. Gov. Paul Johnson's denying James Meredith admission to Ole Miss. The repetition of the girls' confession, flowing with Kennedy's blood and guilt imagery, evokes the hate chanting of bigots who spat on, verbally assaulted, and even hurled death threats at black students daring to integrate white schools. Dressed in their finest Sunday organdy dresses, the black students in *Lesson* are similarly disenfranchised in the privileged domain of the white educational system, a bloody lesson many black children learned in the 1950s, 1960s, and well beyond.

Kennedy's schoolroom setting, moreover, becomes a historically appropriate site for her apocalyptic parable about desegregation in the 1950s/1960s. The seven girls, religious as well as educational scapegoats, witness the violence at the intersection of white culture and religion and the African American desire for emancipation and equality. Like many black students bused to formerly all-white schools, Kennedy's seven pupils do not find their classroom a place of belonging, equality, and learning, as civil rights legislation intended. Instead, their schoolroom, like Blake and Kay's chapel home, is metamorphosed from a sanctuary to a prison where students are condemned for committing one of history's most publicized crimes—murdering Caesar. They are unwelcome, outcasts in racial America. Their schoolroom is a ghoulish site where they are shamed simply for being the Other by their teacher, the Great White Dog, the gatekeeper and enforcer of racist codes of education. The girls must *"stand in the aisle, backs to [the audience]* ." They must write one hundred times: *"I killed the white dog"* and *"it was the Ides of March"* (44). Kennedy turns the *"three blackboards"* and the *"imagery tablets"* on which they write into instruments of humiliation for their disobedient actions. At the end of the play, *"Pupils still stand, skirts covered with bright blood, heads hung"* (46).

The girls' homework itself is a further confession of how and why they are accused of being unfit for and unwelcome in the world of white classical education. The numerous references to Caesar and Calphurnia symbolize the girls' perceived complicity in the seminal crime of destroying (polluting) the classics of a white educational system for which they are judged unfit. Similarly, in *The Owl Answers*, Sarah Passmore, a young black student, is spurned by the white patriarchs of English literature—Chaucer, Shakespeare, Tennyson—when she travels to London to seek their blessing. Kennedy's own experiences studying the classics shed revealing light on *Lesson* and its civil rights background. Like these seven black girls, Kennedy recalled that "at 22 I felt excluded from American society. I wasn't aware of it at the time but the themes in Greek classics—loss of heritage, loss of power ... these things meant something to me" (quoted in Pierre 62). Significantly, Kennedy framed her exile in terms of the classical literature she read but which rejected black pupils who sought entry into white schools. But, ironically, while the White Dog denies these black girls the right to learn and to profess the classics, Adrienne Kennedy distinguished herself in high school as an excellent Latin student and went on to write adaptations of the Orestes and Electra myths, as dramatized by Euripides, and *Oedipus Rex* itself. The ultimate biographical victory of *Lesson*, then, is that Kennedy herself overcame the language of bigotry.

3

One of Kennedy's most provocative plays, *Sleep Deprivation Chamber*, examines the dynamics of racial violence in urban America in the 1990s. Her title tropes the hallucinatory atmosphere of her entire canon. The spirit of Emmett Till, whose name Kennedy invokes at the beginning of *Sleep*, presides over the play as a young black boy (age 14) who had suffered because of the ghastly cruelty of the white legal system. An intensely autobiographical work, *Sleep* is based upon a nightmare her son and co-author Adam (called Teddy Alexander in the play) experienced after being stopped by an Arlington, Virginia police officer on January 11, 1991 for a missing tail light and was then falsely charged with resisting arrest and attacking an officer. Speaking to Mr. Edelstein, Teddy's defense counsel in *Sleep*, the prosecuting attorney, Ms. Wagner, contends that "Officer Holzer pursued your client for three blocks with his lights and siren on and then chased him down a dead-end street. Mr. Alexander was belligerent and hostile and then assaulted Office Holzer. The charge is clear-cut and we are very confident that the court will return a guilty verdict" (38). Teddy and his mother (Suzanne, Kennedy's persona and alter ego) countered that Teddy is innocent. In a letter to Gov. Wilder of Virginia, Suzanne pointed out that "my son ... was knocked to the ground and beaten in the face, kicked repeatedly in the chest and stomach and dragged in the mud by an Arlington policeman ... This occurred in his father's front yard on Riverdale Street ... The Arlington police arrested my son, then concocted a totally false story and charges" (11).

In the pounding stichomythia of conflicting testimonies running throughout the play, Kennedy unravels the competing cultural memories at work in *Sleep*. As in her earlier plays, she excavates different ways of remembering history. The way the dominant white (legal) culture recalls an event—the arrest of Teddy Alexander—is very different from the way an African American family remembers the same incident. While white memory perpetuates the disenfranchisement of black men and women, stripping away their legal and sexual agency, for Suzanne and her African American family, the memory of her son beaten by the Arlington police is treacherous, "just as surely as [what] happened in the Deep South in the 1930s or during Emmett Till's time" (*Sleep* 8).

Characteristic of Kennedy's works from the 1960s and 1970s as well, *Sleep* immerses audiences in a nightmarish blur of history and fantasy. It is a "read-through sleep," to use an illuminating phrase from Arielle Greenberg's poem "Sleep Deprived Manifesto" (2006). Steeped in jurisprudence, blood, and madness, *Sleep* incorporates a series of documents related to the case—numerous letters from Suzanne on behalf of Teddy to county, state, and federal officials, painful excerpts from testimony taken from Teddy and Holzer at the trial—along with dream sequences from Suzanne's nightmares, student reading of a bigoted police manual, and scenes from a production of Shakespeare's *Hamlet* Teddy is directing at Antioch College. Although set in a suburb of Washington, D. C. and on a college campus in Ohio, *Sleep* forces us into Kennedy's hallucinatory world of fright and revenge. The historical (legal process, space, people) mixes with the surreal (dreams, projections of self into literary scripts, terrifying imagery), a pattern shaping *People* and dramatized in *Funnyhouse, The Owl Answers*, and *Motherhood 2000* (1994).

In one dream sequence, for example, Suzanne sees Teddy standing in Yorick's grave, a victim of the Hamlet-like madness infecting Arlington. Several times Teddy describes how Holzer "struck me in my face with his hand or with a flashlight and knocked me to the ground [and] the sucker punched me" (18), adding that, "The officer was pushing me on top of the car and because I had been kicked in the chest I had a very difficult time breathing ..." (33). This is the stuff out of which nightmares are made. Again and again, as we hear testimony or listen to Suzanne's letters, we are trapped in the torture chamber of the mind. Police brutality has murdered sleep. After giving pre-trial testimony, Teddy panics: "As I sat in that chair, my mind filled with every graphic image of prison life. Every prison movie, prison documentary and prison story I had ever seen or heard blanketed my thoughts and sent absolute horror and fear to my heart" (19). Suzanne sums up the nightmare feeling of a black mother caught in prejudiced white history—"I kept dreaming of suffocation" (20). Violence is the language in which Kennedy's characters cry for justice.

The events in *Sleep* (and the layers of terror in which they are submerged) are scripted immediately out of travesties of civil rights in contemporary America. Yet at its deepest level, the violence that engulfs the Alexanders, a prominent and influential African American family, is rooted in the memory of police brutality of earlier decades. The beating that Teddy received at the hands of a corrupt Arlington police officer looks back to Jim Crow law and order that blacks encountered at sit-ins and protest marches in the 1950s/1960s—whips, water hosings, billyclubs, ferocious dogs, Bull Connor's Birmingham. This is the police violence, triggered by white racial anxiety, that has invaded African American nightmares for centuries. As the embodiment of a punishing white historical force, the Arlington Police Department posed a seemingly unconquerable threat for the Alexanders. Edelstein, who prosecuted policemen before, warns Suzanne, "I do not think in the end it will come out fairly." Unfortunately, too, Teddy's mother knows that "Few people win cases against the police" (25). Patrice, Teddy's sister, similarly worries that though her brother may be able to bypass a trial by a judge, "Juries in the eastern district of Virginia tend to side with the police" (39). *Sleep* challenges the *status quo ante* of protecting unjust empowerment.

On another level, Kennedy's play decries the horrors of racial profiling, highly publicized in the 1990s, that singled out black drivers to be stopped and questioned more often than white ones and to receive much harsher treatment. *Sleep* attacks highway apartheid. Two earlier incidents of racial profiling threaded into *Sleep* put Holzer's white-sanctioned crime into an unequivocal civil rights context. In one of the non-trial scenes interspersed throughout *Sleep*, Teddy stands on stage directing a group of student actors who read descriptions from a police manual that exemplify racial profiling. In a series of short, alternating lines, labeled "Blacks" or "Whites," students recite from the manual: "Blacks: Common use of threats to gain respect and fear from others" while we hear "Whites: Posture is 'Do not make threats unless you are prepared to carry them out'" (26). Or, in another example, "Blacks: Public acting up especially when confronted by authority" as opposed to "Whites: Respect for authority" (24). The police manual is a damnable script for a color-coded system of justice Kennedy protests.

In another pre-trial scene, reversing these stereotypes as well as dramatizing an earlier instance of racial profiling, Teddy remembers that when he and his cousin were in Los Angles and asked the police for directions, the two young black men were accosted by white officers. "Get the fuck out of the car, niggers," yells one policeman. Then "the officers pull Teddy and his cousin out of the car and threw them against the wall" (50). Asking what they are doing in this white part of town, the "officer pulls out his gun and places it against Teddy's temple," shouting, "Nigger, I'll blow your head off. Where did you get the Jaguar," which belonged to Teddy's cousin who lives in Beverly Hills. The officer then "*violently body searches Teddy. He grabs him under his testicles and in the crevice of his buttocks several times*" and screams, "Beverly Hills? You niggers better not be lying" (50). This incident in Los Angeles, which foreshadows Holzer's treatment of Teddy in Arlington, underscores the perversion of civil rights African Americans have suffered. Black men have been victimized by the police and the media who together have repeatedly commodified their bodies as erotic and lawless sites to be interrogated, contained, and disciplined, the more violently the better. Following this formula for racial profiling, lynching-style justice in 1990s America, the white officers who stopped Teddy and his cousin saw them not as law-abiding citizens innocently asking for directions but as de facto felons who deserved to be intimidated and sexually violated simply because they were black.

A widely publicized case of police brutality occurring a few years before *Sleep* was staged provides a historical antecedent for Teddy's nightmare ("Human Rights Watch"). Rodney King, a black man, was beaten by four white officers in Los Angeles in 1992, for failing to stop after being pursued. This case, and the bloody incidents it spawned, became the subject of Anna Deavere Smith's widely praised and performed play *Twilight: Los Angeles 1992*. Like many victims of racial profiling, King was cited for non-compliance, a charge leveled against Teddy as well. The police brutality King suffered was videotaped, as was Teddy's, eliciting national horror. Reflecting the same righteousness for her son's vindication, Suzanne stresses the importance of the tape to Edelstein, "But what about the videotape that Teddy's father took of the event?" (25). Unfortunately, Edelstein claims, it is "dark and it has only the very end of the incident. You must get hold of your emotions" (25). The four officers in the King case were acquitted by a jury in April 1992, a decision that precipitated riots in east Los Angeles with 54 murders and over 13,000 arrests. Like the Los Angeles policemen in 1992, Holzer also evaded conviction, getting a verbal slap from the judge—"I hold police officers to a higher standard" (72)—for an offense that warranted far greater punishment. Ultimately, though, King's case, like Teddy's, was victorious, for three of the Los Angeles police officers were convicted, and Adam Kennedy subsequently won a civil suit against Arlington, Virginia. To be sure, there are significant legal differences between the two events/cases. But what happened to Rodney King in Los Angeles serves as a cultural template for the police brutality that victimizes the Alexanders (Kennedys) in *Sleep*. History and nightmares are indivisible another time in Kennedy.

Beyond question, Adrienne Kennedy stands as one of the most daring African American women playwrights for both her dramatic techniques and her representation of history. Her complex and provocative canon of experimental plays has influenced subsequent generations of playwrights, female and male, white and black, from Ntozake Shange to Tony Kushner (Vorlicky). Because of her haunting poetry, non-linear, looping plots, and tragically grotesque heroines, Kennedy has prompted numerous playwrights to think differently about time, place, and character (Kolin, "Revisiting *Funnyhouse*" 167). But also worth our attention, as this essay has argued, is her sustained commitment to publicize the horrors of civil rights that have plunged her characters into a phantasmagoric world of self-doubts, betrayals, and tortures—the consequences of being black in a prejudiced America. When Kennedy thinks of racial crimes in white America, she has remembered, and dramatized, the nightmares of its black victims, past and present.

Note

1 Except for *Sleep Deprivation Chamber*, all page references to Kennedy's plays were to *The Adrienne Kennedy Reader*, edited and listed under Sollors, Wener.

Works cited

Armstrong, Lisa. "*Funnyhouse*." *New York Amsterdam News* (2 February 2006).

Baraka, Amiri. *Dutchman and The Slave*. New York: Morrow/Apollo, 1964.

Barnes, Clive. "*A Rat's Mass* Weaves Drama of Poetry Fabric." *New York Times* (1 November 1969): 24.

Bean, Anne-Marie. "Introduction." *A Sourcebook of African American Performance: People, Plays, Movements*. New York: Routledge, 1999.

Brown, E. Barnsley. "Passed Over: The Tragic Mulatta and (Dis)integration of Identity in Adrienne Kennedy's Plays." *African American Review* 35 (Summer 2001): 281–96.

Byrant-Jackson, and Lois Overbeck, eds. *Intersecting Boundaries: The Plays of Adrienne Kennedy*. New York: University of Minnesota Press, 1992.

Childress, Alice. *Trouble in Mind*. In *Black Drama in America: An Anthology*. Darwin T. Turner, ed. Washington: Howard University Press, 1971. 75–133.

Curb, Rosemary. "'Lesson I Bleed': Adrienne Kennedy's Blood Rites." *Women in American Theatre*. Helen Krich Chinoy and Linda Walsh Jenkins, eds. New York: Crown, 1981. 50–7.

Cummings, Scott T. "Theatre: Invisible Career: Adrienne Kennedy Steps into the Lights." *Boston Phoenix* (31 March–6 April 2000): 7.

Fanon, Frantz. *Black Skin, White Masks*. New York: Grove, 1967.

Goldsby, Jacqueline. *A Spectacular Secret: Lynching in American Life and Literature*. Chicago: University of Chicago Press, 2006.

Greenberg, Arielle. "Sleep Deprived Manifesto" (poem). *Denver Quarterly* 41.1. (2006): 41.

Grimké, Angelina Weld. *Rachel: A Play in Three Acts: 1920*. College Park, MD: McGrath, 1999.

Hansberry, Lorraine. "Lynchsong." http://www.americanlynching.com/literary-old.html#hansberry. Accessed December 20, 2006.

—— *Raisin in the Sun*. New York: Prentice Hall, 1994.

Hawthorne, Greta McCullom. *Black Holocaust in 1984: An Alternative*. New York: Hearthstone, 1980.

Human Rights Watch. "Los Angeles: Background." http://www.hrw.org/reports98/police/uspo72.htm. Accessed November 10, 2006.

Jones, Del. *The Black Holocaust: Global Genocide*. Philadelphia: Del Jones Communications Unlimited, 1992.

Jones, Suzanne W. *Race Mixing: Southern Fiction Since the Sixties*. Baltimore: Johns Hopkins University Press, 2004.

Kennedy, Adrienne. *People Who Led to My Plays*. New York: Knopf, 1987.

Kennedy, Adrienne with Kennedy, Adam. *Sleep Deprivation Chamber*. New York: Theatre Communications Group, 1996. ——

Sollers, Werner, ed. *The Adrienne Kennedy Reader*. Minneapolis: University of Minnesota Press, 2001.

King, Martin Luther. *Words that Changed a Nation* 1963. http://transcripts.cnn.com/TRANSCRIPTS/0702/17/siu.html. Accessed February 7, 2007.

Kolin, Philip. "Revisiting *Funnyhouse* : An Interview with Billie Allen." *African American Review* 41.1 (Spring 2007): 165–75.

——"Tennessee Willliams's '*Big Black: A Mississippi Idyll*' and Race Relations, 1931." RE:AL 20.2 (Fall 1995): 8–12.

—— *Understanding Adrienne Kennedy*. Columbia: University of South Carolina Press, 2005.

Komunyakaa, Yusef. "Tu Du Street." *Contemporary American Poetry*. A. Poulin, Jr. and Michael Waters, eds. Boston: Houghton Mifflin, 2006. 268.

Leverette, Tru. "Travelling Identities: Mixed Race and Fran Rosso's *Oreo*." *African American Review* 40.1 (Spring 2006): 79–91.

Margolick, David. *Biography of a Song* : "Strange Fruit." New York: Harper Collins, 2001.

Matthews, Donald. "The Southern Rite of Human Sacrifice." *Journal of Southern Religion* 3 (2000): http://jsr.fsu.edu/matthews.htm. Rpt. in *Black History Bulletin*. 65.3–4 (1 December 2002): 20–48.

Metress, Christopher, ed. *The Lynching of Emmett Till: A Documentary Narrative*. Charlottesville: University of Virginia Press, 2002.

Omni, Michael and Howard Winnant. *Racial Formation in the United States from the 1960s to the 1980s*. New York: Routledge, 1989.

Pierre, Karly. "Adrienne Kennedy Hears Ancient Voices." *American Theatre* (October 2000): 62.

Powell, A. D. "Where Are Lousiana's 'Race Flagging' Files?" *The Multiracial Activist*. July–October 2005. www.multiracial.com/site/content/view/38/37/. Accessed December 2, 2006.

Robinson, Charles F. *Dangerous Liaisons: Sex and Love in the Segregated South*. Fayetteville: University of Arkansas Press, 2003.

Sivils, Matthew Wynn. "Reading Trees in Southern Literature." *Southern Quarterly* 44.1 (2006): 88–102.

"Six Dead After Church Bombing." *Washington Post* (16 Sept. 1963). WashingtonPost.com/wpsiv/national/longterm/churches/archives1.htm. Accessed September 20, 2006.

Smith, Anna Deavere *Twilight: Los Angeles, 1992*. New York: Dramatists Play Service, 2003.

Tapley, Mel. "*Funnyhouse of a Negro* Reveals America's Obesessions." *New York Amsterdam News* (September 30, 1995): 21.

Till-Mobley, Mamie and Barr, David III. *The Face of Emmett Till*. Woodstock, Il: Dramatic Publishing Company, 2006.

Vorlicky, Robert. "Blood Relations: Adrienne Kennedy and Tony Kushner." *Tony Kushner: New Essays on the Art and Politics of the Plays*. James Fisher, ed. Jefferson City, NC: McFarland, 2006. 41–55.

Wells, Ida B. *On Lynching: Southern Horrors, the Red Record, and Mob Rule in New Orleans*. Manchester, New Hampshire: Ayer, 1990.

Werner, Craig. *Playing the Changes: From Afro-modernism to the Jazz Impulse*. Urbana: University of Illinois Press, 1994.

Williams, Tennessee. "Big Black: A Mississippi Idyll". In Tennessee Williams: Collected Stories. New York: New Directions, 1931.

—— *Sweet Bird of Youth*. In *The Theatre of Tennessee Williams*. Vol. 4. New York: New Directions, 1971.

Wood, Jacqueline. "Weight of the Mask: Parody and the Heritage of Minstrelsy in Adrienne Kennedy's *Funnyhouse of a Negro*." *Journal of Dramatic Theory and Criticism* 17 (Spring 2003): 5–24.

6 "Boogie woogie landscapes"

The dramatic/poetic collage of Ntozake Shange

James Fisher

In February 2006, poet and playwright Malick Browne's *Real Black Men Don't Sit Cross-legged on the Floor: A Collage in Blues* opened at New York's Abrons Arts Center, depicting in an "impressionistic collection of events and images" the "African-American experience." Described favorably by *New York Times* critic Andrea Stevens as reminiscent of *for colored girls who have considered suicide/when the rainbow is enuf* (1975), a poetic work which presented "the tribulations and few triumphs of being black and female in a bigoted world" (Stevens B3), *Real Black Men* owes much to this source. Similar to *for colored girls* in its use of a small ensemble cast and its depiction of the experience of African American history in a visceral, as well as intellectually and emotionally challenging, theatrical experience, *Real Black Men* is one of many non-traditional dramatic works inspired, in part, by *for colored girls*. Ntozake Shange (1948–), author of *for colored girls*, pioneered a new dramatic form in her first produced "choreopoem," a bold mixture of character, poetry, song, and dance which might more accurately be labeled a dramatic/poetic collage, an expression conveying the unique mixture of language, theatre, movement, and music that has become more the rule than the exception in theatrical explorations of the experiences of black Americans. Without question, the influence of *for colored girls* is far-reaching and enduring, not only to black artists but throughout American theatre in general.

The appearance of black women dramatists on the U.S. stage did not truly begin until the middle of the twentieth century, but the evolution in dramatic style resulting from the accomplishments of black women playwrights contributed to revolutionary changes in American theatre after 1960. Lorraine Hansberry's *A Raisin in the Sun* (1959), the first play by an African American woman to win critical and commercial success on Broadway, is also the first play featuring black characters and their concerns to be embraced not only by black audiences, but by predominantly white Broadway audiences. Hansberry's universal reach results, in part, from both the tolerance plea she makes and the fact that her style is, to mid-twentieth century audiences, a familiar one. Striking a carefully considered balance between what Diana Adesola Mafe describes as "the 'universal' and the 'particular'" (Mafe 30), Hansberry invites white audiences into the world of the racial "Other," humanizing black culture and promoting tolerance. Her mastery of realistic/naturalistic devices gives way to an overtly poetic style evident in the work of the most significant African American women dramatists of the nearly fifty years since her appearance, Adrienne Kennedy, Alice Childress, Suzan-Lori Parks, and Shange. These and other black women playwrights present visions of the African American experience less concerned with universal tolerance pleas, instead turning inward to depict the particularities of each author's experience of life within a racially divided society. Adopting poetic voices (and some, like Shange, employing song and dance), black women dramatists craft highly individual modes of expression through which they reveal the emotional and intellectual texture of being black in late twentieth century America. Although Kennedy was assailed over the perception that she presents blackness as a negative, her nightmarish poetic dreamscapes have slowly won appreciation even if her plays have been less understood and appreciated by non-blacks. Shange, who was profoundly influenced by Kennedy, broke through racial parochialism with *for colored girls* (1975), a work similar to Kennedy's in a dramaturgical approach radically different from the Hansberry model.

Born Paulette Linda Williams in Trenton, New Jersey, to a surgeon and social worker, Shange experienced a comparatively comfortable early life, much like that of Hansberry, who was to some extent similarly shielded from the worst excesses of racism. However, when Shange's family moved to St. Louis and she was bused to a German–American school as part of Southern desegregation laws, she first encountered racist attitudes, experiences later chronicled in her novel *Betsey Brown* (1985). Despite discouragements from racist teachers, Shange excelled in literature, influenced by white American authors including Mark Twain and Herman Melville, but also the major black writers of the Harlem Renaissance, most especially Zora Neale Hurston, who Shange would later describe as a literary foremother. Shange graduated with honors from Barnard College in 1970 and went on to complete a graduate degree in American Studies at UCLA in 1973. Experiencing bouts of depression during her college years, resulting in part from an unhappy first marriage, she recognized in herself a deep-seated anger over racism and the secondary status of women in American life. Renaming herself Ntozake Shange, a name derived from the Xhosa language, she fully embraced her African heritage. Ntozake, translated as "she who comes with her own things," and Shange, meaning "one who walks like a line," proved apt names for a young artist innovating dramatic depictions of the racial divide in the U.S.A.

Following graduation from UCLA, Shange taught literature and culture at different universities and danced with several companies, including the Third World Collective, Raymond Sawyer's Afro-American Dance Company, and the West Coast Dance Company, experimenting with integrating poetry with movement. In collaboration with Halifu Osumare's

The Spirit of Dance, Shange crafted a theatre piece on the origins of black dance in West Africa before establishing her own troupe, prophetically named For Colored Girls Who Have Considered Suicide. A year after her UCLA graduation, Shange completed seven poems modeled on Judy Grahn's *The Common Woman* (1969), in which she depicts a range of experiences and emotions of black women (all nameless), and these poems became the pattern from which she designed the dramatic/poetic collage of *for colored girls*. Throughout her writing life, Shange would frequently publish poetry, often later adapting it to the stage, as with *The Love Space Demands: A Continuing Saga* (1987). A work in three parts, with the second (*The Love Space Demands*) and the third (*I Heard Eric Dolphy In His Eyes*) constructed in dramatic form. More a performance piece than a play, it was performed with three musicians and three actors/dancers exploring what Shange describes as the space between reality and possibility. More importantly, this combination of poetry, music, dance, and theatrical embellishments was a continuation of experimentation that took shape in *for colored girls*.

for colored girls began its stage life off-Broadway at New York's Studio Rivbea on July 7, 1975, where it met with critical approval. The production transferred to the Public Theatre on June 1, 1976, and moved on to Broadway's Booth Theatre on September 15 of that same year. In all, *for colored girls* gave an impressive 867 performances in New York, leading to a cast album and a PBS-TV "American Playhouse" film in 1982. *for colored girls* won numerous honors, including an Obie Award, an Outer Critics Award, an Audelco Award, and a Mademoiselle Award, as well as nominations for a Tony Award, a Grammy for the cast album, and an Emmy for the television film.

What is surprising about the success of *for colored girls* is that Shange assaults gender and sexual barriers, as well as racial ones, to present a portrait of black womanhood for black women. And despite these largely uncharted themes in the history of American drama, *for colored girls* was embraced by an audience well beyond its intended demographic. The play's success is even more surprising considering the fact that many critics described *for colored girls* as more poetry than drama, and Shange as more poet than dramatist. Poetic drama has rarely found a receptive audience in U.S. drama. There is little doubt that Shange's work is entirely its own thing, and perhaps achieves universality through its uniqueness and specificity, and through a merging of various forms of expression creating a new form. *for colored girls* is as much poetry as drama, as much dance as theatre, as much music as language. The merger of poetry with drama (or dance with theatre, or music with language) is not new—theatre history reveals frequent mergers of some or all of these components. However, Shange's choreopoetic amalgam of these components, like Kennedy's dramatic dream spheres, displays originality in its use of these eternal tools as a liberation of emotional complexities and human circumstances from the confines of either realistic drawing rooms or the self-conscious theatricalisms of Brechtian epic theatre. Shange crafted a new form to fit her themes and to develop a language to speak to her target audience.

Shange's achievement as a dramatist spreads across thirty-plus years and her subsequent plays have generally received mixed reviews, with critics divided over this choreopoetic style and some of Shange's themes, particularly what was seen as her harsh depiction of black men. The variety of Shange's work, including adaptations of plays by Bertolt Brecht, British playwright Willy Russell (whose themes often center around the struggles of working class women), and her own novels and poetry, remains consistent in melding lyrical language, theatrical elements, dance, and music to examine particularities of black life with an unwavering emphasis on the experiences of young black women. As Martin Gottfried wrote at the time of the premiere of *for colored girls*, the:

> essence of the show remains its pure and perfectly captured blackness. Black language, black mannerisms, black tastes and black feelings have never been so completely and artistically presented in a Broadway theatre except for Melvin van Peebles's *Ain't No Way to Die a Natural Death* [sic]. This is truth, energy and strength, theatre on the highest level, musical and choreographic to its roots.
>
> (Gottfried 201)

This sentiment was expanded on by Clive Barnes, who enthused that *for colored girls* "could very easily have made me feel guilty at being white and male. It didn't. It made me feel proud at being a member of the human race, and with the joyous discovery that a white man can have black sisters" (Barnes 4).

That none of Shange's post-*for colored girls* drama has achieved anything approaching the widespread popular response it received suggests that there is some particular aspect of her first produced play that touches audiences, in both its content and its originality of presentation, that is not present in subsequent plays. However, this may not be the case, for all of Shange's plays, some superior in quality to *for colored girls*, offer variations on its themes and are similarly addressed to an audience of black women. She has seldom strayed from the concerns of young black women coming of age, relations among black women (and women in general), racism in America, and the complex struggle of blacks, male or female, within that society to attain self-actualization. An examination of Shange's work reveals that she is, as she described herself, "a poet or writer/rather than a playwright" (*Three Pieces* ix), and although there is much truth in this, Shange's dramatic achievement reveals a writer whose exploration of the borders between drama and poetry is singular, not to mention influential, within contemporary American theatre.

for colored girls was initially performed in cafés and poetry centers in California before Shange and choreographer Paula Moss brought it to

New York for performances at the Studio Rivbea where its reception led to successful runs at the Public Theatre and on Broadway. The seven actress/dancers who performed *for colored girls* are identified by the colors of a rainbow that pointedly includes brown among its hues. Shange stresses that the play's title identifies the audience she was speaking to and for, young black women of color. Aiming to provide guidance in the complex transition from adolescence to womanhood for this target audience, Shange concludes that their lives and experiences have not previously been explored in dramatic terms, a point she makes at the beginning of *for colored girls*: "somebody/anybody/sing a black girl's song/bring her out/to know herself/to know you/but sing her rhythms/carin/struggle/hard times/sing her song of life/she's been dead so long/closed in silence so long/she doesn't know the sound/of her own voice/her infinite beauty" (*for colored girls* 2).

The other portion of the play's title, *when the rainbow is enuf*, is similarly informative. The rainbow, a wonder of color following a storm, binds Shange's work to Hansberry, who uses a rainbow metaphor in *A Raisin in the Sun* to describe Walter Lee Younger's coming into his manhood following a painful journey of self-discovery. Shange appropriates Hansberry's metaphor, but it is used for the women of *for colored girls* who transcend the silence that protects them and makes them invisible (and is thus a form of oppression) and uses pain to build a new strength and bond of sisterhood from their shared experiences. As Neil A. Lester writes, the rainbow symbolism is "a visual manifestation of women's spiritual beauty and eventual self-actualization. That a rainbow is not monochromatic by definition affirms the diversity of black females' experiences socially, culturally, and individually" (Lester 26).

For Shange's women, a positive identity is achieved through their "sexuality, spirituality, and pride" (Mafe 44), coupled with resistance to the oppressions inherent in stereotypical images of black women, not to mention women of all races. Shange's emphasis on performance is, in and of itself, an expression of that sexuality, spirituality, and pride, and the original production of *for colored girls* mirrored the triumph of black women performers within American theatre, calling to mind artists like Ethel Waters, who effortlessly mastered song, dance, and dramatic expression in a time when being a black woman otherwise placed her at the bottom of the socio-economic pecking order. Deborah R. Geis writes that Shange's use of choreopoetic monologues is a means to place "the narrative weight of a play upon its spoken language and upon the performances of the individual actors" (Geis 210) and, as such, is essential to understanding Shange's dramatic mission. Geis stresses Shange's emphasis on the performative qualities of monologue in liberating the actors so that they might offer more than one character and experience, embracing a "storytelling" approach, each woman in the ensemble may contribute from a position of individual performance strength, whether in song, dance, acting, or any combination of these areas.

Critics chided Shange for a lack of traditional character development in *for colored girls*, as well as her subsequent works, but they miss a central point of her overall achievement by failing to recognize that she consciously chooses to eschew realistic approaches to character or structure, as does Kennedy, in order to achieve a more free-flowing means of merging the emotional terrain of young black women with essentially non-realistic means of expressing it through dance, music, and poetry. More significantly, the unidentified figures in *for colored girls* suggest a further liberation, one from the representational demands of the well-worn realistic/naturalistic stage. As Elizabeth Brown-Guillory simply states it, "Shange's theatre pieces generally do not conform to traditional dramatic structure" (96–7), and those critics unable or unwilling to accept her work as "theatre" or "drama" on her terms miss the fact of her transformation, or transmutation, of familiar performance techniques to suit her ends. Shange's dramatic/poetic collage grows out of an intentioned avoidance of a too rigid structure for, as John Timpane writes, she insists on "the rough edge, the open, the fragment" (Timpane 203), which, among other things, ties her creations to Kennedy's and is part of the inspiration she herself supplies subsequent dramatists, especially Pulitzer Prize winner Suzan-Lori Parks.

Thematically, Shange is intently focused on the progression of young, vulnerable women from childhood innocence and fear to a womanhood informed by experiences both positive and negative. Their strength emerges from a triumph over suffering and rejection, but also from the joy of adolescent wonder and sisterhood. There is an emphasis on complex and contradictory feelings about coming-of-age, but also on confusing feelings regarding love, sex, and rejection, of "not being wanted/when I wanted to be wanted," and growing past such feelings. One of the women, who has risen above the despair of rejection, speaks of her former lover, saying, "this note is attached to a plant/i've been waterin since the day i met you/you may water it/yr damn self" (*for colored girls* 10). Beyond this, darker currents emerge in accounts of date rape, as well as other forms of oppression, and in these areas the play generated controversy.

Some critics questioned Shange's "perceived attack upon the chauvinism of males" (Hill and Hatch 401), particularly black males, in *for colored girls*. Even other playwrights, including women of color, rebutted *for colored girls* in their own works, including Angela Jackson, whose play, *Shango Diaspora: An African-American Myth of Womanhood and Love* (1982), insists that *for colored girls* "was not meant to create healthy dialogue between the sexes, but was presented in such a psychotic manner as to foster animosity … and divide the African family" (cited in Hill and Hatch 426). The vehemence of Jackson's reaction, and that of several critics, suggests that Shange touched a raw nerve on both sides of the racial and gender divides, but an over-emphasis on Shange's depiction of men in *for colored girls* overlooks her true achievement on several levels, one of which includes reclamation of black-inspired music and dance as an African American heritage.

There is little doubt that *for colored girls* is a potent forerunner of "def" poetry and rap music, as well as subsequent theatrical works including *Bring in Da Noise, Bring in Da Funk* (1996) and Suzan-Lori Parks's *Top Dog/Underdog* (2002), and Parks's subsequent plays, as well as Tony Kushner's *Caroline, or Change* (2003), which features a black woman character as its protagonist, using musical idioms from both black and white cultures (composed by Jeanine Tesori) to explore the emotional turbulence within the battered, bitter soul of a thirty-five year-old black maid working for a white Jewish family in Louisiana at the critical historical juncture of John F. Kennedy's assassination, the Civil Rights movement, and the escalating conflict in Vietnam. Shange's achievement also stems from her intent to depict "unexpressed experiences held in the hearts by many black women" (Hill and Hatch 426), which Parks and Kushner, in their highly individual ways, do as well.

Male stories are by no means Shange's concern beyond the impact of men on the lives of her young women characters, although in later works she offers more varied portraits of black males, finding in them emotions similar to those of her women. In *for colored girls*, however, black males, as well as the domination of white society, provide major obstacles for Shange's women, and she lambasts all of them in a stream of commentary on the resulting diminishment of the human spirit, as when "lady in blue" says, "when i walked in the pacific/i imagined waters ancient from accra/tunis cleansin me/feedin me/now my ankles are coated in grey filth/from the puddle neath the hydrant [...] i usedta live in the world/now i live in harlem and my universe is six blocks" (*for colored girls* 28). This diminishment results from economic deprivation, degradation, fear, confinement, and the resulting general erosion of hope, but also from more immediate oppressions including rape and other forms of violence.

Suicide, as directly suggested by the play's title, is also a concern in *for colored girls*. Shange's women consider it as an option, but suicide is a solution to be rejected in favor of finding strength of spirit through expression as a means of escaping the oppression that implanted thoughts of suicide in the first place. As the "lady in red" makes clear of her individual triumph over adversity and her personal journey of self-awareness, "i found god in myself/and i loved her/i loved her fiercely" (*for colored girls* 51). Any triumph of spirit is darkened by imminent dangers in *for colored girls*, but facing and surviving those dangers, and containing and controlling them by expressing them, is the path to womanhood Shange charts.

Black women dramatists since Hansberry deal with these subjects to a greater or lesser extent, but Shange is most closely related to Kennedy, who similarly creates a dramatic/poetic space for her metaphysical travelers, dream walkers who break through a membrane of racial and personal history, wandering through a nightmarish no man's land where shards of black experience and individual despair are illuminated. Shange's use of dance, and other non-realistic elements like those evident in Kennedy's harrowing dreamspheres, is aimed at establishing a "freedom to move in space, to demand of my own sweat a perfection that could continually be approached, though never known, waz poem to me, my body and mind ellipsing" (*for colored girls* ix).

Shange's innovative structure, coupled with her introduction of themes of rape, abortion, drug use, child abuse, and corporate and state sanctioned racism, remains consistent throughout her work, even as she expands her creative template. One consistent concern is Shange's resistance to working in the realm of commercial theatre, although, ironically, the Broadway success of *for colored girls* meant that mainstream theatre more frequently makes use of Shange-style nonlinear structures and similarly merges various performative elements with an awareness of play as play, moving past the didacticism of Brecht's epic theatre and the technological spectacle of Robert Wilson. Shange's discomfort with the presentation of *for colored girls* on Broadway, which she herself performed in, resulted from a general mistrust in the commodification of artistic endeavor, but especially from the fact that by placing the play in a Broadway theatre, with its significantly higher ticket prices, it was being taken away from economically deprived black women, the audience for whom Shange had created it in the first place. Her concern is no affectation, for to Shange creative success can only be achieved outside the realm of commercialism and by speaking to and for those without an officially sanctioned cultural voice. As Maxine, in Shange's *spell* #7, says, "as a child i took on the burden of easing the ghost-colored folks' souls and trying hard to keep up with the affairs of my own colored world" (*Three Pieces* 50). Like Kennedy, Shange intends to keep her attention on her "own colored world."

In presenting that world, Shange treads a fine line because of the particularity and techniques of her work. *for colored girls* found a universal audience like Hansberry, but the parallel in their work is that it might aptly be described as universal because it is particular. Hansberry, in a 1961 interview, dispensed with the "universality" issue, stressing that "we don't notice the Englishness of a Shakespearean fool while we're being entertained and educated by his wisdom; the experience just happens" (Bigsby 92), a notion with which Shange might have sympathy, for her aim of speaking directly to young black women does not exclude non-black women or, for that matter, men. The wisdom of her women is there for all to receive, but Shange cares only to speak directly to women of color. The mobility and newness of Shange's dramatic/poetic collage allows this universality to grow from the basic human need for expression of experience. Shange culls many aspects of literary, mythical, and performance traditions, as Carol Allen writes:

> from ancient myths (African, early English, and Greek), new-world myths (tall tales, slave narratives, literary/dramatic hybrids, and frontier narratives) to historical pageants, passion plays, African masking rituals, and expressionistic drama. To these ingredients, African-American

women writers add their own panache and healthy store of culturally specific aesthetics (shout outs, dance moves, emotionally laden epiphanies, advance and retreat, comedy, and sensuality).

(Allen 255)

In doing so, Shange strives to tap into the fundamental human need to understand the self through the imitative arts, a point she underscores in discussing her approach to writing, which, she notes, is a:

cerebral activity. For me it is a very rhythmic and visceral experience. Dance clears my mind of verbal images and allows me to understand the planet the way I imagine atomic particles experience space. I am not bogged down with the implications of language. I am only involved in the implication of movement which later on, when I do start to write, become manifest in the rhythms of my poetry.

(Betsko 365)

Allen omits mention of white appropriation of black performance traditions, but Shange exhibits a keen awareness of the legacy of blackface and minstrelsy, practices at once an oppression and a celebration of African American creativity. Leaping ahead chronologically, but importantly in understanding the evolution of Shange's work, *spell #7: a geechee quick magic trance manual* (1978), makes overt reference to the minstrel tradition through the presence of a large blackface mask that dominates the scene, as she describes in her stage directions, an image intended to encourage the audience to "integrate this grotesque, larger than life representation of life" (*Three Pieces* 7) into their response, for, as Karen Cronacher writes, the minstrel mask was and is "a sign of white domination in the field of entertainment" and Shange's mask is a reminder of a range of racial stereotypes typified by minstrelsy which she subverts to address different "racial, cultural, political, and class" (Cronacher 177) experiences. To this end, Shange also appropriates a minstrel show structure, including an interlocutor, lou the magician, who engages in patter with the ensemble of performers, but also provides commentary and perspective. lou, the progeny of a family of "retired sorcerers/active houngans and pennyante fortune tellers" (*Three Pieces* 8), recounts that his father was once asked by an unhappy black child to make him white, but lou's father insists "aint no colored magician in his right mind/gonna make you white/I mean/this is blk magic/you lookin at/and I'm fixin you up good and colored/and you gonna be colored all yr life/and you gonna love it/being colored/all yr life" (*Three Pieces* 8).

spell #7 proceeds to explore this overarching theme through characters identified as "actor," "actress," "dancer," etc., all joined together to debate relations between black women and men, their work as artists, and their place in American society. The characters learn to embrace their racial heritage within the context of what they have suffered in a white-ruled society, a theme carried over from *for colored girls*. It is, in its essence, the overarching theme of all of Shange's work, whether she is examining it through the experiences of young black women, as in *for colored girls*, or as she finds it in slavery, the great progenitor of racial conflict in America, and its theatrical legacy in minstrelsy. Like Anna Deveare Smith's *Fire in the Mirror* (1990), focusing on the Crown Heights riots, *spell #7* offers discordant vignettes of racial strife in a white-dominated society. Also, Shange reconsiders the blackface tradition in the way August Wilson applies jazz to expand the boundaries of his more traditionally structured dramas; the inspirations for blackface minstrelsy and jazz come from African Americans, both were appropriated by whites, and both have been reappropriated by blacks as a means not only of reclaiming their creations and heritage, but as a way of achieving a sense of cultural power in the present.

The title of *spell #7* refers to a magical "spell" permitting its characters freedom of expression; this obvious device represents a central pillar of Shange's thematic construction, the search for a means to liberate. lou calls the audience to "come with me/to this place where magic is/to hear my song/sometimes i forget and leave my tune in the corner of the closet under all the dirty clothes/in this place/magic asks me where i've been/how i've been singin/lately i leave my self in all the wrong hands/in this place where magic is involved in undoin our masks/i am able to smile and answer that" (*Three Pieces* 27). In this magic place, Shange's characters confront racist attitudes more directly than in *for colored girls*, in which the concerns are gender politics and issues of personal fulfillment. However, at one point, as the characters explore their various perspectives on the dilemma of African Americans, Shange allows the women figures to address their competitiveness for opportunity, but despite these tensions the women come to place a higher value on sisterhood and self-actualization than on economic or creative opportunity.

Some of the most compelling moments in the poetic vignettes of *spell #7* stem from Shange's sardonic humor, as when one character recalls that as a child she thought black children did not get polio because she never saw any black faces on TV telethons. Another character speaks of having a baby named "Myself," but when the child begins crawling the woman's happiness wanes because she realizes that once the child can crawl it is no longer hers, it belongs to itself. A few sketches are overtly comic, including one in which black men try various seduction methods to attract the women or another segment about the identifying black trait of kinky hair, with one character speaking of brushing her hair day and night, in a mirror, a store window, while on the telephone, and waiting in an unemployment line. She fears she will brush her hair so much that it will get straight and heavy, causing her to fall.

Rife with outright humor and grim irony, *spell #7* also presents perspectives on black men, as when one male character points out that "we don't exist unless we play football or basketball or baseball or soccer" (*Three Pieces* 46).

There are varied digressions into the legacy of stereotyping and the original play ends with a stage direction indicating that the minstrel mask remains visible after the final blackout as lou the magician repeats a variation on his line, "crackers are born with the right to be alive/i'm making ours up right here in yr face/and we gonna be colored and love it" (*Three Pieces* 52).

With the original production of *spell #7*, critics again decried a lack of three-dimensional characters; for example, Christopher Sharp complained that Shange "values her verse much more than she values her characters" (Sharp 109), while others lamented what was described as an absence of traditional dramatic structure. Richard Eder commented on the response of Shange's audience, which he compared with the intensity of a revival meeting. John Simon condemned the "maniacal egocentricity" that in his view made *spell #7* "every bit as bad as *for colored girls*" (Simon 57), but his dyspeptic, and undoubtedly racist, response was generally not supported by other critics, including Don Nelson, who applauded Shange's "ability to make the word flesh, to fuse idea and character so that it comes out humanity" (Nelson 108). *spell #7* inevitably found less commercial success than *for colored girls* in its 1979 New York Shakespeare Festival production at the Public Theatre, perhaps because audience members were less interested in a work exploring the seemingly unresolvable conflicts between blacks and whites than they were in the more personal gender issues of *for colored girls*.

Prior to *spell #7* Shange had written only the comparatively minor *A Photograph: A Still Life With Shadows/A Photograph: A Study of Cruelty*, which had been produced by the New York Shakespeare Festival to less than favorable reviews. A sketchier, less focused work, it is, nonetheless, a continuation of both Shange's themes and dramatic experimentation. The piece's five characters have names and all occupy an old San Francisco flat belonging to sean, a photographer. Haunted by a difficult relationship with a nearly absent father who abused his mother, sean is in relationships with three different women and produces commercially viable photographs, but yearns for artistically satisfying achievements. He comes to learn that his father's abusiveness resulted from abuse he had suffered at the hands of sean's grandfather, raising questions about the legacy of generational abuse. In sean's case, this legacy creates a vulnerability within him which undermines attainment of happiness, but which he has the opportunity to overcome through his relationship with michael, a dancer and the wisest of the young women he is involved with. He begins to understand, like the play's author, that the ability to create liberates one from the pain of the past and a troubled present. As sean watches michael dance, he chants, "you're gonna dance for everybody burdened michael/you can move/you are space and winds" (*Three Pieces* 108). Some critics continued to challenge Shange's dramatic/poetic collage, but Neal A. Lester writes that through:

> minimal attention to traditional plot development, Shange focuses instead on the discussions, attitudes, and behaviors of these black

individuals, particularly as they recognize and acknowledge their sexuality as essential parts of their identities. ... Tensions in the play might arise from the contradictions in the characters' behavior and words, in the absence of a hero with which the audience might identify, and in Shange's unwillingness to resolve identity issues she raises.

(Lester 141)

Although some reviewers continued to question Shange's ability to create fully-dimensioned characters in a traditional sense, Richard Eder found michael "a grave and captivating seer," but called the play itself "unconvincing" (Eder, "Sovereign Spirit" C11).

In 1978, Shange's *boogie woogie landscapes* was first performed as a one-person show in the "Poetry at the Public" series at the New York Shakespeare Festival. Shange's *boogie*, a term which she uses to define her chorepoetic style, also liberates her from the word *play* and the traditionally realistic/naturalistic requirements bound up in it for American dramatists. A revised and expanded version of *boogie woogie landscapes* was produced as a benefit for Frank Silvera's Writers Workshop at the Symphony Space Theatre in June 1979 followed by productions at the Kennedy Center for the Performing Arts in 1980 and the Mark Taper Theatre Lab in Los Angeles in 1982, under the title *Black and White Two-Dimensional Planes*. In *boogie woogie landscapes*, Shange weaves expressionistic techniques into her dramatic/poetic collage, probing the terrors and dreams of layla, a young black woman described as an "all-american colored girl" (*Three Pieces* 113). layla's subconscious emotions and past life are illuminated in a series of poetic and musical sequences performed by a series of "night companions (dream-memories)" who present, as Shange writes in her stage directions, the "geography of whimsy, fantasy, memory and the night" (*Three Pieces* 113). Shange's dream-like figures and the fears engendered by the night sweats layla experiences seem inspired by Kennedy's nightmare dreamscapes, but Shange emphasizes the revelations of selfhood layla experiences through the "sense of dislocation and confusion" (*Three Pieces* 113) engendered by these shadowy figures. The third person narrative of these non-traditional characters is a variation on Shange's usual style; here, instead of the characters speaking directly of their experiences as in her earlier plays, layla's experiences are transmitted indirectly through the night companions to proffer a more reflective and objective examination of her experience. And layla's experience is, of course, based directly on Shange's own. *boogie woogie landscapes* draws heavily on Shange's childhood and early adolescence, suggesting that she never strays far from her recurrent themes of a young black woman's experiences, both those from her own life and from observation of others. *boogie woogie landscapes* attempts a deeper probing into Shange's own psyche, from which she reveals the critical transition point of a young woman's life, the experience of the simultaneously joyful and fearful transformation into adulthood. As Shange writes, "everything in boogie woogie landscapes is the voice of layla's unconscious/her unspeakable realities/for no self-respecting afro-american girl wd reveal so much of herself of her own will" (*Three Pieces* xiv).

boogie woogie landscapes was published in a collection simply titled *Three Pieces* in 1981, along with *spell #7* and *a photograph*, and Shange's foreword to these plays underscores her mission as a black "poet in American theatre" self-challenged with developing "an independently created afro-american aesthetic" (*Three Pieces* ix). *boogie woogie landscapes*, more than many of Shange's post-*for colored girls* dramatic works, reveals her desire to experiment. Holding firm to her ongoing thematic concerns and autobiographical resources, Shange's experimentation with form on the fragile border separating poetry from theatre, song from speech, and action from dance is intended to locate a means of liberating the black experience, and expressions of it, from the "straight theatre" of Hansberry or the "coon shows" which "were somebody else's idea" (*Three Pieces* x). Her kinship with Kennedy, particularly, is evident in this mission, but Shange's dramatic/poetic collage is a path she forges from her own imagination, constructing it from both the positive and the negative cultural wreckage of race relations in America. Simply stated, Shange is seeking a means to "create an emotional environment" in theatre which is "an all encompassing moment/a moment of poetry/the opportunity to make something happen" (*Three Pieces* xi), and despite critical brickbats focused on her uniquely individual approach, Shange holds firm to an aesthetic based on a rejection of traditional dramatic forms, including the creation of three-dimensional "real" characters in a linear naturalistic play.

At the beginning of the 1980s, Shange continued to experiment with form by putting her dramatic/poetic collage to use in the realm of adaptation. Her first such attempt, Bertolt Brecht's *Mother Courage and Her Children*, won an Obie Award when it was produced at the New York Public Theatre. Brecht's original play is set in the early seventeenth century during the Thirty Years' War, but Shange shifts it to just after the American Civil War, remaking Mother Courage as a former slave selling her wares to combatants in the Plains war against the Indians. Critic Mel Gussow acknowledged "certain relocation problems," but found Shange's adaptation a "true cultural and political transplant" and a "considerable dramatic achievement" (Gussow 20), a view countered by his colleague Frank Rich, who felt that the adaptation failed to serve either Brecht or Shange, noting that a "black writer indeed has no obligation to answer to white writers, living or dead, and for Ntozake Shange it seems a waste of talent and energy to do so" (Rich D33). Shange also adapted Willy Russell's play *Educating Rita* in 1980 for a production staged at Atlanta's Alliance Theatre in 1982. Her 1984 collection of poems, *From Okra to Greens* (1984), was expanded as a stage piece entitled *from okra to greens/a different kina love story: a play with music and dance* (1985), a section of which had previously been produced under the title *Mouths* at New York's The Kitchen in 1981. With this choreopoem, Shange moves even further from traditional dramatic structures.

Focusing on two central figures, Okra, a black woman, and Greens, a black man, she explores the terrain of a relationship from the first meeting through several stages, including infidelity, and, finally, to hard-won reconciliation. Along the way, digressions of a more political nature are sprinkled in, expanding her consistent concerns to include a plea to American blacks to develop a strong community that includes a bond with peoples of color throughout the world.

Shange's second novel, *Betsey Brown*, published in 1985, is an autobiographical coming-of-age story of a black thirteen-year-old girl living in St. Louis in 1957 and is a variation on her recurrent themes of racial inequality, family dysfunction, and the complex transition from girlhood to womanhood. Shange adapted the novel to the stage in 1989 as *Betsey Brown: A Rhythm and Blues Musical*, although in this period Shange shifted her energies toward literary pursuits and teaching. She did not completely move away from the stage, as demonstrated with the short play, *Daddy Says: A Play* (1988), later expanded as a teen novel (2003), and a few subsequent works. In all cases, Shange continued her experimentation in the theatrical realm, expanding on the dramatic/poetic collage she pioneered. In *Daddy Says*, two young girls devastated by the death of their mother, a female broncobuster, grapple with conflicted feelings of pride in their mother's non-traditional achievements while wishing she might have chosen a more typical (and safer) career. Shange presents a reasonably sympathetic portrait of the father, but finds him unable to cope, as he himself acknowledges, "Well how am I s'posed to talk to two girls 'bout/this woman business" (*Daddy Says* 248). The unhappiness and confusion of their loss is mitigated, to some extent, by Cassie, their father's new friend, a mature woman who provides them guidance and comfort, recalling that she did not have such support in her own youth. She also sets the girls' father straight: "You don' wanna woman good as you/smart as you/brave as you? Whatchu gonna do wit' them girls, huh? Give 'em some make-up and mo' free time so they can get pregnant and drop outta school ... ?" (*Daddy Says* 244).

Shange's works, finally, are all of a piece; each individual play is a dramatic/poetic collage, but these individual pieces stitched together form one large dramatic/poetic collage, a rainbow of complex emotional colors expressed through language, movement, and music, emphasizing variations of a dominant theme. In the way that the eight nameless individually "colored" girls of her first play form a complete rainbow, Shange's individual plays form something of a theatrical rainbow—and a more complete presentation of her themes. Her goal in writing inherently autobiographical works is a "journey of a visual artist from adolescence to womanhood," a depiction of the experiences of:

> adolescent girls and young women ... because we know so little about ourselves; in a literary sense, there are so few of us. And one of the

reasons I try to investigate girls from different backgrounds and girls with different senses of success is because I want to make sure that we all know that none of our desires are illegitimate.

(*Resurrection* 323)

During the 1990s and beyond, Shange has focused more on teaching and smaller-scale experimentation in her occasional stage work. In *The Resurrection of the Daughter: Liliane* (1994), Shange creates a character whose "vulnerability and audacity" provide "the right to discover whatever it is we are, without having to deal with what the world thinks we are" (*Resurrection* 324). Celebrating literary foremothers—Zora Neale Hurston, Lorraine Hansberry, Adrienne Kennedy, among others—Shange herself emerges as a profound influence on a subsequent generation of black women playwrights inspired by her dramatic/poetic collage, most particularly Suzan-Lori Parks, who continues to lead her generation away from mainstream American theatrical traditions toward techniques in service of those themes particular to the experiences of blacks, especially black women. From *for colored girls* to *The Resurrection of the Daughter: Liliane*, and the more recent *Lavender Lizards and the Lilac Landmines: Layla's Dream* (2003), Shange, through her varied and deeply personal writings, but especially in the rainbow of her dramatic/poetic collage, informs her theatrical progeny of where black women and black artists have been. Working from a poetic sensibility and the tender emotional complexities of coming-of-age black girl/women, Shange recounts where her African American forebears and sisters have been, who they were and who they are, what they feel as they come into their own as women, and, most significantly, what they may become as women and artists.

Works cited

Allen, Carol. *Peculiar Passages. Black Women Playwrights, 1875–2000*. New York: Peter Lang, 2005.

Barnes, Clive. "Stage: *Black Sisterhood,*" *New York Times* (2 June, 1976): 4.

Betsko, Kathleen and Koenig, Rachel. *Interviews with Contemporary Women Playwrights*. New York: Beech Tree Books, 1987.

Bigsby, C. W. E., ed. *The Black American Writer. Volume 1: Fiction*. Baltimore, MD: Penguin, 1969.

Brown-Guillory, Elizabeth. *Their Place on the Stage: Black Women Playwrights in America*. New York: Praeger, 1990.

Browne, Malick. *Real Black Men Don't Sit Cross-legged on the Floor: A Collage in Blues*. 2006.

Cronacher, Karen. "Unmasking the Minstrel Mask's Black Magic in Ntozake Shange's *spell #7*," *Theatre Journal*, 44.2 (1992): 177–93.

Eder, Richard. "Sovereign Spirit," *New York Times* (22 December, 1977): C11.

——"Stage: Ntozake Shange's Dramatic Poetry in *spell #7* at Public," *New York Times* (4 June, 1979): C13.

Geis, Deborah R. "Distraught Laughter: Monologue in Ntozake Shange's Theatre Pieces," in *Feminine Focus: The New Women Playwrights*. Enoch Brater, ed. New York and Oxford: Oxford University Press, 1989. 210–25.

Gottfried, Martin. "'Rainbow' over Broadway," *New York Post* (16 September, 1976): 201.

Grahn, Judy. *The Common Woman* 1969.

Gussow, Mel. "*Stage: Mother Courage*," *New York Times* (14 May, 1980): 20.

Hansberry, Lorraine. *A Raisin in the Sun* 1959.

Hill, Errol G. and Hatch, James V. *A History of African-American Theatre*. Cambridge and New York: Cambridge University Press, 2003.

Jackson, Angela. *Shango Diaspora: An African-American Myth of Womanhood and Love* 1982.

Kushner, Tony. *Caroline, or Change* 2003.

Lester, Neal A. *Ntozake Shange: A Critical Study of the Plays*. New York and London: Garland, 1995.

Mafe, Diana Adesola. "Black Women on Broadway: The Duality of Lorraine Hansberry's *A Raisin in the Sun* and Ntozake Shange's *for colored girls*," *American Drama* 15.2 (2006): 30–47.

Nelson, Don. "Shange Casts a Powerful 'Spell,'" *New York Daily News* (16 July, 1979), cited in *New York Theatre Critics' Reviews* 40 (1979): 108.

Osumare, Halifu. *The Spirit of Dance*.

Parks, Suzan-Lori. *Top Dog/Underdog* 2002.

Rich, Frank, "'Mother Courage' Transplanted," *New York Times* (15 June, 1980): D5, D33.

Shange, Ntozake. *From Okra to Greens* 1984.

——*from okra to greens/a different kina love story: a play with music and dance* 1985.

——*The Love Space Demands: A Continuing Saga* 1987

——*Daddy Says: A Play*, in *New Plays for the Black Theatre*. Woodie King, Jr., ed. Chicago, IL: Third World, 1989.

——*for colored girls who have considered suicide/when the rainbow is enuf*. New York: Macmillan Publishing Co., Inc., 1977.

——*The Resurrection of the Daughter: Liliane* in *Moon Marked and Touched by Sun. Plays by African-American Women*. Syndé Mahone, ed. New York: Theatre Communications Group, 1994.

——*Three Pieces*. New York: St. Martin's Press, 1981.

——*Betsey Brown* 1985.

——*Betsey Brown: A Rhythm and Blues Musical* 1989.

——*Daddy Says* 2003.

——*Lavender Lizards and the Lilac Landmines: Layla's Dream* 2003.

Sharp, Christopher. "spell #7: A Geechee Quick Magic Trance Manual," *Women's Wear Daily* (4 June, 1979), cited in *New York Theatre Critics' Reviews* 40 (1979): 109.

Simon, John. "Fainting Spell," *New York Magazine* (30 July, 1979): 57.

Smith, Anna Deveare. *Fire in the Mirror* 1990.

Stevens, Andrea. "40 Years of Black Male History in 2½ Hours," *New York Times* (9 February, 2006): B3.

Timpane, John. "'The Poetry of a Moment': Politics and the Open Form in the Drama of Ntozake Shange," *Modern American Drama: The Female Canon*. June Schlueter, ed. Rutherford, NJ: Fairleigh Dickinson University Press, 1990.

7 The feminist/womanist vision of Pearl Cleage Google

Beth Turner

As a third-generation black nationalist and a radical feminist, the primary energy that fuels my work is a determination to be a part of the ongoing worldwide struggle against racism, sexism, classism and homophobia. I approach my work first as a way of expressing my emotional response to oppression, since no revolution has ever been fueled purely by intellect, no matter what the boys tell you; second, as a way to offer analysis, establish context, and clarify point of view; and third, to incite my audiences or my readers to action. ("Artistic Statement" 46)

(Pearl Cleage)

Beginning in 1983 with the New York production of her play *Hospice*, Pearl Cleage has established herself as one of the foremost African American dramatic voices in contemporary American theatre, with seven prominently produced plays. Her best-known play *Flyin' West*, portraying four African American pioneer women, has been widely produced across the country in both Black theatres, such as St. Louis Black Repertory and Pittsburgh's Kuntu Repertory, and White regional theatres including The Kennedy Center and San Diego Repertory Company, giving rise to Howard Pousner's assessment in the *Atlanta Journal/The Atlanta Constitution* that *Flyin' West* is "one of the most popular plays of recent years in American theater—with 15 productions and counting" (M4). Her plays, *Hospice* and *Blues for an Alabama Sky*, have also enjoyed considerable popularity on the regional and university stage. According to Freda Scott Giles, "Cleage has achieved a rare plateau for an African-American playwright: consistent professional production" (Giles 29). Additionally *Blues for an Alabama Sky* was chosen as the United States' official theatrical presentation for Atlanta's 1996 Cultural Olympiad's Olympic Arts Festival.

The fact that five of her plays have also been commissioned is further affirmation of her dramatic vision: a feminist/womanist perspective "ensconced within the framework of the well-made play" (Cleage, "Artistic Statement" 46). In 1992 Pearl Cleage's two one-acts *Chain*, and *Late Bus to Mecca* were commissioned and developed in conjunction with the Women's Project and the Southeast Playwrights Project of Atlanta, and co-produced by the Women's Project and the New Federal Theatre at Judith Anderson Theatre in New York City. Her three full-length plays, *Flyin' West*, *Blues for an Alabama Sky*, and *Bourbon at the Border* were all commissioned and produced by the Alliance Theatre in Atlanta.

In her articulation of feminist opposition to the interlocking oppressions of sexism, racism and classism, Cleage's work resonates with the spirit of both Ntozake Shange and Alice Childress. In fact, seeing Shange's *for colored girls who have considered suicide/when the rainbow is enuf* brought about an epiphany for Cleage. She recalls, "Ten minutes into the piece, I started weeping in surprise and gratitude and I wept throughout the play. It was like hearing my own voice in seven different bodies ... seeing that play changed my life" ("Playwright's Choice" 20). However, her interest in the well-made play as the vehicle for expressing feminism aligns Cleage's work more squarely with that of Alice Childress in plays such as *Trouble in Mind* and *Wine in the Wilderness*. Childress's skill at recreating historical period in *Wedding Band*, set in 1918, is also echoed in Cleage's body of work that actually constitutes a considerable portion of a historical cycle: *Flyin' West* is set in 1898; *Blues for an Alabama Sky* in 1930; *Late Bus to Mecca* in 1970; *Hospice* in the 1980s; *Chain* in 1991; and *Bourbon at the Border,* set in 1995 but with considerable back story from the 1960s. However, unlike August Wilson, who completed a twentieth-century historical cycle, Cleage is actually very wary of the idea of committing to such a life-defining project. Pearl Cleage, whose interest in writing began early in her life, just wants to keep writing.

Born in Springfield, Massachusetts in 1948 and raised in Detroit, Cleage was the second daughter of Doris Graham Cleage, a teacher, and Albert Cleage, a charismatic, activist preacher who founded the Freedom Now party in Detroit. She marveled at her father's mastery of the spoken word and learned precociously to understand linguistic power. Similar to her father, who had himself been involved in community theatre (Greene 27), Cleage was endowed with a strong dramatic sensibility that led her, even as young as seven years of age, to compose post-Thanksgiving dinner skits. She wrote her first complete play in the fourth grade. By the time she entered Howard University, where she would study under three extraordinary African American playwrights—Owen Dodson, Ted Shine and Paul Carter Harrison—she was fully committed to playwriting.

Cleage came to Atlanta, at the age of twenty, to complete her BFA at Spelman and has made the city her home ever since. While living in Atlanta, she has been a columnist/contributor to the *Atlanta Tribune*, *Ms*, and *Essence* as well as the founding editor of *Catalyst*, a literary magazine. On the political front, she served as the press secretary to Maynard Jackson, Atlanta's first Black mayor. The author of six prominently produced and published plays, Cleage has also written books of poetry, short stories, essays and novels. Much to theatre's loss, for the past ten years, she has devoted herself to the writing of literary fiction. As much as she loves the collaborative artistic process of theatre, she became dismayed by the artistic compromises that the cutbacks in theatre funding began to impose. She says, "With a novel you can control everything—the quality was guaranteed by me" (Personal interview). Excelling as a novelist, she has had an immensely fruitful period during which she has published five full-length novels: *What Looks Like Crazy on an Ordinary Day* (1997), an Oprah's Book Club selection; *I Wish I Had a Red Dress* (2001); *Some Things I Thought I'd Never Do* (2003); *Babylon Sisters* (2005); and *Baby Brother's Blues* (2006). Cleage is married to Zaron W. Burnett, Jr., a novelist and theatre artist with whom she frequently collaborates, most notably on the "Live at Club Zebra!" performance series. She is also the mother of one daughter, Deignan, by a previous marriage, and the grandmother of one granddaughter.

While the focus of this chapter is on Pearl Cleage's published plays, it would be remiss not to mention some of her dramatic work that remains unpublished. Included among these are plays written during her college days: *Hymn for the Rebels* (1968) and *Duet for Three Voices* (1969), both produced at Howard University; and *The Sale* (1972), mounted at Spelman College. Her unpublished work also consists of plays that have been produced professionally: *puppetplay* (1981), *Good News* (1984), *Essentials* (1985), and *Banana Bread* (1985), all produced at Just Us Theater in Atlanta; and *Come and Get These Memories* (1987), produced by the Billie Holiday Theatre in Brooklyn.

Of the latter, the most significant play, in terms of national recognition, is *puppetplay*, chosen by the prestigious Negro Ensemble Company to open its seventeenth season in New York City in 1983. A play about a young woman's devastating love relationship, Cleage represented the woman's psychic distress by splitting her into two characters: Woman One, played by Seret Scott, and Woman Two, performed by Phylicia Ayers-Allen (later Rashad). Using a seven-foot puppet to represent the male character, Cleage's intentions remained unclear and at first *New York Times* critic Mel Gussow wrote that the play "is a look at a futuristic world that turns people into robots and allows puppets to become a kind of silent ruling class" (I 73).

Since it is vitally important to Pearl Cleage that audiences understand her work, in her next play, *Hospice*, she abandoned the experimentation she used in *puppetplay*, later admitting "I like old-fashioned, well-made plays, where there's a lot of talk. I'm not an avant-garde kind of a person" (Greene 35). Cleage's love of the well-made play dates back to her undergraduate years at Howard University where, among the work of great Black writers, she was also introduced to Ibsen's plays. She enthuses, "I am a die-hard Ibsen fan. ... I love the complexity of the women characters in those plays" (Personal interview). Eschewing postmodern distrust of the empathetic force of realist theatre on the audience, Cleage embraces this quality instead.

She asserts, "Using traditional forms gives me more power in taking the audience's defenses away" (Giles 28), thus making it an important tool for promulgating the feminist ideology that drives her writing.

Woodie King, Jr. introduced Pearl Cleage's work to New York by producing the premiere performance of *Hospice* in 1983 as a part of his Women's Series at the New Federal Theatre in Lower Manhattan. *Hospice*'s winning of five AUDELCO Awards in November 1983 (the Audience Development Committee, founded by Vivian Robinson in 1983 for the promotion and recognition of excellence in Black theatre, has held an Award Ceremony, similar to the Tony Awards, in November every year since its founding), combined with the poor critical reception that greeted the NEC production of *puppetplay* that same month, further affirmed Cleage in her use of realism. *Hospice*, directed by Frances Foster, an original member of the Negro Ensemble Company, also featured two female characters: Alice Anderson performed by Lee Chamberlain and her daughter, Jenny, played by Joan Harris. On curtain rise, it becomes obvious that the existential frame for this play is impending birth and imminent death: Jenny's body bulges with the infant to whom she is about to give birth at any moment, and Alice's chemotherapy-induced bald head attests to her impending death from cancer. On a major threshold, each woman has independently sought her own private hospice in the solace of the family home, thought to be unoccupied. Alice in particular is discomfited to find Jenny there. It has been twenty years since she abandoned the then ten-year-old Jenny to the care of her husband and departed for Paris to pursue her dreams of being a poet. Jenny sees their chance encounter as a possible opportunity to recuperate what she believes is missing from her life—her mother's wisdom. But for Alice all that matters is "[t]he parts of my body that are going to start hurting again in a few minutes" (60). Even as she approaches her death, Alice remains a woman who refuses to comply with societal dictates of motherhood. She sharply counters Jenny's insistence on a mother–daughter bond by saying: "That sepia-tone photograph you've been carrying around in your head for twenty years hasn't got anything to do with me. I wasn't that way then, and I'm not that way now" (67). She coldly adds, "I couldn't stand to look at you" (69).

Cleage admits that Alice "is not a mother I would want to be. ... But I'm often annoyed by the image that black women have of being all-knowing, all-patient, all-hardworking. ... We get to have great mothers and we get to have really selfish mothers"(Greene 38). In Alice, Cleage has fashioned a character that definitely flies in the face of the "controlling image" (Collins 67) of the Black woman as the all-sacrificing "superstrong Black mother" (quoted in Collins 116). A life of self-abnegation was not the path for Alice. Married at the age of seventeen to an older charismatic civil rights activist (based on Cleage's own father), Alice's dreams of being a poet were being obliterated by her husband's priorities and needs. In what is usually a male literary narrative, Cleage has Alice leave child, husband, home and identity to travel to Europe to pursue a successful career as a published poet and a new exoticized subjectivity as Simone. In so doing, Cleage creates a character that stretches beyond the borders of normative gender restrictions to exist as a fully-realized human being, even at the expense of family life.

By the end of the play, Alice and Jenny come to a détente—a moment of mother–daughter bonding achieved minutes before Jenny is whisked off to deliver her baby. But it is in no way a fairy tale ending. Alice's oblique declaration of love, "I was always some place loving you, Baby" (72) as well as her last lines of the play wherein she wearily and cynically warns herself, "Don't fool yourself, Miss Alice. Just don't fool yourself" (72), suggest that she may have fabricated the tale of motherly love Jenny so craved. Although Alice might deny it, this untruth told by her—a woman who sacrificed home, family and country to avoid living a lie—to a daughter about to face the harrowing joy of childbirth, is ultimately her most worthy expression of maternal caring.

As is the case for most of her writing, the inspiration for her next works, the double-billed one-act plays, *Chain*, and *Late Bus to Mecca*, came from contemporary life around her. In the case of *Late Bus to Mecca*, it was the Muhammad Ali–Jerry Quarry fight held in Atlanta in 1970. For *Chain*, it was an article in *The New York Times* about a young Puerto Rican family whose daughter was a crack addict. As a last resort, the parents had chained her in the house, resulting in their being arrested. Cleage converted the family to a fictional Black family from Alabama and fashioned a one-character play evocative of Anna Deavere Smith's innovative solo performances. This depiction of the ravages of drug addiction was performed by Karen Malina White. It opens in a dark void that is breached only by a slide projection reading "Day One." It is the first of seven projections that will mark the beginning of each of seven days/scenes. As the slide disappears, total darkness returns and with it "a loud scream" followed by "sounds of someone scuffling, struggling, trying to escape and being caught. Only one voice is heard—the voice of Rosa Jenkins" (275). Although it is clear that there is a skirmish going on, the cause of the struggle is completely unknown, adding to the frightening nature of the sounds. When words are finally delivered, they are equally perplexing and disturbing:

> Rosa: (Screaming, crying, pleading in the darkness): What are you doing? No! Stop it! Don't Daddy! Please don't! ... Wait, Daddy! Wait! Don't do it! ... Daddy, please! Please! (275–6)

This pleading is followed shortly by loud sobbing. The dark theatre and stage allows for vivid imaginings by the audience. What is happening? Is a young girl being molested or raped by her father? As the audience sits in the darkness, phenomenologically suspended in a liminal moment, they anticipate a grim site/sight upon the rise of the lights. When the lights finally rise, the audience sees sixteen-year-old Rosa Jenkins lying in a heap in the middle of an apartment living room. It is not long before the audience discovers that Rosa is attached to the radiator by a long thick chain. Such a chain is rife with signification, a metonym for slavery in conjunction with an African American body. Connotations of animality also emerge, with the stage directions even stating: "She is like a caged animal, and she growls in her throat in a way that expresses wordless rage and frustration" (277). In Cleage's depiction, Rosa, enslaved by crack cocaine, has been reduced to a chained animal.

By the time the lights rise on the seventh day/scene, her parents have removed the chain as a reward for her progress. In this decision, Cleage reveals their naiveté about the insidious nature of addiction. As Rosa struggles with her craving for drugs, there is a poignant moment towards the end of the play when she actually takes the chain out again, and "places the shackle around her wrist like a bracelet. She is painfully aware of the safety the chain offers by taking away her choices" (308). But before she can resolve to re-shackle herself, there is a furtive knock at the door, marking the arrival of her boyfriend, and a new supply of crack.

As with Cleage's two previous plays, male characters are missing from the stage; we learn about the men in her life only through Rosa's eyes. With the story of Rosa's boyfriend Jesus, Cleage broaches the seedy side of sexual politics—voyeurism, sexual exploitation, and rape. An emotionally disso-ciative crack addict, Jesus is able to sell and use dope dispassionately. While he is nominally Rosa's boyfriend, he is emotionally and sexually distant, never engaging in physical intimacy with her but teaching her to masturbate for his voyeuristic pleasure. He just as dispassionately leaves her as collateral for the money he owes two drug dealers—highlighting her status as a commodified object. The dealers are about to rape her when her father intervenes. Rosa recounts:

> My daddy crazy. They coulda blown him away with his Alabama ass. ... He was beatin' on that door like he was packin' a Uzi and he didn't have shit. Not even no stick or nothin'. He just standin' there talkin' shit about: 'Where my baby girl at? Where you got my Rosa?' And I'm hollerin': 'Here I am Daddy! Here I am!' (302)

Back at home, her father weeps and Rosa is very moved by his tears. "That hurt me worse than anything. ... I love my daddy" (299). Even so, the allure of crack is stronger.

Atypical of her later work, Cleage uses nonrealist conventions in this play. Projections not only announce each scene but in one ironic moment, Rosa's boyfriend's name, previously heard only in its Spanish pronunciation, "Hey-suess," appears in a projected letter that begins "Dear Jesus," sounding more like the beginning of a child's prayer than a plea for drugs.

Cleage also breaks the fourth wall in the play. On several occasions Rosa directly addresses the audience, to ask for a light for her cigarette. She later further implicates the audience in the action by identifying them as surrogates assigned by her father to watch her while he is at work. Failing in this assignment as much as her father, the audience watches helplessly as Rosa opens the door and whispers Jesus's name with hope and anticipation.

While differing thematically, *Late Bus to Mecca* is connected to *Chain* through stylistic conventions. The first moments of the play also occur in the darkness with, however, much less ambiguous sounds; in this case, bus engines and announcements of departures and arrivals serve to establish the ambiance of a bus station. A line of script projected at the beginning of each of the thirteen scenes again breaks the darkness and serves as a caption for the short snapshot-like scene that follows. However, rather than creating a Brechtian alienation effect, these projections are invitations to the audience to engage with the narrative of what is also essentially a one-woman monologue; while Cleage puts two women on the stage in this play, one is mute. Both characters, Ava Johnson, a prostitute, originally performed by KimYancey; and a Black Woman (ABW), a mute, homeless woman, played by Claire Dorsey, are in their twenties. Focusing on the issue of class oppression, Cleage is determined to prevent the stereotypic portrayal of these characters. In a special "Note to the Director" she states, "We cannot allow class distinctions, superficial moral judgments and personal prejudices to divide and conquer us. ... Ava must be an admirable and likable character so that the audience's identification with her can help them confront and release their own class prejudices." Likewise, ABW "is specific. She is not The Black Woman. She is *a* black woman [my italics]" (312).

The play takes place on October 24, 1970, two evenings before Muhammad Ali's momentous return to the ring to fight Jerry Quarry in Atlanta (the Black Mecca) after having been banned for three years in retaliation for his conscientious objection to the Vietnam War. Like innumerable real life stories that unfold in the shadows of historic events, Ava and ABW are caught up in their own personal drama. Ava's pimp is planning to have Ava and her same-sex lover Sherri perform sex with dogs for the prurient amusement of his clients that same week-end. Nauseated by this proposal, Ava has come to the Detroit Greyhound Bus Station to escape with Sherri to Atlanta where she believes that one week of working the fight crowd will enable both of them to retire from prostitution and go to beauty school. Having bought two tickets, Ava installs herself near ABW to await Sherri, who never arrives. In the interim, Ava slowly builds a relationship with the near catatonic ABW, who, although she never speaks, does accept Ava's offer of Sherri's unclaimed ticket at the end. This is a tremendous gesture of agency on the part of this deeply emotionally crippled woman, and a confirmation that Ava, prostitute notwithstanding, has taken the humane stance Cleage promulgates for her feminist subjects.

Cleage ends the play with the projection of seven pedantic slides: "The Lessons"; "Take care of your sisters"; "Be resourceful"; "Make a plan"; "Make a move"; "Don't do animals" (339) with the final slide showing all six previous messages together as the lights go to black.

This dramaturgical choice makes *Late Bus to Mecca* the most didactic of Cleage's body of published plays. Revealing the tension between her activist agenda and her artistic sensibilities, she says, "I'm always conscious of trying not to write an issue play because I think that's not why people come to the theatre. ... They will go there with you but you gotta ... make some story that they're interested in first" (Personal interview). She concedes, however, that *Chain* and *Late Bus to Mecca* are "morality plays" (Miles 265).

By the time Pearl Cleage wrote *Flyin' West* in 1992, she was more at ease with her ability to have her audience "get it" without resorting to such didactics. Commissioned by the Alliance Theatre of Atlanta and directed by Kenny Leon, this two-act historical melodrama tells the story of four African American women pioneers: seventy-three year old Miss Leah, played by Carol Mitchell-Leon; two sisters, Fannie Dove, age thirty-two, and Minnie Dove Charles, age twenty-one, played by Elizabeth Van Dyke and Kimberly Hawthorne respectively; and an adopted sister, Miss Sophie, age thirty-six, played by Sharlene Ross. For the first time in her body of work, Cleage also introduces two male roles: homesteader Wil Parrish, played by Charles Donald, and Minnie's abusive husband, Frank Charles, originated by Peter Jay Fernandez. Although ostensibly a story about the tribulations of these pioneer women, Cleage admits that the play is also "a way to talk about contemporary issues, like race, gender, class, feminist issues" (Monroe 31).

The inspiration for *Flyin' West* came to Cleage from several sources. Most dramatically, while driving in her car, she heard the voice of a Miss Leah saying lines that remain in the play, "We can't let nobody take our babies. We've given up all the babies we can afford to lose" (Greene 41). Cleage says, "I realized she was a homesteader. I went and read the Homestead Act of 1860 and then went and read diaries and journals and tried to look at movies about women on the frontier" (Greene 41). Her research led her to set the play on a homestead outside of the all-Black town of Nicodemus, Kansas in 1898. Additionally, Cleage was also highly influenced by the famed Black anti-lynching activist and journalist Ida B. Wells, whose editorial, denouncing the lynching of a Memphis friend and urging Black folk to leave Memphis for the West, led to a mass exodus of about seven thousand people, including single women. Amazed by Wells's influence, Cleage decided to have the family of three young women be "Exodusters," as the Memphis migrants were called.

The action of the play is set into motion by the arrival from London of the youngest sister Minnie with her mulatto husband Frank. It is soon discovered that Frank physically abuses his wife. Having lost his bid for his share of the inheritance from his deceased slave-owning father, Frank intimidates his pregnant wife, by means of a severe beating, into signing the deed for her part of the homestead over to him. It is his intention to sell the land to White speculators and thereby recoup the funds he has lost in his inheritance battle. Understanding that Frank represents a threat not only to Minnie's life but also to all of their hard-fought dreams, the women assess their options. The adopted sister, Sophie, who throughout the play is most comfortable with a rifle in her hand, states:

> You know as well as I do there are no laws that protect a woman from her husband. Josh beat Belle for years and we all knew it. ... It wasn't a crime until he killed her! I'm not going to let that happen to Min. ... I'm going to step out on my front porch and blow his brains out. (76)

To protect Sophie from certain imprisonment, the women decide to kill Frank with a poisoned apple pie made by elderly Miss Leah from a secret recipe passed down from Africa. This action resonates with historical and cultural significance. Freda Scott Giles states "Cleage's use of the poisoned pie carries two threads of meaning. The first is connected to the retention of knowledge from the African motherland, passed through the oral tradition, which fosters self-preservation, especially if kept concealed from the oppressor. The second thread is connected to the folk tradition of victory over oppression through covert confrontation" (Giles 29). This stunning resolution to the sisters' dilemma evokes a wide range of reaction by audiences, including, not infrequently, requests for the recipe.

The last scene of the play takes place seven months after Frank's death. It is a celebratory scene. Everyone, except Miss Leah who is babysitting, is excitedly getting ready to go to a town dance. Of this ending, Cleage says:

> There had to be a little coda there that said [the killing] was a terrible moment but it was the right thing to do. And here's how we know. ... They're going to the party. The baby's been born. The baby's fine. Miss Leah is going to tell this child the story of its life. Sophie's under the full moon, saying 'My land is safe.' It was the right decision based on the world of that play.
>
> (Personal interview)

If in this tale of domestic abuse Cleage creates an unsavory man as her first male character, she balances her depiction of Frank with that of Wil Parrish, the epitome of responsible Black manhood. Wil is a man who is ready to partner with, rather than dominate, these pioneer women when his help is needed. Wil understands the threat Frank poses to the sisters and their dreams and, stepping up to the plate, he offers to undertake the deed of killing Frank in the masculine ritual of man-to-man confrontation. Yet, when the women present him with their alternate plan, he embraces it without struggle and assists them in a supportive role. Wil's respectful attention to the desires of these women also renders him worthy of a love relationship with Fannie.

Cleage's inclusion of a positive male character marks her movement from a strict radical feminist to a womanist perspective. The nature of this shift is evident in Michael Awkward's description:

> Black womanism demands neither the erasure of the black gendered other's subjectivity ... nor the relegation of males to ... limiting positions. What it does require ... is a recognition on the part of both black females and males of the nature of the gendered inequities that have marked our past and present, and a resolute commitment to work for change. ... [I]t heartily welcomes—in fact, insists upon—the joint participation of black males and females as *comrades*. (99)

With Frank, Cleage absolutely refutes the right of Black men to convert their suffering from racial abuse into violence against women; in Wil she shows that Black men can embrace full subjectivity for women and partner with them towards mutually affirming goals. While Cleage's activist perspective is omnipresent in the play, it is beautifully woven into a compelling plot, making *Flyin' West* her most skillful blending of ideology and art.

With *Blues for an Alabama Sky*, also produced by the Alliance Theatre and directed by Kenny Leon in 1995, Cleage continued in the vein of writing historical dramas. *Blues for an Alabama Sky* is the story of four Harlem residents in 1930: Angel Allen, a singer and a former prostitute, originated by Phylicia Rashad; her gay friend Guy Jacobs, formerly a male prostitute but now a dress designer, played by Mark C. Young; Delia Patterson, a social worker and family planning activist, played by Deidrie N. Henry; and Dr. Sam Thomas, a doctor at Harlem Hospital, performed by Bill Nunn. They are joined by a recently arrived widower from Alabama, Leland Cunningham, performed by Gary Yates, whose eventual attraction to Angel fatefully embroils him in the lives of the four Harlemites and propels the play into a tragic spiral. For the first time, Cleage has created more male roles than female, allowing for multiple explorations of sexual politics, reproductive rights and homophobia in this explosive drama.

While Cleage has said that her plays usually begin with her characters, her long interest in the Harlem Renaissance may also have served as a source of inspiration for *Blues for an Alabama Sky*. Cleage's fascination with the Harlem Renaissance was sparked by her parents during her childhood. She says, "My mother was a big fan of Langston Hughes ... she had met Hughes and talked about him. So, it was always a period that was alive for me" (Personal interview). Her initial exposure was also strongly reinforced at Howard University by her teacher, Harlem Renaissance playwright Owen Dodson. In *Blues*, abundant references to famous Black personalities of the era such as Josephine Baker, Rev. Adam Clayton Powell, and Langston Hughes deepen the play's connection to the period, but these legends never appear as characters.

Cleage's choice of the Harlem Renaissance in this period may also have been influenced by her decision to introduce a gay character. By setting the play in Harlem in 1930, when, according to Eric Garber, founder of the Gay, Lesbian, Bisexual and Transgender Historical Society, Harlem was "a gay liberated capital," Cleage was able to provide a compatible background for Guy, and a platform from which she could address issues of sexual orientation and homophobia. As Garber states: "[T]he major male figures of the period were gay or bisexual: Alain Locke, Countee Cullen, Langston Hughes." Garber even mentions the buffet flats ("rental units notorious for cafeteria-style opportunities for a variety of sex") (www.glbtq.com/literature/harlem_renaissance.html), organized by Langston Hughes and Richard Bruce Nugent, that Cleage has Guy attend in *Blues*.

The story centers on Angel and Guy who both escaped prostitution in Savannah and migrated to Harlem for a better life. Guy has been Angel's safety net throughout the many vicissitudes of her life in Harlem, providing shelter and nurturance when needed. As the play opens, he is rescuing her from the latest crisis in her life. Having learned that her Italian gangster boyfriend has married another woman, she has spent the evening trying to drown her sorrows in alcohol. As the curtain rises, Guy is seen navigating a very drunk Angel down the streets of Harlem at 3 a.m. with the assistance of a stranger, Leland, who has offered to help.

Leland, a fundamentalist Christian, ill-advisedly falls in love with self-absorbed, worldly Angel. It is a relationship built on self-delusion and deception. Grieving from the recent death of his wife in childbirth, Leland is swept away by Angel's physical similarities. Angel, for her part, sees in Leland the possibility of acquiring some stability and security in her life. Giving up on what she decides is Guy's unrealistic dream of becoming a dress designer for Josephine Baker in Paris and on his promise to take her there with him, Angel becomes pregnant by Leland. However, when Guy is actually summoned by Josephine Baker, Angel's ever present self-interest takes precedence and she presses her friend, Dr. Sam Thomas, to perform an abortion on her. Later, frustrated at still not being able to unfetter herself from Leland despite her "miscarriage," she heatedly reveals the facts of her abortion to him. In his fury, Leland turns on Sam, and shoots him to death.

Like Alice in *Hospice*, Angel provides a complicated image of Black womanhood. Cleage says "I'm used to writing black women characters, even when they do something wrong, it's because of oppression or something that's happened to them. Angel has those reasons, but is also prepared to manipulate people. ... [S]he was not the person you needed to emulate as a black woman in the audience" (Greene 40). Yet, Cleage also provides a Black female figure whom the audience can emulate. Guy's next door neighbor, Delia, is an activist social worker, who is striving to assist Margaret Sanger in opening a family planning center in Harlem. Through her character and that of Sam Thomas, Cleage is able to broaden the issue of reproductive rights beyond Angel's personal story. Having moved a long way from her earlier "morality plays," Cleage does not insist on an untroubled "right" answer here. Delia does succeed in helping Sanger to open the clinic but someone burns it down before the play ends. (Historically, the clinic endured for five years.) Sam, who does not take abortion lightly, performs one on Angel and dies for his action. The life of a doctor in exchange for the life of a fetus—these issues and their consequences still rage.

In Sam and Delia, Cleage also depicts a romantic pairing that resembles the wholesomeness of the nascent relationship between Wil and Fannie in *Flyin' West*. Delia, still a virgin at the age of twenty-five, has devoted much of her life to the welfare of the Black community as a social worker. Sam, for his part, has done the same. He works long hours, delivering babies (seven in two days) and trying to save people injured in gun shootings and other acts of violence. He is weary but he still finds joy in music and in the successful outcome of a dangerous birth. Love has eluded the both of them, but in the course of the play their feelings for each other manifest. On the threshold of consummating their love, Delia wistfully mentions that she had promised herself she would never marry a doctor. Sam, a bluesman at heart, responds lovingly: "I'll stop practising. I'll wear two-tone shoes and play the baritone sax" (163). Their burgeoning love makes Sam's death all the more tragic.

With Guy and Leland, Cleage is able to explore issues of homophobia and gender oppression. Leland, again blinded by his own misconceptions, does not recognize Guy as a homosexual until he hears one of Guy's accounts of an evening at Langston's. Outraged at the idea of men flirting with men, Leland blurts out "I don't know how sophisticated New York people feel about it, but in Alabama, there's still such a thing as abomination" (158). Leland is not alone in his intolerance. Guy is also attacked by a group of young thugs when he leaves his apartment in "tuxedo pants, a formal shirt with an ascot and a silk smoking jacket" (151) to get some sugar for a tea he is throwing. Although Cleage presents Guy as a dandy in his taste in clothing, she does not stereotype his character. He is centered, loyal, fun-loving, talented, exuberant and fully able to handle himself in a physical fray. The blood on his shirt after the attack is not his own and he boasts, "If you ever see me in a fight with a bear, you help the bear" (152). Portraying Guy as a fully developed and sympathetic character was crucial to Cleage. She asserts:

> [T]he black American community is very, very homophobic. But I've never seen a production where people did not embrace Guy. ... That these straight black men in the audience, who I know are homophobic in their real lives, would applaud and say 'Go on, brother,' all of that is wonderful.
>
> (Greene 37–8)

Cleage has aptly named her play *Blues for an Alabama Sky* as it evokes the blues sensibility that is so prevalent in this story. The potential for happiness is present in everyone's life as is the possibility of tragedy. With Sam's death, tragedy washes over all the characters. However, Guy's long-held dream of Paris has come true. He takes Delia with him, leaving Angel behind to contemplate her next move in the wake of the disaster she has wreaked on everyone around her.

As with her previous full-length plays, *Bourbon at the Border* was commissioned and produced by Alliance Theatre. It premiered in 1997, directed by Alliance artistic director, Kenny Leon. It is the last play by Pearl Cleage's to be produced thus far and it marks the end of an amazingly fruitful collaboration between her, the Alliance and Kenny Leon, who is no longer artistic director there. Faithful to her writer's mission "to tell the truth"("First Person Singular" 135), Cleage removes all nostalgic rose-colored glasses in *Bourbon at the Border*, as she unabashedly examines the darker side of the Civil Rights Movement. She asserts, "There's this feeling that everyone in the civil rights movement was either martyred and killed or they not only *survived* but went on to be elected mayor or go to Congress. It's a feeling that everybody involved was a great warrior" (Binelli L1). By opening a window onto the lives of two former Civil Rights activists who, some thirty years later, are still struggling unsuccessfully with the effects of the violence they endured during the Freedom Summer of 1964, Cleage uncompromisingly lays that myth to rest.

Part murder mystery, part romantic tragedy, *Bourbon at the Border* is set in a Detroit neighborhood that is "neither particularly fashionable [nor] particularly safe" (189), and is remarkable only for the view it provides of the Ambassador Bridge that crosses to Canada. Although the play takes place in 1995, the roots of the story extend back to the Freedom Summer in Mississippi in 1964 when James Cheney, Michael Schwerner, and Andrew Goodman were murdered. In her "Playwright's Notes" Cleage contextualizes the time period by describing the details of that fateful summer and the impact of the racial climate of that time, particularly on the psyche of young Black people. She quotes an excerpt from *Dutchman* for which LeRoi Jones (Amiri Baraka) received an Obie Award that same year. In it Jones identifies Black America's distilled rage as the source of its genius in blues and jazz and prescribes murder as a cure for Black America's insanity: "Bird [Charlie Parker] would've played not a note of music if he just walked to East Sixty-Seventh Street and killed the first ten white people he saw. Not a note! ... Murder. Just murder! Would make us all sane" (192).

During that fateful summer, Charles, a student activist at Howard University (played by Terry Alexander) had recruited May (performed by Carol Leon-Mitchell) for the ride to Mississippi to help register Black folks to vote. While there, they were captured by racist police, who threatened to rape May if Charles didn't whip her. When she was beaten within inches of her life, they still raped her so savagely in front of him that she was never able to conceive children. After May returned home, Charles was recaptured, and tortured for two weeks. He emerged with his leg broken in three places and his mind compromised. Feeling alienated from their families and friends by their experiences, they clung to each other, eventually marrying and moving to their apartment on the border of Canada. May reminisces that Charlie "used to say we were like desperadoes, drinking bourbon at the border and planning our getaways" (263). They were able to hold everything together for a while and then it got so Charlie found he could not touch her without crying. He has been suffering from depression, mental breakdowns and suicide attempts ever since.

The play, which also involves May's upstairs neighbor Rosa St. John (played by Andrea Frye) and her boyfriend, Tyrone Washington (performed by Taurean Blacque) depicts the first three weeks following Charlie's latest release from a mental hospital. With Tyrone's aid, Charlie has obtained a position as a truck driver and everything seems to be coming up roses. The happy picture is marred only by the background violence of their environment: a White man mysteriously killed but not robbed, and a young woman who jumps to her death from the bridge when road rage led a man to beat her. A second murder takes on more significance but still seems like background context—a metaphor for the violence that still exists in American life. However, eventually with the death of a third White man, one for each week since Charlie's release, it becomes clear that there is a serial killer who is slashing the throats of these men and it is Charlie. Caught in the matrix of violence, Charlie was trying, as LeRoi Jones' prescribed in *Dutchman*, to restore his sanity by taking out his rage on random White men who were about the current age of his former Southern torturers. As the police close in, the last scene reveals Charlie and May huddled together, in the face of hopeless odds, reciting the details of their fantasy about a free life in Canada, a scene evocative of the last moments of Alice Childress's *Wedding Band*.

This is by far Pearl Cleage's darkest and most tragic story and it left audiences conflicted. Despite Charlie's murders, the audiences were sympathetic towards him because of all he had suffered in helping to bring about civil justice for Black people. They yearned for a redemptive ending for Charlie and May—the escape to Canada and a peaceful healing of their lives—but Cleage was not going to let the virulence of American racism off that easily. Racism does warp and kill, and those caught in its clutches can not always be redeemed. Addressing her audience's disappointment, she says, "I know exactly what black people want from a black writer. They want an interesting story where we win at the end. And sometimes that's what I'll write, and everybody's happy, and sometimes it's *Bourbon at the Border*. Audiences felt betrayed when they saw it; they wanted *Flyin' West*" (Greene 43).

Writing the truth in the face of possible audience disapprobation is the mark of a playwright possessing maturity and integrity. But for Pearl Cleage, writing has always been about truth-telling and activism. A staunch opponent of racism, sexism, classism, homophobia, with a lucid understanding of how one oppression cannot be battled without engaging the others, Pearl Cleage has remained true to her principles. Her transition from a strictly feminist stance to the more broad-based womanist position is a part of her maturation and has come from a realization that, as bell hooks says, it is "possible for black women to love black men and yet unequivocally challenge and oppose sexism, male domination and phallocentrism" (108).

Although Pearl Cleage's diverse writing interests take her away from playwriting at times, her love of the genre remains. Indeed, she will return to the theatre with the production of a new one-act play, *The Song for Coretta*, which is scheduled to premiere at Spelman College in February. She says there is also one other full-length play germinating. Perhaps 2007 will mark the beginning of still another fertile era of playwriting by this talented writer, who has been one of the most prolifically produced contemporary African American playwrights writing in the tradition of her noteworthy feminist/womanist forebears—Alice Childress and Ntozake Shange. Based on the precarious health of American theatres vis-à-vis the robust publishing market, the likelihood of such a rebirth seems slim. Still, one can hope.

Works cited

Awkward, Michael. "A Black Man's Place in Black Feminist Criticism," in *The Black Feminist Reader*. Joy James and T. Denean Sharpley-Whiting, eds. Malden, MA: Blackwell Publishers, 2000. 88–108.

Binelli, Mark. "Pearl Cleage on the 'Border'." *Atlanta Journal-Constitution*, Arts Section (11 May 1997): L1.

Childress, Alice *Trouble in Mind: A Comedy-Drama in Two Acts* in *Black Theatre: A Twentieth-Century Collection of the Work of Its Best Playwrights*. Lindsay Patterson, ed. NY: Coward, McCann and Geoghegan, 1975. 135–74.

——*Wine in the Wilderness: A Comedy-Drama*. NY: Dramatists Play Service, Inc., 1969.

——*Wedding Band: A Love/Hate Story in Black and White*. NY: Samuel French Inc., 1973.

Cleage, Pearl. *Hymn for the Rebels* 1968.

——*Duet for Three Voices* 1969.

——*The Sale* 1972.

——*puppetplay* 1981.

——*Good News* 1984.

——*Essentials* 1985.

——*Banana Bread* 1985.

——*Come and Get These Memories* 1987.

——"Artistic Statement." *Contemporary Plays by Women of Color: An Anthology*. Kathy A. Perkins and Roberta Uno, eds. New York: Routledge, 1996. 46–7.

——*Blues for an Alabama Sky* in *Flyin' West and Other Plays*. NY: Theatre Communications Group, 1999. 87–186.

——*Bourbon at the Border* in *Flyin' West and Other Plays*. NY: Theatre Communications Group, 1999. 187–270.

——*Chain* in *Flyin' West and Other Plays*. NY: Theatre Communications Group, 1999. 271–308.

——*Flyin' West* in *Flyin' West and Other Plays*. NY: Theatre Communications Group, 1999. 1–86.

——*Hospice* in *New Plays for the Black Theatre*. Woodie King, Jr., ed. Chicago: Third World Press, 1989. 45–72.

——*Late Bus to Mecca* in *Flyin' West and Other Plays*. NY: Theatre Communications Group, 1999. 309–39.

——"Playwrights Choice." *Black Issues Book Review* 3.4 (2001): 20–4.

——Personal interview. 9 August 2006.

——*What Looks Like Crazy on an Ordinary Day*. NY: Avon Books, 1992.

——*I Wish I Had a Red Dress*. NY: William Morrow, 2001.

——*Some Things I Thought I'd Never Do*. NY: One World Books, 2003.

——*Babylon Sisters*. NY: One World Books, 2005.

——*Baby Brother's Blues*. NY: One World Books, 2006.

Cleage, Pearl and Burnett, Jr., Zaron W. *Live at Club Zebra!: The Book*. Vol. 1. Atlanta: Just Us Theater/Club Zebra, 1988.

Collins, Patricia Hill. *Black Feminist Thought: Knowledge, Consciousness, and the Politics of Empowerment*. New York: Routledge, 1991.

Eric Garber, "A Different Kind of Roots: African American Resources in the Archives." *Our Stories Newsletter*, http://www.glbtq.com/literature/harlem_renaissance.html (accessed 23 October 2006).

"First Person Singular: Pearl Cleage." *Essence* 35.11 (March 2005): 135.

Giles, Freda Scott. "In Their Own Words: Pearl Cleage and Glenda Dickerson Define Womanist Theatre." *Womanist: Theory and Research* 2.1 (1996–1997): 28–35.

Greene, Alexis. "Pearl Cleage." *Women Who Write Plays: Interviews with American Dramatists*. Alexis Greene, ed. Hanover, NH: Smith and Kraus Inc., 2001.

Gussow, Mel. "Theater: *Puppetplay* with Negro Ensemble." *New York Times*, (27 November 1983), I 73.

Jones, LeRoi. *Dutchman*, in *Dutchman and The Slave: Two Plays*. New York: Morrow Quill Paperbacks, 1964.

hooks, bell. *Feminist Theory: From Margin to Center*. Cambridge: South End Press, 2000.

Miles, Julia, ed. *Playwriting Women: Seven Plays from the Women's Project*. Portsmouth, NH: Heinemann, 1993.

Monroe, Steve. "Black Women as Pioneers." *American Visions* 9.5 (1994): 31.

Pousner, Howard. "I Have Always Known I'm a Writer." *Atlanta Journal/The Atlanta Constitution* (19 March 1995): M4.

8 "We must keep on writing"

The plays of Aishah Rahman

Brandi Wilkins Catanese

The title of this essay comes from Aishah Rahman's 1989 essay "Tradition and a New Aesthetic." Born in 1936, Rahman has fulfilled this mandate, working steadily for over three decades to create an impressive bibliography of plays that address the complex interworkings of race, class, gender, and spirituality within and beyond the U.S.A. As the author of four full-length plays, two musical dramas and a libretto, several one-act plays, and a memoir, with a novel and a documentary film in progress, Rahman is a prolific artist helping both to create and to document the vibrancy of black culture and, in particular, to draw attention to the unique plight of black women within our society. A Professor of Literary Arts at Brown University, Rahman has also been instrumental in developing the work of new playwrights, as evidenced by her editorship of *NuMuse, An Anthology of New Plays* (1994) from Brown University. The length of her own dedication to the theatre and the breadth of her influence on younger generations of playwrights make her an important figure in African American dramatic literature and history.

As many scholars have noted, one of the most consistent features of Rahman's work is her translation of a jazz aesthetic into the realm of playwriting. Rhythm, improvisation, and repetition with revision all structure Rahman's plays, as evinced in her production notes informing actors and directors that, for example, the monologues in *The Mojo and the Sayso* (1987) are "conceived as a riff on a specific instrument ... rooted in classical jazz rhythms" (40). However, Rahman's use of jazz tropes is not merely the sign of a personal affinity with the form; rather, as Thadious Davis suggests, "plac[ing] her characters within a framework of jazz articulation ... has specifically African American historical connotations" (68). In her own words, Rahman further defines this aesthetic as "acknowledg[ing] the characters' various levels of reality [... and] express[ing] multiple ideas and experiences through language, movement, visual art and spirituality simultaneously" (quoted in Mahone 283). Best known for what Margaret Wilkerson refers to as her 1977 "underground classic" (197), *Unfinished Women Cry in No Man's Land While a Bird Dies in a Gilded Cage*, Rahman's other works offer just as many provocative insights into the workings of power within American culture. Her first full-length work, *Lady Day: A Musical Tragedy* (1972), ambitiously tackles the economic and sexual exploitation of black women and the centrality of jazz and blues to black life. Since that time, Rahman's other works have addressed such varied topics as police brutality, intraracial skin color prejudice, the Clarence Thomas confirmation hearings, black sexual politics, and the role of Christianity within the black community. After a focused consideration of *Unfinished Women*, the remainder of this essay will explore three recurrent themes in Rahman's full length works: black iconography, black spirituality, and black gender politics.

Signifying on tradition: *Unfinished women*

Although it was not her first play, I begin my analysis with *Unfinished Women,* both because of its prominence within Rahman's body of work and because it demonstrates another essential feature of her oeuvre: intertextuality, or the African American rhetorical tradition of signifyin(g). *Unfinished Women Cry in No Man's Land While a Bird Dies in a Gilded Cage* earns its canonical status not only by staging timely concerns about black women, motherhood, and freedom, but also by responding to the concerns expressed in earlier works of African American drama. In describing it as a "polydrama," Rahman claims the play's debt to jazz:

> [t]he two settings—Hide-a-Wee Home for Unwed Mothers and Pasha's boudoir—should be played and intraplayed with the dramatic image of Bird and Bird's music being the fundamental notes that both parts bounce off on creating tensions between them, while at the same time weaving the seemingly disconnected parts into one 'polydrama' (4).

From the outset, the fusion of these narratives enables Rahman's work to reflect the varied experiences of marginalized people within American culture: her emphasis on polydrama suggests that neither world depicted onstage can be understood without the other. *Unfinished Women* stages as simultaneous the day on which jazz great Charlie Parker dies and the day on which the female residents of the Hide-a-Wee Home for Unwed Mothers must decide whether or not to give up their newborn children for adoption. By staging these crises adjacent to and through one another, the hope, frustration, brilliance, and despair of the two scenarios rely upon one another to achieve their full dramatic meaning, a tactic which localizes the intertextuality that Rahman also accomplishes on a larger scale.

For those familiar with African American drama, one of *Unfinished Women*'s most striking features is its obvious connections to both LeRoi Jones's *Dutchman* and Adrienne Kennedy's *Funnyhouse of a Negro*. Jones won the 1964 Obie Award for Best American Play for telling the story of the young, middle-class black man Clay's fatal seduction by white society, embodied by Lula, the redheaded murderess. Near the end of *Dutchman*, Clay harshly condemns Lula for her presumption of familiarity with black culture, telling her, "Charlie Parker? Charlie Parker. All the hip white boys scream for Bird. And Bird saying, 'Up your ass, feeble-minded ofay! Up your ass'" (390). Rahman's play seems to take this quote as inspiration, and functions as both an extension of and complement to Jones's earlier critique. While Rahman's own 1972 one-act *The Lady and the Tramp* borrowed *Dutchman*'s conceits of public transit and murder to examine relationships between black men and black women, in this full-length play she revisits the loaded pairing of black male and white female characters. She ponders the bond that unites Charlie Parker and Pasha, his European lover, and depicts the violence in their relationship as an intricate form of psychosexual torture that the couple inflict upon one another. Focusing on the dominant society's marginalization of her characters—including jazz legend Parker—Rahman also offers a feminist rejoinder to Jones's earlier work, underscoring the importance of including black women's unique concerns in any critique of blacks' place in American society.

Also achieving acclaim (and an Obie Award for Distinguished Play) in 1964, Adrienne Kennedy's *Funnyhouse of a Negro* has come to be seen as a counterpoint to *Dutchman*'s indictment of white America's mores in both form and content. Kennedy focuses on Sarah, a light-skinned black woman who desperately embraces those aspects of her lineage and cultural literacy that link her to Europe while disavowing her African heritage as beastly. By allowing Sarah to narrate her conception as an act of rape inflicted upon her fair (almost white) mother by her savage black father, Kennedy also relies upon the controversial trope of white femininity threatened by black masculinity, but she chooses to stage the consequences of such encounters for the middle class black woman rather than man. Furthermore, Kennedy completely rejects the tenets of realism, crafting a surrealist narrative in which a fragmented protagonist shares the stage with a grotesque Jesus, European royalty, and slain African leader Patrice Lumumba. A decade later, Rahman's Hide-A-Wee Home for Unwed Mothers offers an important supplement to Kennedy's depiction of black women by rejecting realism to give voice not only to the crises of the socio-economically privileged, but also to those women of lower status who are thus triply marginalized—by race, gender, and class. The character Paulette comes from an upper middle class black family who will not accept her back into their domestic unit until she gives away her child, but there are many other types of women in the home as well. Consuelo's Puerto Rican mother encourages her to make a family with the white father of her child in order to experience upward socio-racial mobility; Mattie is a tough young girl whose pregnancy is the result of a rape that steals her sexual innocence and destroys her ideals of romantic love; and Midge deals with the hostility of the other girls who believe that her whiteness insulates her from the pressures that the rest of them face.

The final young woman, working class character Wilma, expands Rahman's representation of black womanhood and provides the conceptual link between the play's two worlds. Wilma juxtaposes what she perceives as Charlie Parker's freedom with her own sense of confinement as a black woman, asserting, "Secretly, I always wanted to be a man 'cause they can do things and go places. Bird is the man I wanted to be" (21). Additionally, Bird ushers her into a historical understanding of her difficulties as a potential black mother: during the sexual encounter in which she conceived her child, "the sound of Bird's horn [... tugged] at me, taking me back to a memory I was born with ... I took a journey I could no longer avoid and along the way I helped a woman toss her newborn baby overboard a slaveship ... I took my place in the circle of black women singing old blues" (22). Likening her decision to give away her child to the decision of black women during the Middle Passage (and slavery) to commit infanticide rather than expose their children to the horrors of enslaved life, Rahman uses Wilma to make clear that the intervening centuries have done little to improve the choices available to black mothers in America. Joyce Meier describes this claim as a "painful undertow in black American theatre" (135), linking Rahman's play to other works, including Alice Childress's contemporaneous *Mojo* and Angelina Weld Grimké's earlier *Rachel*, that depict black women rejecting the task of motherhood for a variety of reasons, all of which relate in some way to the oppressive forces that limit life chances for black women and their children.

Rahman exposes the irony of Wilma's investment in Bird as a symbol of freedom through the scenes that take place in Pasha's boudoir. The fame that music has brought him, the attention of a white woman (supposedly our society's greatest prize for men), and the numbing succor of drugs all fail to make Bird feel as free as Wilma believes him to be. Among other things, Rahman offers an economic critique of the plight of black artists. Parker's renown is not equated with financial freedom, as he declares, "Clubs are named after me. Musicians make it ... imitating me. And I can't even give it away ... I ... am ... Charles ... Parker, Jr. ... and I beg people to let me play" (28). Bird experiences acutely the consequences of turning black expressive culture into a commodity that can be reproduced outside of the context within which it was created: his name and style become a brand that eclipses his individual virtuosity, robbing him of his financial and artistic independence. Likewise, Pasha's boudoir is the gilded cage in which Bird will ultimately die: sumptuous yet stifling, the room and its owner offer comforts at great price. Rahman exposes the irony of Bird's nickname, his lack of access to his name's symbolic portent, and emphasizes the manifest unfreedom that he experiences at his peculiar intersection of race, gender, and genius.

However, throughout the play, Rahman also denaturalizes white womanhood, especially white motherhood. Pasha's wealth and privilege do not grant her her deepest wish: to have a child with Parker, who repeatedly refuses her pleas. Left without a biological child, Pasha spends much of the play with a needle, thread, and cloth, trying literally to fabricate the baby that would offer fullness to her life. Her failures demonstrate that although she finances the melodrama she enacts with Bird, she does not control its script. Her counterpart in the Hide-A-Wee Home is Midge, a white woman trapped by society's general disdain for unwed mothers and the specific censure she would face as the white mother of a mixed race child. Lashing out at her housemates, she asks, "Look at you all standing around and wondering what kind of white girl would end up in a place like this. You think you have a monopoly on pain?" (26). The inclusion of both Pasha and Midge as failed mothers works against the historical paradox which sees black women simultaneously as natural caretakers of others' children and yet as matriarchs who nurture pathology within their own family units. If white families are held up as the norm to which the rest of society must conform, and white mothers in particular are seen—through the emphatic disavowal of black domestic labor—as emblematic of an appropriate female domesticity, these characters' failures help to remove white women from the pedestal that centers their experiences while silencing women of color.

Unfinished Women's conclusion demonstrates Rahman's polydramatic jazz aesthetic most clearly and affirms Wilma's role as the figure that connects the two worlds through a bittersweet optimism. The final scene is described by Rahman as "nearest to a spontaneous jazz piece. [… It] bursts into music and voices … weaving in and out of, on top and below, each other, accelerating in pace, volume, and intensity" (34). Bird, Pasha, and the young mothers share the stage, experiencing their individual crises. While each young woman lingers in the fears, hopes, or disappointments that will motivate her decision, Pasha speaks reverently about her unrealized role as a mother, and Bird experiences his transition into eternity; words lose their definition and become infinite sounds that complement Wilma's birth cries. By the end of the scene, Bird's "breaking into song" and Wilma's "wish [to] sing" are one, and the play concludes with the question, "While unfinished women cry in no man's land/The Bird dies in a gilded cage/Could a baby's cry/Be Bird's musical notes/That hang in the air … forever?" (36). Although Bird's life ended prematurely, the spirits of resistance and survival to which his music gave sound live on in the world, both through the loyalty of his fans and through the birth of new children, who repeat the cycle of existence but with the possibility of a different ending. This conclusion allows Rahman's polydrama to challenge the notions of resolution that are intrinsic to the well-made play, conforming to unities of time and place.

Resurrecting icons

Rahman's project of resurrecting black culture represents an attempt to restore some of the humanity that the constant commodification of blackness within American culture undoes. In addition to Charlie Parker, Rahman has rescripted the lives of many other cultural icons, some literally (e.g., Billie Holiday in *Lady Day* and Zora Neale Hurston in *Tale of Madame Zora*), and others figuratively (e.g., Anita Hill in *Only in America*, Clifford Glover in *The Mojo and the Sayso*, and George Jackson in one play from *The Mama* trilogy). In each instance, her plays acknowledge the larger significance of the historical figure's life, making clear why these individuals have become iconic within black cultural politics. Indeed, Rahman's first full-length work established her reputation through this concern. Premiering in 1972, *Lady Day: A Musical Tragedy*, challenged the myths surrounding legendary jazz and blues singer Billie Holiday's life. The musical begins by emphasizing the dire historical moment into which Holiday was born: as the character Flim Flam sings, 1915 "Was a bad time O Lord/To born a woman black and bid her sing" (5). Only one song would be available to her. However, rather than allowing the causes and particularities of Holiday's tragedies to become irrelevant at worst and salacious trivia at best, *Lady Day* takes pains to explain the conditions of which Holiday's music is an elliptical record. First, Rahman addresses Holiday's childhood: "Raped at ten, the law declared her guilty/Sent her to a Catholic institution/Arrested once again/For teenage prostitution/Black woman's beauty/Is her enduring pain" (5). Sexual violence and exploitation robbed Holiday of her childhood, traumas which set the tone for the rest of her life. According to Rahman, *Unfinished Women* "juxtaposes the oppression of the artists and women in American society" ("Tradition" 24), but *Lady Day* stages their confluence within one life.

Anticipating subsequent denunciations of "the traffic in women," Rahman examines the overlap between sexual and economic oppressions of women through the depiction of Holiday's relationship with her lover and business manager, a composite character who represents the many men who treated Billie Holiday badly in romantic and professional dealings. In a key scene, Dan Sugarman uses their sexual relationship as the means to control Holiday's professional career, demanding that Billie sign a contract that will end her dreams of controlling her own artistic destiny. She asserts, "I want to own my own club and publish my own songs" (21), and in return Sugarman threatens that if she refuses to "do the singing while I [manage] your affairs" (21), he will continue to be unfaithful to her. Although she depicts Billie sacrificing artistic and economic independence in order to preserve a romantic relationship, Rahman makes clear, in light of the instability of her childhood, that what Holiday actually craves is peace and security. As she signs the contract, she expresses the emotional terms of the deal for her: "No more arguments between us, please? I hate being without you, even for one minute" (21). As his name suggests, Sugarman is also exposed as the person who introduces Holiday to heroin after she pledges her obedience to him, a betrayal that accelerates the downward spiral of her life.

In addition to highlighting Sugarman's role in her demise, Rahman stages Holiday's prison sentence for drug possession in order to offer a critique of the second-class citizenship blacks continue to endure in America. Beginning with the drippingly ironic trial scene, in which "Billie is handcuffed to the [American] flag" (27), we see the judicial system's presumption of black guilt, and unwillingness to serve anything other than a punitive function. Holiday's repeated pleas that she is unwell are ignored, and instead the Judge repeatedly asks her, "Are you guilty or are you guilty?" (28), imposing a juridical script with only one outcome for a black woman who has signed away her freedom to others. Holiday is condemned with the judgment, "You have defied American society/Offended Christian morality/ For this crime—you must pay some time/A year and a day—now take her away!" (29). In the abject space of the jail cell, Holiday commiserates with her cellmate, claiming, "Being born black, well, that's tears enough to start with, but being Black and a woman is a special kind of pain" (30).

Audiences are forced to see Holiday as a woman whose life emblematizes both the possibilities and the penalties of black womanhood. Her talent allows her to express her resilient spirit while also holding out the promise of upward social and economic mobility, but the combined forces of racism and sexism deny her control over her creative gifts, and by extension, over herself. This systemic suffocation, rather than the specific effects of drugs and alcohol on her body, is the true cause of her death, the true tragedy of *Lady Day*, which explains why Rahman identifies the time of this play as "Yesterday, today, but not tomorrow" (1). The pronounced exclusion of tomorrow serves both to underscore the loss of *Lady Day* and to call into question the obsolescence of the types of tragedies that Holiday endured both as a black woman and as an artist within American society. Why, Rahman seems to be asking, can't we imagine a tomorrow in which this story would make no sense?

In *Tale of Madame Zora* (1985), directed in its Ensemble Studio Theatre premiere by Glenda Dickerson, Rahman shifts her attention to novelist, playwright, and anthropologist Zora Neale Hurston. Again, Rahman harbors no hagiographic intentions, but instead wishes to examine the controversies surrounding Hurston's legacy. The conceit of the play is "the annual Lie Swapping Barbecue Festival in Eatonville, Florida, 1963" (1). Locating the play in Hurson's hometown, Rahman establishes a vivid, dynamic environment in which she can honor Hurston by staging the rich folk cultures that were so important to Hurston's work while also addressing the very serious matter of who gets to tell the definitive story of Hurston's life? With the richness of her characters, from the master of ceremonies Black Herman to the rivals Cora Mae and Happy Sweet, Rahman's Eatonville maintains the idiosyncracies typical of such Hurston plays as *Color Struck* and *Polk County*, and reflects her stated intention to "incorporate the blues of the rural south with the oral tradition" ("Tradition" 24). The play offers a celebration of Zora as one of what Glenda Dickerson refers to as "a pantheon of bad girls and hard-headed women ... the dark, dangerous, unruly presence against which normalcy is defined" ("Focus" 50), and of which Dickerson celebrates Rahman herself as a fellow member. In a more subtle deployment of her signature jazz aesthetic, the musical rejects divisions between the past and the present, placing the ghost of Zora onstage simultaneously with the competing narratives of her life, which are themselves woven into an elastic present tense with her 1960s admirers and detractors.

Because her heyday was the Harlem Renaissance and the play is set on the cusp of the shift from Civil Rights to Black Power agendas, questions of racial authenticity and the politics of representation loom large in Rahman's efforts to understand Hurston's life. First, in relation to the Harlem Renaissance, the community questions the influence of Hurston's anthropology professor Franz Boas upon her work, particularly her investment in the supposedly objective truths of anthropology. Turning Zora into a native informant, Boas sends her into the streets with calipers to get measurements of at least five hundred black Harlemites, so that he might "show the world how false theories of racial inferiority are" (18). In Rahman's play, Hurston does this with aplomb, even convincing one man to submit to the calipers by offering him the chance, in trade, to measure her behind. This scene is cannily juxtaposed with the sonic backdrop of nascent black nationalism: snatches of Garveyite rhetoric—"Up ye mighty race ..."—call into question the propriety of Hurston's phrenological expeditions on behalf of a white man, however well-intentioned.

The other, most pressing question about Hurston's authenticity—as measured by race loyalty—came from her relationship to white Harlem Renaissance patrons after she left the safety of academia. After a scene in which various Renaissance artists subjugate themselves to the "Godmother's" expectations of their art—primitive and uneducated, as she wishes to see them—Zora's spirit calls out to the community, and by extension, to the audience: "You out there, suppose I turned up my nose at white folks and their gifts. No folklore collecting, no writing ... nothing ... I wouldn't be able to do it ... That's the way it was back then ... youngeyes!" (24). Not only does Rahman's Zora defend her actions, she calls into question the racial basis of the claims against her. When an audience member claims to be tortured by her obsequious ways, she rails against him and his elitism, charging, "How dare you turn your noses at me ... I write about black folks you never met and wouldn't know how to act if you did" (26). As she did earlier with *Unfinished Women*, Rahman affirms the validity and necessity of representing blacks other than those of the respectable middle class.

The play culminates with a ritualized representation of Zora's death, in which each of the main characters declaims a facet of her complicated life, and Dr. Mo, the root doctor, offers one of the final lines: "In every tale there are two truths. But turn a tale bottoms up and what you got is the second truth. Another truth. Still the truth. But not the same" (47). With these words, Rahman focuses her attention on our present-day efforts to "turn a tale bottoms up," emphasizing that it is our constantly evolving definition of black cultural politics that motivates us alternately to emphasize, occlude, and augment Zora's story. We, rather than she, continue to change. Our enunciated memories of Zora offer a palimpsest of our shifting investments in her work. Additionally, the conceit of the Lie Swapping Festival, the collaborative and competitive approach to telling her life story, and the challenges that the spirit of Zora makes from the grave all conspire to emphasize orality's central place within black culture. As a ritual itself, *Tale of Madame Zora* celebrates the retelling of black histories as a restored behavior that, with each redoing, helps to reconstitute the community.

The old world meets the new: Spirituality

The recurring role of spirituality in Rahman's work attests to her abiding interest in writing plays that can transcend the distance between her American context and "those cultures of the African diaspora and others that [she] feel[s] spiritually connected with because of common group experiences" ("Tradition" 23). It helps to locate Rahman's African American characters within a larger diasporic cultural framework, one that acknowledges the survival of cultural practices that predate the transatlantic slave trade, thereby affirming the specificity of African American culture as one that is informed by but not synonymous with the practices of the dominant American culture. Rahman penned the three-act *Voodoo America* (1968) during her time at Howard University, and then explicitly returned to these themes decades later with her libretto *Anybody Seen Marie Laveau?* (1999). In an interview with Thadious Davis, Rahman calls the work "a libretto in search of a composer" (quoted in "Writing" 69); for this reason, it has received staged readings but no full production to date. The libretto tells the story of Marie Laveau, the near-mythic nineteenth-century voodoo priestess, and her struggle to retain primacy in the face of threats from folkloric African trickster High John the Conqueror, and from the encroaching Union army occupation of New Orleans. As a whole, the libretto serves to underscore the cultural hybridity lying at the core of American society, exploding the myth of what David Theo Goldberg refers to as American monoculturalism. It also pays tribute to the inventiveness of diasporic Africans who created their own spiritual systems responding to their conditions in the New World. Rahman places the opera in "1862 when Union forces occupied the rebel city of New Orleans [and] The Crossroads where African Gods and Catholic Saints merge" (1), and this merger is physicalized through characters that shift, as they see fit, between identifying as Yoruban and Vodun deities and as Catholic saints.

By setting the opera during the period of the Civil War, Rahman immediately places questions of black freedom and American national values at the forefront of the narrative. The Union occupation of New Orleans ostensibly represents a commitment to black freedom, but the aptly named character General Ben

Only demonstrates the conditional liberation that his army has to offer, one that requires submission to the emphatic hierarchy of whiteness over blackness, masculinity over femininity, and Christianity over other belief systems. For most of the opera, Only attempts to thwart Marie Laveau as the symbol of the city's unruly multiplicity, even sacrificing his wife for her religious treason, but by the libretto's end Laveau's force is undeniable. Her union with High John the Conqueror affirms the place of African traditions within this American context, and General Only abandons his strict beliefs exclaiming, "All saints and gods bless New Orleans ... MARIE LAVEAU HAS GOT THE POWER!" (68). With this final triumph over the reductive racial and spiritual logics of the Unionist army, the opera imagines a different America, one in which the refrains of "only white," and "only Christianity" are supplanted by a celebration of the many races and spiritual practices that comprise our national culture.

The Mojo and the Sayso approaches the same theme but in a different fashion: turning her attentions to the black family, Rahman creates what critics celebrated as an "emotionally true and theatrically arresting" depiction of one family's journey from unfathomable grief to truth and reconciliation (Vaughan 609). Premiering in 1988, the play was inspired by the real-life 1973 murder of 10-year-old Clifford Glover by a plainclothes police officer who believed Glover and his stepfather to be armed robbery suspects. *Mojo* took root in Rahman's imagination at the time when Glover was killed, and though it took many years to germinate, Rahman felt she had no choice but to write the play: "After [she] investigated and did some research, [she] knew the family were people who were voiceless. And [she] had to give voice to them" (quoted in Mahone 283). Through her play, an individual tragedy—and the journey toward healing—becomes emblematic of larger issues facing the black community.

As the beginning of the play makes clear, young Linus's death has ripped the Benjamin family apart, sending each member running in a different direction to seek comfort. Acts Benjamin, the father, puts all of his energy into rebuilding cars. Racked by guilt over his failure to protect his son, he chooses never to discuss the night of the murder, and instead works to complete "the dream car of [his] mind" (43). As a talismanic symbol of unfettered mobility crafted from what others would consider junk, Acts's unfinished car represents the escape from grief that he cannot achieve through other means. As with the bird imagery in *Unfinished Women*, mobility is a dream of freedom, deferred. By contrast, his wife, Awilda, insists that "LINUS IS NOT DEAD [... a]s long as I remember him, Linus is alive" (45). Her commemorative strategies align her with African oral traditions, in which *nommo*, or the generative power of the spoken word, structures what is real and what is not, separating the living from the dead. However, the place where Awilda acts on this African desire is within the Judeo-Christian church, which supplants her nuclear family in her attentions, and which forces the play toward an unanticipated resolution.

While Acts and Awilda retreat from one another into their respective avocations, their surviving son, Walter, experiences a crisis of masculine identity. Walter too rejects the domestic unit, changing his name to Blood, which both completes the fracturing of the family that Linus's death initiated, and describes very clearly his desire for revenge against the world whose violence took away his brother. Aligning himself with the radical activism of imprisoned George Jackson and his brother Jonathan, both of whom were slain by the state, Blood aspires to be "a righteous gunman ... Alone and armed ... Beyond fear" (58). Rahman dedicates the play to "George Jackson, Clifford Glover, and all the Others" (38), reminding us of the senseless deaths, both venerated and anonymous, that continue to take black men away from their communities prematurely. Blood's desperate efforts to become a gun-wielding revolutionary gesture tragically to the other side of America's war on black men. The police officer's bullet cuts short Linus's boyhood (and manhood) as well as Blood's boyhood. The loss of his brother forces Blood into adult feelings too soon, temporarily forcing him into a nether space in which he is allowed to be neither child nor man.

The play's title refers to a fatherly exchange between Acts and Walter. He begins by informing Walter that "in order to survive. You gotta have a little gris-gris to depend on. It could be anything. A prayer, a saying, a rabbit foot, a horseshoe, a song. A way of looking at life, a way of doing things, a way of understanding the world you find yourself in" (62). This appeal to a metaphysics that transcends everyday practices is one of the intimations that Rahman plans to challenge the safety of orthodox Christianity within the play. Acts repeats this advice minutes later when he assures Blood that "[t]he right Mojo will give you the sayso. Put you in the driver's seat" (65). Despite this advice, Acts, like the rest of his family, has chosen an inappropriate mojo: he sees his car as the thing that will give him control over his life, Awilda clings to the church as her salvation, and Blood believes his weapons will give him a sense of purpose. By the play's conclusion, they come to recognize that their shared mojo is the truth.

This journey toward truth begins with the ceremonial expulsion of lies offered in the name of traditional Christianity, personified by Awilda's unscrupulous pastor. When Awilda seems poised to make a disastrous decision that will enable the pastor to profit from the family's tragedy, Blood initiates what he describes as a native Mexican ritual that will "releas[e] the lies from [the pastor's] flesh" (70). By forcing the pastor to remove layer after layer of artifice, Blood reveals the depth of the Pastor's dishonesty: he is exposed as materialistic, perverse, hypocritical, and inhuman. The entire family renounces him, condemning the pastor as a vulture and thereby relieving themselves of the illusions and dishonesty that have been layered over their grief. Acts speaks candidly about Linus's death for the first time and the family's transformation begins: Acts's car comes to life, Awilda sheds her mourner's garb, and Walter renounces his *nom de guerre*, declaring, "No more pain, no more blood" (73). The car, named Mojo 9, becomes a literal vehicle for the family to escape their stagnation, and the play ends with a sense of futurity that the rest of the play lacks. *Mojo* offers a shift from the pessimism of *Lady Day*, in which Billie Holiday's death proves the triumph of hegemonic forces over her life. In this instance—which actually rewrites the tragic exploitation of the real-life Glover family—Rahman offers an escape from the values that threaten to destroy the black family, although it is worth noting that the family's healing sends them out of America and into Mexico. The "absurdity, fantasy, and magical mayhem" that are, in Rahman's words, "intrinsic to the script" (40), offer a productive challenge to the ideological imperatives of naturalistic theatre, underscoring the fact that black life in America demands recourse to alternate cosmologies, both in living everyday life and in the telling of black stories.

Gender politics

While Rahman's black feminist sensibility is apparent throughout her body of work, two plays that pay special attention to black women's plight within American society are *Chiaroscuro* (2000) and *Only in America* (1997). Each play offers a critique of normative practices that disempower black women, whether they be intraracial beauty politics or legislative and cultural politics. In each instance, Rahman is willing to indict black cultural mores as one of the culprits, colluding with a racist American value system that constantly proves Zora Neale Hurston's allegation that the black woman is the mule of the world. Rahman articulated this black feminist stance in her 1979 essay, "To Be Black, Female, and a Playwright," when she noted the specific difficulties black women faced, being "judged differently and more harshly—by both women and men—than ... their male counterparts" (256). Rather than simply "[protest] that [black women's] humanity was far more diverse than indicated by the sexless matriarchs and prostitutes [white] writers had popularized" (258), Rahman has dedicated her career to writing against these traditions within and outside of the black community that collaborate to silence black women.

Rahman's 2000 play *Chiaroscuro: A Light (and Dark) Comedy*, takes its name from the art term that describes the skillful manipulation, usually in painting or drawing, of lightness and darkness. In Rahman's work, it refers to the practice of colorism within the black community, whereby light-skinned blacks (especially women) are seen as more attractive than dark-skinned blacks, and therefore implicitly deserving of preferential treatment both within and outside of the black community. Rahman sets her light and dark comedy on a fantastical cruise ship, placing three light-skinned black women (one of whom is light enough to pass for white) and three dark-skinned black men in an environment in which their prejudices can collide. The potential couples are hosted by Paul Paul Legba, a trickster spirit, who plays ship steward on a vessel with "the ambiance of la belle époque, iron neck collars, beautiful jam-packed holes, graceful branding irons refurbished, human stench, luxurious cruise ships ever built rechristened" (2). With this description, Rahman suggests early on that the issues *Chiaroscuro* will tackle are central to the way that Africans were introduced into the new world, frustrating any sense that the cultural legacies of enslavement have entirely disappeared from contemporary black life.

Rahman employs a metatheatrical technique to highlight the longstanding cultural bias that effectively erases black women by fixating on the desirability of white women—even within the black community. At the play's climax, Legba has induced the singles to perform in a production of *Crazy for You*, an adaptation of Shakespeare's *Othello*. In this instance, however, he draws their attention to the black woman who is not represented on the ship: the dark-skinned, "average" black woman, whom the ship's passengers each silently pity for her lack of beauty. The play within a play helps to suggest the performativity of racialized sexual identity, as the singles demonstrate their mastery of the roles they are meant to play within the script, and none are disturbed by the invisibility of the "Shaneekwa"s of the world, whose "hue seems not the color of love" (68). For example, Russ, whom Rahman describes as "looking for the right kind of woman" (1), knows full well how to play Othello; his acculturation into American society has fostered a preference for women who look nothing like him. Likewise, La Honda and Sienna, the two women who may be light-skinned but could not actually pass for white, accept their self-abnegating roles within the production, demonstrating their resignation to the pigmentocracy that makes them fit only for secondary status.

Gina Rose, the fairest woman on the ship, finally breaks from the colorist script when her body betrays her: after being "gifted" with the role of Desdemona, that icon of desirability, her body begins to transform, revealing "her natural darker self" (72), and she becomes vulnerable to her shipmates' disapproval. Paul Paul Legba reveals the true stakes of their voyage when he declares himself "a lowly steward on the slave ship of your mind" (73): the entire journey is a litmus test, assessing the distance each guest has traveled from the mental slavery of color consciousness. In the end, even Paul Paul Legba sheds his disguise, revealing himself to be Mama Legba, and her role in helping the singles to discover, challenge, and resolve their relationships with one another becomes more pertinent: in rejecting the beauty of their African ancestry, color-conscious blacks cut themselves off from value systems that precede slavery. Light-skin privilege, Rahman asserts, perpetuates the intraracial schisms that blacks have long been trying to undo and abets the dominant culture's efforts to marginalize black aesthetics in general and black women in particular.

In a different vein, *Only in America* reinterprets a controversial moment in black and American history: the Clarence Thomas/Anita Hill hearings. During the 1991 Senate hearings meant to confirm Clarence Thomas as the second black judge on the U.S. Supreme Court, Anita Hill came forward to testify about the episodes of sexual harassment that she allegedly endured working for Thomas at the Department of Education and the Equal Employment Opportunity Commission. Her testimony came under great scrutiny, Thomas was voted onto the court in spite of her charges, and Hill's career suffered for her candor. *Only in America* retells this story in abstract terms, making significant changes to the storyline that underscore the broader implications of Hill's experience. More forthrightly than any of the other full-length works in Rahman's oeuvre, this play offers a traditional black feminist critique of the intersectionality of black women's oppressions within and their unique angle of vision on American culture.

In this fantastical play, Anita Hill becomes Cassandra, and Rahman describes her as one who "understands words but cannot speak" (78). This character choice links her not only to the literal and figurative silencing of Anita Hill, but also to her namesake figure from Greek mythology, whose punishment for rejecting the attentions of the god Apollo was to have a gift of prophecy that would never be trusted by those to whom she spoke. As with *Chiaroscuro*'s reference to *Othello*, the Cassandra of Greek myth allows Rahman both to demonstrate the durability of certain cultural stereotypes and to highlight the by-now rote nature of these relationships between men and women in our society. Cassandra's antagonist within the play is given the punning name Oral: he taunts her with his sexual advances, but also with his access to speech, to legitimacy and intelligibility within the mainstream culture. Oral's verbal domination of Cassandra can also be connected to French feminist critiques of phallocentrism, in which speech is understood to be an extension of the sexualized power that men wield over women and in society at large.

In addition to exposing black women's plight as instruments of (black) male power grabs, *Only in America* offers a sharp critique of the competing camps that gathered to support Hill and Thomas, respectively. The fact that Hill was championed by (white) feminists and lambasted by black (male) leaders for discussing "family matters" in public and thereby undermining the political prospects of all blacks meant that she was unable to stake any political claim as a black woman, and to explain the unique convergence of race and gender in her experiences of private sexual harassment and public intimidation. Within the play, Rahman translates these competing camps into Scatwoman, the black cleaning lady intimidated by Oral into denying what she sees and knows to be inappropriate behavior, and Lili, the white speech therapist who translates Cassandra's unintelligible sounds into English and tries to teach Cassandra to speak for herself in public.

In the final minutes of the play, Rahman specifically draws upon Cassandra's Greek legacy, as she describes her own fate: "You will speak the truth/that no one will want to believe/ ... /There is no rape among us./She who cries 'rape'/works against us/Dishonors our House/Discredits the race" (109). As did the mythological Cassandra, Rahman's character understands that her fate is to speak the difficult truths that challenge her community's understanding of itself. The concluding moments of the play allow

Cassandra to move from simply asserting her individual voice to speaking on behalf of many nameless and voiceless women who have been targeted by systemic violence: she "see[s] violence/Against dark women/Oppressed men/Downpressing oppressed women" (113), and despite Oral's persistent efforts to cast doubt upon her knowledge and her experiences, she continues to speak. The play ends in bittersweet triumph: the voice of oppression has been silenced for the moment, but the question remains; what to do with the power to speak when so much of what needs enunciating is so painful? *Only in America* is not a facile piece of black feminist theatre; instead, it initiates a conversation about the intraracial politics, what Cornel West refers to as the racial reasoning that privileges race-based solidarity over ethical assessment, that have just as profound an impact on black women's lives as do the external pressures of racism.

Lasting significance of Rahman's black aesthetic

Any one of the concepts that structure this essay's review of Rahman's work (intertextuality, jazz aesthetics, black iconography, alternate spiritual epistemologies, and gender politics) offers a useful perspective from which to locate Rahman within the larger community of (African) American (women's) drama. An emphasis on intertextuality, for example, allows us to recognize the relationship between Rahman and playwrights such as George C. Wolfe, whose own *Colored Museum* (1986) responds to *Unfinished Women* itself: in the monologue "Permutations," a young pregnant girl named Normal Jean tries to imagine her pregnancy as something wonderful, and looks forward to the day when her baby is born from an egg, a bird that will be free to fly in ways that she never could. Rahman and Suzan-Lori Parks share several interests: Parks too rejects realism, speaking of the jazz technique of "rep and rev," or repetition and revision, that structures her work, and has produced several plays that revisit cultural icons (e.g., the Venus Hottentot, the black welfare mother, the black minstrel figure) in order to reframe the constitutive role of blackness within Western culture, while making specific interventions into our understanding of black women's experiences. Anna Deavere Smith also shares Rahman's interest in restaging real-life events: her postmodern documentary theatre pieces deny simple resolution in favor of dissonant juxtapositions that enable new ways of recognizing the convergences of racism, sexism, and classism within our society.

From the beginnings of contemporary African American drama, in which the realistic works of Lorraine Hansberry and Alice Childress achieved acclaim; through the nascent experimentalism of the 1960s, when Adrienne Kennedy's surrealist black feminism rose to prominence, and the stirrings of black feminist performance in the 1970s, with artists including Ntozake Shange and Robbie McCauley creating new forms in their efforts to "sing a black girl's song;" and into the present moment, when the postmodern eclecticism of Glenda Dickerson and other artists "create[s] meaning by resisting resolution [... and allowing room for] unarticulated resonance" (Haring-Smith 50), Aishah Rahman has remained an influential force within the field. The constant evolution of her work allows Rahman continually to "[recommit] to being present, to a fierce simultaneity, to a raucous multivocality, to an activist spirituality, to the bringing together of sometimes disparate aesthetics and ideas, to a pleasure in the sensuality of honesty—of sweat and spit and venom and blood" (Dickerson 50). Likewise, Rahman expresses a persistent devotion to the possibility of a culturally autonomous black theatre: one that recalls both DuBois' four-part mandate regarding location, audience, subject, and authorship and August Wilson's turn of the twenty-first century demands for a self-determining black theatre. By constantly contributing to African American drama as both a working playwright and as an educator and mentor to younger artists, Aishah Rahman repeatedly earns her place as a documentarian of the shifts in black expressive culture and, to borrow Margaret Wilkerson's phrase, "continue[s] to offer creative defiance to a world in need of [her] vision" (xxv).

Works cited

Childress, Alice. *Mojo and String: Two Plays*. New York: Dramatists Play Service, 1971.

Davis, Thadious. "Aishah Rahman's *Writing in the Dark*: the presence of an absence." *Obsidian III: Literature in the African Diaspora* 1.1 (1999): 56–72.

Dickerson, Glenda. "Focus On Aishah Rahman: Sweetpeas and Black-Eyed Susans: (Other) Women in the News." *Obsidian III: Literature in the African Diaspora* 1.1 (1999): 50–5.

Grimké, Angelina Weld. *Rachel: a play in three acts*. College Park, MD: McGrath Publishing Company, 1969. 1920.

Haring-Smith, Tori. "Dramaturging Non-Realism: Creating a New Vocabulary." *Theatre Topics* 13.1 (2003): 45–54.

Hurston, Zora Neale. *Color Struck*. *Black Female Playwrights: An Anthology of Plays before 1950*. Kathy Perkins, ed. Indianapolis: Indiana University Press, 1989. 89–102.

——*From Luababa to Polk County: The Zora Neale Hurston Plays at the Library of Congress*. Baltimore: Apprentice House, 2006.

Jones, Joni L. (Iya Omi Osun Olomo). "Why Devise? Why Now?: Riffing on the Syllabus." *Theatre Topics* 15.1 (2005): 49–50.

Jones, LeRoi. *Dutchman*. *Black Theatre USA: Plays by African Americans, 1935–Today*. James V. Hatch and Ted Shine, eds. New York: The Free Press, 1996. 381–91.

Kennedy, Adrienne. *Funnyhouse of a Negro* in *Black Theatre USA: Plays by African Americans, 1935–Today*. James V. Hatch and Ted Shine eds. New York: The Free Press, 1996. 333–43.

Mahone, Sydne, ed. *Moon Marked and Touched by the Sun: Plays by African-American Women*. New York: Theatre Communications Group, 1994.

Meier, Joyce. "The Refusal of Motherhood in African American Women's Theater."
MELUS 25.3–4 (2000): 117–39.

Rahman, Aishah. *Anybody Seen Marie Laveau?* Alexandria, VA: Alexander Street
Press, 2005.

——*Chiaroscuro: A Light (and Dark) Comedy.* Alexandria, VA: Alexander Street
Press, 2005.

——*The Lady and the Tramp.* 1972.

——*Lady Day: A Musical Tragedy.* Alexandria, VA: Alexander Street Press, 2005.

——*The Mama: A Folk's Tale.* 1968.

——*The Mojo and the Sayso. Plays by Aishah Rahman.* New York: Broadway
Play Publishing, 1997. 37–74.

——*NuMuse, An Anthology of New Plays.* Providence: Brown University, 1994.

——*Only in America. Plays by Aishah Rahman.* New York: Broadway Play
Publishing, 1997. 75–116.

——*Tale of Madame Zora.* Alexandria, VA: Alexander Street Press, 2005.

——"To Be Black, Female, and a Playwright." *Freedomways* 19.4 (1979): 256–60.

——"Tradition and a New Aesthetic." *MELUS* 16.3 (1989–90): 23–6.

——*Unfinished Women Cry in No Man's Land While a Bird Dies in a Gilded Cage.
Plays by Aishah Rahman.* New York: Broadway Play Publishing, 1997. 1–36.

——*Voodoo America.* 1968.

Vaughan, Peter. "Penumbra's 'Mojo' surreal, successful." Review of *The Mojo and
the Sayso*, by Aishah Rahman. Penumbra Theatre Company, St. Paul, MN. *Star
Tribune* 20 March 1992: 24E.

Wilkerson, Margaret, ed. *Nine Plays by Black Women.* New York: Mentor, 1986.

Wolfe, George C. *The Colored Museum.* New York: Broadway Play Publishing, 1987.

9 Glenda Dickerson's Nu Shu

Combining feminist discourse/pedagogy/theatre

Freda Scott Giles

To speak when one was not spoken to was a courageous act—an act of risk and daring ... The punishments I received for "talking back" were intended to suppress all possibility that I would create my own speech

(bell hooks)

The performance is not usually held up as a legitimate mode of historiography ... But performance can demonstrate aspects of and ideas about history that are less possible in print ... performed history can actively place the past in the community context of the present time.

(Charlotte Canning)

In the course of conducting research for her most recent "performance dialog," *Sapphire's New Shoe*, Glenda Dickerson learned about a secret language among Chinese women, Nu Shu. Forbidden for centuries from learning to read and write, the women of Jiangyong developed their own writing system as a means for communication and mutual support outside of the purview and control of men. This hidden language often existed in plain sight, sewn onto garments or woven onto strips of cloth.[1] Such a transgressive, liberating act of creating a means and place for speech in the face of repression might serve as a metaphor for Dickerson's goal in developing "miracle plays" and "performance dialogs" over the course of the past three decades. Like Nu Shu, her stage language is created by women; unlike Nu Shu, it is a language meant to be read across boundaries of gender, race, and nationality. It is a language meant to get knowledge produced by women who may not necessarily be scholars acknowledged as scholarship. Dickerson's production techniques create a space for melding womanist performance and feminist scholarship in the academy, a space traditionally resistant to nontraditional production and presentation of knowledge. Instead of writing plays, Dickerson, in collaboration with actors who are familiar with her techniques, builds theatre pieces that enter into a dialectic with contemporary history, politics, and feminist thought, as well as with the audience.

Dickerson's techniques in building her performance works are decidedly feminist. They follow the usual feminist precepts of rejecting linear narrative and the genre of realism as constructions that have failed to provide the open space needed for a multidimensional, comprehensive feminist discourse. In every work, Woman is in the subject position, never in the peripheral, object position. However, in describing Dickerson's methodology for making her theatre, and for making her theatre her own, it might be helpful to consider some remarks from Michelle Cliff's essay, "Object Into Subject: Some Thoughts on the Work of Black Women Artists." Early in her essay, Cliff expands on the metaphysical and psychological explanation of racism as a personal and political practice, offered by white author Lillian Smith. Smith's study of a variety of psychological and philosophical theories led her to trace the origins and manifestations of racism to the "mythic" mind: " that place where dreams, fantasies and images begin: where they take form as art, literature, politics, religion." (271–2) The mythic mind is the seat of the creative act. Its framing and supporting structure is reason. Within the mythic idea of white racism, the irrational obsession with skin color is constructed within a frame of rationalization, i.e., white supremacy— and is imbedded in institutionalized segregation: "An insane idea now exists with a reasonable reality, not an irrational dream." In the process, the objects of racism are rendered Other, denied self-definition, self-realization, and selfhood. Their cultural values are ignored and their cultural products are recast by the dominant culture to serve the purpose of objectification. They are rendered silent. Cliff goes on to state that in the process, white and Black women alike remain objectified and divided. The white woman, objectified to serve the dominant patriarchy, has complied in the objectification of the Black woman, first and foremost, historically, through the process of slavery. In this process, the female slave endured, and sometimes, rebelled: "with magic, poison, force, even with spit" (278). Learning to read and write, as well as preserving and sustaining her own cultural forms, became further avenues for subversion and rebellion.

It is here that we return to Dickerson's theatre. In constructing her works, she examines her own "mythic mind" and that of other women of color. She does not seek to reflect that mind back to the audience, as Adrienne Kennedy does in her expressionistic works, nor does she offer her own ideas, imagination, and experiences as poetry, or choreopoems as Ntozake Shange does. Though she is often compared to these two artists, Dickerson seeks to ground the "mythic mind" of the woman of color in material history and current events, not only as consciousness raising, but as a catalyst for political/social action. She seeks to include the audience in the performed experience, setting up a dialectic with the performed work, which itself is a dialectic with history, memory, and culture. Her work usually contains a pastiche of Western, Eastern, and African mythology, historical events, poetry, and religious rituals and iconographies. In a literary sense, it may be described as a mythopoetic theatre framed in the reality of Black women's experiences. Dickerson is unwavering in her determination to cast the creative imaginations and histories of Black women as reflective of the universal experience of humanity, thus giving voice to those who are silenced by sexism and racism while deconstructing and demolishing objectification, as formed through stereotypes of African American women. She is persistent in insisting that the political and social realities of women of color be foregrounded on a resonant plane of myth and imagery. Cultural production by and about women of color, from kitchen objects to religious practices, folklore, art, literary productions, music, and movement are integrated into oral histories, historical narratives, and reports of current events. Dickerson pursues change in the way Black women's experiences are perceived, not only in the realm of art, but in the academy. Their resonant experiences serve as a platform for neglected academic discourse; the production of knowledge is incomplete without them. Her persistence of vision and her attachment of her artistic creations to the pursuits of the academy in service to reclaiming and reconstructing the way women's contributions are perceived and interpreted, set her apart as a theatre artist. Throughout her career, in the production, direction, and performance of her own work, Dickerson has melded the professional theatre with theatre in the academy in a unique way.

Like Cliff, Dickerson has adopted Aunt Jemima, as depicted by the visual artist Betty Saar, as an iconic image central to her work. Saar's mixed media construction, "Liberation of Aunt Jemima," shows a familiar view of the mammy figure as a cookie jar (a source of nourishment), a face on a pancake box, holding a white baby, and posed with a broom. However, Aunt Jemima is also depicted holding a pistol and a rifle, one of her skirts shaped as a Black fist. Aunt Jemima is an icon of survival and resistance, the instrument of her own liberation.

Dickerson's decision to forge a career as a theatre director might, in itself, be described as a transgressive act. As Sue Ellen Case noted in *Feminism and Theatre*, despite significant gains for playwrights and actors, relatively few African American women have been able to break through as professional directors (104). Dickerson attributes her gift for stage direction to her grandmother's power to influence and shape her environment (Dickerson, "Wearing Red" 154). The roots of Dickerson's directing methodology go back to her theatre training at Howard University, where she earned her B.F.A. in 1966. After graduation with an M.A. in Speech and Theatre Arts at Adelphi University, Dickerson returned to Howard to teach in the Department of Speech and Drama. Poet, playwright, stage director and teacher, Owen Dodson (1914–1983), a member of the Howard faculty, became a significant instructor and mentor. Dodson combined a practitioner's knowledge of the theatrical with his poetic sensibilities. Later, in 1981, Dickerson would pay tribute to him by founding the Owen Dodson Lyric Theatre (ODLC), a touring theatre company housed in various locations in New York City (including, for a period, Vinette Carroll's Urban Arts Corps theatre space in lower Manhattan), that performed together for seven years. Dickerson describes the ODLC as serving as a modern-day collective griot.[2]

Her appreciation for ritual, myth and folklore became a through-line in her creative work.

In 1971, Dickerson earned an Emmy Award nomination for her direction of a televised performance of Alice Childress's classic comedy/drama, *Wine in the Wilderness*, followed in 1972 by a Peabody Award for her conceptualization and direction of "For My People," a program of African American poetry produced for station WTOP in Washington, D.C. From 1973–1976, Dickerson served as the first Drama Department Head at D.C.'s Duke Ellington High School for the Performing Arts. Subsequent academic appointments include Fordham University, Mason Gross School of the Arts, Rutgers University, State University of New York at Stony Brook, and chairing both the Departments of Theatre Arts and of Television, Rutgers University, Newark and later, the Department of Drama and Dance, Spelman College, Atlanta, Georgia. Dickerson currently heads the Center for World Performance at the University of Michigan, Ann Arbor. Her professional theatre work and her scholarly research have taken her all over North America, to the Caribbean, Europe, Japan, and Africa. Her experiences brought her insight into the universality of the language of oppression and of women's experiences: "... the anguish of women is echoed around the world and resonates from continent to continent" (Dickerson, "Cult" 184).

Though her university and professional work often called for her to direct realistic plays, Dickerson chafed under the restraint of realism. As she experimented with forms to reflect her ideas, she steadily built a body of work that tended toward the stylized and expressionistic: "Aunt Jemima tapped my shoulder and told me that well-made—in my case—was a phrase which best modified beds" (184). Her experiments during the 1970s often took the form of poetry framed into narratives; she called these productions "miracle plays:"

> I define a miracle play as a tapestry for the stage ... these miracle plays recognize myth as the original mother tongue. My miracle plays embody history, culture, literature, symbols, dreams, and inspiration ... They explore archetypes as they are revealed through the lives of drylongso[3] people (180).

The Unfinished Song (1970), *Jesus Christ Lawd Today* (1972), and *Owen's Song* (1978), based on Owen Dodson's poetry, would fall under this category. Each of these works consisted primarily of performed African American poetry enriched by folkloric references and music. Another of these works, *Magic and Lions*, produced in 1977 at the Women's Interart Theatre in New York, became a watershed experience. Dickerson created a ritual, combining ancient Dogon (a people located in Mali) and Egyptian mythology, to return ancient Egyptian gods and goddesses to contemporary times, using the language of Ernestine Jackson's poetry and a fictive language created by the actors, along with original music. The poetry took on entirely new resonances as performed and reacted to by the "gods." Audiences responded well to the production, but Dickerson came to a realization about her need to move further in a new direction. She viewed the framing of her narrative of that show as "my last obeisance to a patriarchal world-view in a miracle play" (185). She thought that rituals and myths from historic or traditional sources privileged male hegemony. The "miracle plays," combining poetry, myth, and ritual, would move toward the realm of everyday women's worldviews and lives, and place women squarely in the foreground.

In the midst of turning her own creative process toward these new miracle plays, Dickerson was offered the opportunity to direct a Broadway show, *Reggae*, written and produced by the same production team that created *Hair*. At the time, 1980, Dickerson was only the second African American woman to direct a Broadway show.[4] The producers and Dickerson experienced creative differences; *Reggae* closed after twenty-one performances. That experience served to reinforce her determination to make a different kind of theatre. In 1981, she conceived a production based on the poetry of Alexis DeVeaux, entitled *NO*. The official title became, *"NO!" a new, experimental work of neoliterary events, political messages and innovative stories for the stage.* Later, another title, *NO! A Parlor Reading*, was used. That title signified an atmosphere of elegance and sensuality, of women with "The courage to 'wear red', to redefine, rediscover, reclaim that which has been misdefined for us ..." (Dickerson, " Wearing Red" 155). Mel Gussow, in a positive review of the performance for the New York Times, compared *NO* to Shange's *for colored girls* (14). Dickerson, however, is careful to note that her work is different in form and execution from Shange's choreopoem design. As Dickerson and Breena Clarke later wrote, the miracle play process "should not be considered choreopoetic, though it employs the poetic voice ... [it] is expressed through culturally specific archetypes and calls upon a racial idiom in verse form ..." (Clarke and Dickerson, "The Triune Voice" 410).

Selected short stories and poetry by DeVeaux were adapted into a series of narratives on women's lives that included honest and realistic portrayals of sexual and psychological abuse, as well as celebrations of female heterosexual and lesbian sexuality. *NO* was conceived as an anthem of defiance and resistance to suppression. Dickerson felt liberated by the opportunity to produce and stage the work herself. She "sanctified a sullied space," ("Festivities and Jubilations") a space where Black women were represented on the stage, in a found space on the lower east side of New York, in 1981. The show became a success with audiences and critics.

Her next miracle play, first performed in 1984, *Tarbaby, a paradigm for our time*, was designed as a ritual of affirmation designed to build self-esteem among young women. *Tarbaby* also became a rite of passage for Dickerson as an artist: "I resign from the ranks of directors of plays and become instead a full time PraiseSinger ... I will be concerned not with acts, and scenes and curtains; but with redemption, retrieval, and reclamation" (187).

While teaching at Stony Brook, Dickerson discovered that the nearby community of Setauket, Long Island was home to an African American settlement that may have preceded the Revolutionary War. Organizing a group of student volunteers to assist, Dickerson gathered stories from that community's elders, and collected artifacts for an exhibit. Then she developed a "miracle play" for performance within the exhibit, through which professional and student actors and the audience would interact in absorbing and performing the community's rich history. She took the title of the exhibit and performance, *Eel Catching in Setauket*, from an 1845 painting by William Sidney Mount (1807–1868), "Eel Spearing in Setauket," in which a foremother of one of the storytellers, Rachel Holland Hart, is depicted. Dickerson altered her title to reflect a less violent image, that of capturing the substance of a community, rather than the image of hunting and conquering.

Two years of preparation culminated in public performances in 1988. The community, the university, and professional theatre practitioners were enmeshed in an interactive theatre event that carried enormous emotional power. Descendants of community founders lent testimony to their own performed stories as the audience walked among the community's displayed treasures. They told stories of how the community was built, the histories of members of generations of founding families who still lived there, and the defining moments for community institutions, like the local African Methodist Episcopal Church.

Dickerson followed up this project with a similar project for the city of Newark New Jersey, *Wellwater: Wishes and Words: a Living Portrait of Newark's People*, in 1992. She followed much the same pattern as *Eel Catching in Setauket*, leading a team of Rutgers University students in conducting extensive research and gathering oral histories on the history of the city. Though the grants she received from New Jersey State Arts Council and the State University of New Jersey were not large enough for her to complete the project with an exhibit of artifacts, the students presented the text as a "work in progress."

Dickerson's next miracle play was inspired by her 1991 visit to Jekyll Island, Georgia, site of Ibo Landing, a cultural icon treated reverentially in Julie Dash's film, *Daughters of the Dust*, which premiered that same year. At the time, Dickerson had not seen the film, but she knew well the story of how African captives disembarked a slave ship there, turned resolutely toward home, and walked into the ocean.

When she made her way to the site, she was forcefully turned away by its white owners. On the island she witnessed golf balls whizzing past hallowed burial grounds and momentous histories relegated to small plaques. She met an African American woman there, Ana Bel Lee, who had become an artist after her retirement as a social worker; her artwork evoked the life and history of the island. Dickerson discovered that, serendipitously, Lee's work would soon be exhibited at Spelman College, where Dickerson had recently accepted appointment as chair of the theatre department. The ensuing miracle play, *Ana Bel's Brush: a Live Oak Drama*, was presented in 1992.

The performance environment was created from Lee's canvasses and artifacts, including her brushes, photographs of her, and other items from her studio, plus pine cones, sand, and moss from Jekyll Island. Her paintings were hung in a nearby gallery. The story of her life was performed by a professional actress, Margurite Hannah, from Lee's oral history, recorded by Dickerson in taped interviews.

As a manifesto for this phase of her work, Dickerson composed an essay, "The Cult of True Womanhood: Toward a Womanist Attitude in African American Theatre," which she performed at the Association for Theatre in Higher Education Conference in 1987. The essay describes her process for arriving at her methodology for creation of a womanist theatre. She begins her discussion with a description of the Cult of True Womanhood, a late nineteenth-century movement, aimed at white, middle class women, urging them toward religious piety, sexual purity, domesticity, and obedient submission to the male prerogative as the only acceptable hallmarks of femininity. Dickerson deconstructs and subverts those ideas and restructures the term as a paradigm for resistance against rather than submission to white patriarchy. Dickerson claims for the Cult of True Womanhood the descendants of women who were "exploited by racism, denied equality by their own husbands, yet determined to educate themselves and their children, take pride in themselves and their history and to 'lift up the race.'" (182) The drama of nommo,[5] the spirit force—expressed through the word, ritual, rhythm, music and dance—is used as the basis for the creation of a theatre language that speaks from, as well as about, the womanist experience. As the editors of *Theatre Journal* noted, the rhetorical style in which Dickerson delivers her ideas offers "an alternative discourse, central to the development of a woman-identified, ethnic language and outside of the white, upper-middle-class, gender marked language of traditional scholarship" (178).

Dickerson bundled her ideas and research from "The Cult of True Womanhood" and another of her essays, "Wearing Red" into a solo performance, *Glenda Dickerson is Spreading Lies: A Space Shuttle for Black Women*. In her role as PraiseSinger and Educator, Dickerson "sprints the Space Race in America." Dickerson's work often refers to space and the uses of space as a race and gender issue. Historically, women of color have been denied space, particularly space in the public sphere. Space itself, whether theatrical space or any other narrative space, must be reconstructed to provide a venue that more appropriately allows appreciation of the scope and diversity of the woman of color's knowledge and experience. In lieu of a lecture, Dickerson exemplifies her work by performing the means through which her work revalues women's history and demands space for both her gender and her race.

The performance of a Dickerson essay often includes audience participation. At a scholarly conference, a staid group of academics may find themselves moving and singing in a circle, chanting an affirmation, or taking part in a ritual honoring the foremothers, singing "May the Circle Be Unbroken." The subject may be feminist historiography and reclamation of the Black woman's identity, supported by critics, historians, and theorists, but the delivery is designed to open the audience to engaging the material through a variety of avenues. Scholar Marvin Carlson likens Dickerson to French feminists, who emphasize the act of speaking in one's own voice: "there is no substitute for hearing Dickerson perform one of her essays, but even on the written page her voice is powerful and distinctive" (Carlson 536).

In 1992 Dickerson collaborated with her longtime friend, author Breena Clarke, on a script for the miracle play, *Re/membering Aunt Jemima: A Menstrual Show*, a womanist deconstruction of the Aunt Jemima stereotype (see Perkins and Uno 34).

Dickerson and Clarke sought to reclaim Aunt Jemima as the Santeria figure La Madama, guardian orisha[6] of the domestic sphere. The desire to contemplate, reexamine and transform the imagery of Aunt Jemima is shared by a number of other contemporary African American literary, visual, and theatre artists. Current theatrical explorations of the image can also be found in George C. Wolfe's *The Colored Museum* (1988) and *The Death of the Last Black Man in the Whole Entire World* (1990) by Suzan-Lori Parks. Dickerson and Clarke expand Aunt Jemima's iconography by connecting her all the way to Africa through a deity in a New World religion.

In order to do so, Dickerson and Clarke invert and reinvent the minstrel show format, expanding the deconstruction to include traditional and modern stereotypes of the African American woman. This strategy of confronting and reappropriating minstrel stereotypes from an offensive rather than defensive position is another post-Afrocentric theatrical strategy, shared with playwrights such as Parks and Wolfe, as well as with Ntozake Shange, as exemplified in *spell #7: a geeche jibara quick magic trance manual for technologically stressed third world people: a theatre piece* (1979), which begins with the company performing in minstrel masks beneath a giant, grinning black mask that hovers over the stage. Confrontation with the minstrel show is particularly significant to the theatre, since this form, in which whites counterfeited black behavior, and forced black performers to do the same, has embedded its images of African Americans into world consciousness ever since its inception in the 1840s.

The minstrel device of the "stump speech," the mangling of language meant to demean the African American's intelligence, is one of the primary means through which Dickerson and Clarke realign language into images descriptive of the power of African American women's experiences and ideas.

Layers of misrepresentation and manufactured shame are peeled away to expose the archetypal black woman who was integral to the Black diaspora's survival. The minstrels become "menstruals," of quintessential female identity, who bend time and space to enact a mythic history of Aunt Jemima, from her travails as a slave through her sufferings in the present. As Kim Euell notes, the menstrual represents the feminine capacity for both pain and creativity (671).

Euell also notes that the play is "double-voiced," a text " talking to other texts, offering critique and revision," as Henry Louis Gates describes in *The Signifying Monkey*. Viewing George C. Wolfe's *The Colored Museum* as the first of a new wave of such texts, (674) Euell describes this new wave as works that ask the audience to participate in a ritual of adjudication and absolution of stereotypes.[7] The major difference in *Re/membering Aunt Jemima* from other works that reclaim and demystify icons is that this work goes a step further toward revision of the icon into a powerful symbol of affirmation (672). Aunt Jemima is not only reclaimed; she is revered.

Raucous humor infuses the action as Aunt Jemima (having been forced to jump the broom with Uncle Ben, among others) gives birth to thirteen daughters, cultural icons in their own right, who range from Pecola, an evocation of Peola, the troubled daughter in Fannie Hurst's *Imitation of Life* (1933) and the Pecola of Toni Morrison's *The Bluest Eye*, to Dorothy (Dandridge), to Sapphire, to Anita, whose fate mirrors that of Anita Hill (reviled for revealing Supreme Court Justice Clarence Thomas' sexual harassment). In a stunning turn from comedy to tragedy, Aunt Jemima— elderly, sick, forgotten, trapped in her pancake box—is shotgunned to death by police who arrive to evict her, a direct reference to the case of Eleanor Bumpurs.[8] Aunt Jemima's last words echo Sojourner Truth's declaration: "Ain't I a woman?" The words recall the legendary incident in which Truth bared her breasts to silence skeptics who sought to discredit her entitlement to speak about women's rights.

As she is eulogized, and the feats and exploits of her daughters are described, Aunt Jemima springs back to life: "Ah can catch bullets with my ass-perity [*sic*]. Sometimes Ah send them back with interest and sometimes Ah transform them into balls of cotton." Aunt Jemima is vulnerable to attack, but she is too resilient to be destroyed. She is capable of just retaliation and able to create a positive, productive outcome from a negative New World experience that began with slavery. As one menstrual explains, "She is with us always and asserts herself in our daily lives and offers us a strategy" (see Perkins and Uno 45).

Theorizing their work, Clarke and Dickerson describe their methodology in the creation and production of *Re/membering Aunt Jemima* as recovering and releasing the Triune Voice, as expressed by the term, I Am/Who Was/Who Am. The I Am represents the subject's act of asserting identity, of taking control of her narrative. In Clarke and Dickerson's work, this means that the woman whose speech is being reified on the stage, whether the speaker of a slave narrative or a "drylongso" woman giving her testimony, has "changed her status from that of an object, owned and identified by another, to the subject of her own discourse" (411). This process leads directly to the Who Was, the voice that "enlarges upon the initial assertions to reflect and comment on the particular circumstances of her bondage." The assertion of identity and testimony of the history become the foundation for the third component, Who Am, which represents the voice of the performer. The performer's voice melds with that of the foremother: "agreeing to embrace them and synthesizing them with the voices of contemporary African American women is the rebellious/revolutionary/emancipatory act of the performer." (Clarke and Dickerson, "Triune Voice" 410–12). As scholar Harry Elam describes, Aunt Jemima and her daughters denote black women's collective identity, consciousness, and shared heritage of struggle and survival, cutting across potentially divisive elements, such as class. Through Aunt Jemima and her daughters, past history is connected holistically to contemporary Black women's experiences (Elam 5)

Dickerson elevated two literary giants to mythic proportions in *Zora and Lorraine and Their Signifyin Tongues* (1995). After steeping herself in the works of Zora Neale Hurston (1891–1960) and playwright Lorraine Hansberry (1930–1965), Dickerson reconstructed their writing into a cosmic argument. No matter that they met at the end of Hansberry's life, while she lay dying in a hospital bed, five years after Hurston died. Naming Hurston the "Grand Signifier" and Hansberry the "Cool Tongued Rebel," Dickerson pits their methods of interpreting the African American experience, and even the fictional characters they created, against each other in a contest of ideas that becomes a celebration of their lives and works. Dickerson celebrates both as warrior women and attempts to give them their due. "As artists," she believes, "we must be on a mission to introduce our students to their culture. There is not the concern for the race that there used to be. We are not the 'race people' we used to be" (Interview 1996).

Dickerson makes it clear that claiming voice and claiming space mean purveying truth rather than denigrating men: "If a woman is speaking her truth, whatever her truth is, it really doesn't have anything to do with men in the sense that it is not for or against men, it is about her ..." (Interview 1996). Some feminists have given the impression that much of the feminist movement is fixated on the victimization of women; womanism resists that notion. The big picture is liberty and justice for all. The goal of freeing society from racism, classism, and sexism is mutually inclusive.

The next phase of Dickerson's work combined the miracle play with street theatre, putting the performance on a level similar to the medieval mystery cycle plays that progressed through the community, stopping at designated stations. For two days during the Centennial Olympic Games (Atlanta, 1996), she executed a site-specific performance event. *Folksay: A Living Exhibit* (later known as *Talkstory of Style and Substance*) brought to life the history of Atlanta's seminal African American community, the

Auburn Avenue district. Using the Wheat Street Baptist Church and the Baldwin Burroughs Theatre at Spelman College as anchors, Dickerson and her actors traversed outdoor sites throughout the neighborhood, recreating historic events that took place there. Many of the tableaux, which evolved into scenes, were based on turn-of-the-century photographs by Thomas Askew, Atlanta's first African American professional photographer. In front of the Odd Fellows Hall, Mamie Smith (1883–1946) and her Jazz Hounds recalled the era of the blues. In front of the Herndon Building, Alonzo (c.1858–1927) and Adrienne Herndon (1869–1910) told the story of how he founded the Atlanta Life Insurance Company and how she designed their historic home only to die just as it was completed. On the street, Mary Combs (n.d.) described how, as the first person of color to purchase real estate in antebellum Atlanta, she waited for it to appreciate in value, then sold it to buy her husband's freedom from slavery. Some audience members knew of the performance ahead of time; many did not, and joined along the way. Auburn's past and present intersected, culminating in a musical celebration in the church.

The current phase of Dickerson's work, the performance dialogs, has become known as *Transforming Through Performing*. The text, a combination of historical documents, testimony, myth, and ritual, is transformed through its performance by women of color into a participatory dialectic with the audience on the universality in women's experience. The performers themselves, through their process of preparation and execution of the performance, are transformed into performance scholars, enabling the audience to synthesize and theorize relationships across history, across cultures, across academic and performance disciplines. Included in each performance is a table setting, as a symbolic evocation of gendered space, of community, and of communal sharing. There is always a ritual, whether a pouring of libation for the ancestors, women who have died the previous year between performances, or oblation to deities of Africa and the African diaspora. Choral speech, chanting, secular songs and spirituals, archetypal characters, and myths, frame, amplify, and enhance the juxtaposition of related historical and contemporary events against testimonies gathered from well-known and little-known women. Each performance dialog is accompanied by a feedback session with the audience, facilitated by a scholar, and follow-up panels that interrogate major themes raised in the performance dialogs. Dickerson views this process as a potential catalyst for social change: the process of transformation is complete when the experience leads to social action, and to a concept of black female identity that includes the insights of artists and of women outside the academy.

Prior to a successful application for a Ford Foundation grant, obtained in 2000, the original plan was for Dickerson, in collaboration with scholar Jacqueline Matisse, to travel to Tanzania to interview Rwandan women displaced by genocidal conflict. However, the narratives collected in Tanzania remain unused; the events of September 11, 2001 intervened.

Dickerson organized a workshop and the first performance dialog, *Kitchen Prayers: Performance Dialog on 9/11 and Global Loss*, was performed as a staged reading in December of 2001, followed by a more fully staged version in May, 2002. The entire trilogy of performance dialogs was first performed in theatres at the University of Michigan, Ann Arbor.

The story of Niobe became the mythic/metaphoric frame for the performance. Niobe, who arrogantly boasted of her children, angered the gods, who cut them down and turned her into a weeping stone. Niobe came to represent the United States. The performance became an effort to process the disaster, through reportorial accounts, first person testimony by performers and audience members, choral speech, folk songs, spirituals, myth, and poetry. The event became a communal meditation on the meaning of a shared traumatic experience. The immediacy of theatrical time, combined with closeness of the audience to the event in time, melded in a unique way. The immediacy of the performance took the audience from the position of spectator to the position of witness.

Margaret Wilkerson describes the term, "kitchen prayers," as one that speaks both of power and of supplication: the kitchen is a gendered space over which the woman exerts unquestioned authority, while a prayer is an expression of humility and aspiration. *Kitchen Prayers* offers a new means for processing contemporary history, especially in terms of current global conflicts (Wilkerson, in "What's Cookin' in the Kitchen"). The participating actors became known as "Prayerful Performers,"[9] and the performances became "performance dialogues," connoting the expectation of audience participation at some point in the performance. During the first *Kitchen Prayers*, audience members were invited to volunteer their own stories of their responses to the events of September 11, 2001. The September 11 anniversary was marked in every subsequent performance.

The controversial nature of Dickerson's work was made imminently apparent when she was invited to mount a series of three performances of *Kitchen Prayers* in Istanbul, Turkey in the summer of 2002. In recognition of their surroundings, the Prayerful Performers added excerpts from Euripides' *Trojan Women* and a section on the constested practice of head covering in Turkey, using the testimonies of Muslim women. The audience responded with shock and anger. Dickerson was likewise shocked that the audience could not accept the potential for African American women to embody a Turkish experience, or to combine disparate women's experiences into a universal statement. The experience proved painful, but useful, as the performers went into another series of workshops (Interview 2006).

Identities on Trial: a Kitchen Protest Prayer premiered in April 2003. As explained in the performance's program, the trial as women's experience is explored in its several forms: as ordeal ("trials and tribulations"), experimentation (a "trial run"), or legal action ("trial by jury"). A direct response against the war in Iraq, the major portion of the work engaged narratives from a United Nations (U.N.) tribunal on women's rights.

Through showing the experiences of Bangladeshi, Roma, Guatemalan, Iranian, Nepalese, and other women through the performance of African American actors, Dickerson reasserts her belief in the universality of oppressed women's experiences and the right of African American women to present them.

The final segment of the trilogy, *Sapphire's New Shoe: the Kitchen Table Summit,* was presented on October 29, 2004, as both a culminating production and a culminating event for the entire project. Sapphire, the iconic stereotype of the termagent black female, was reclaimed as the embodiment of resistance to oppression. Dickerson framed this performance dialog in both the idea of contemporary Nu Shu, a language of resistance for women, and the ritual celebration in honor of the dead by the Boa Morte Sisters of Brazil, whose religious practices combine Yoruba and Catholic cosmology.

The performance begins with Mama Rice (not as "mother" of Condoleeza or Connie, but as a figure likened to a voodoo priestess, who conjures up seemingly disparate women who end up having much in common), adorned in a white costume similar to the ones worn by the Brazilian Boa Morte Sisters, ritualistically setting a table for the ancestors, with a special homage to Saartje Baartman (1789–1815).[10] The first guests to arrive are Condoleeza Rice, Secretary of State, and Connie Rice, her cousin, a human rights activist. They heatedly debate their positions as activist women, from the right and from the left; they become angry, but end up laughing together. They will love each other, somehow, through their differences. Other guests enter at various times, including Contrary Woman, who rails against female genital mutilation and unnecessary hysterectomies, and Bone Woman, based on Dr. Clea Koff, an African American woman who performs forensic identifications of massacre victims at sites around the world, including Rwanda and Bosnia. Miriam Chamani, a contemporary voodoo priestess, enters, discussing the resurgence of interest in voodoo. The audience is invited into the discussion of current events with the question, "Are we better off now than we were on 9/11?" The actors (six women play all the roles) remain in character while interacting with the audience. Madame C. J. Walker (1867–1919), builder of a fortune based on hair care products, enters and reads a portion of Hannah Craft's slave narrative, the controversial book uncovered by historian Henry Louis Gates, seeking a critique. Aunt Jemima enters; since she is a convicted felon, she is denied the right to vote; she talks about slavery in the twentieth century. It is later revealed that Betty Saar rescued her from incarceration in a pancake box. Dr. Ruth Simmons, first African American woman to become president of an Ivy League university, Brown, talks about her efforts to examine Brown's debt to the slave trade and the efficacy of reparations. Other women who participate in the discussion include Essie Williams, daughter of Strom Thurmond; Dr. Dorothy Height, legendary civil rights activist; the former wife of the Beltway Sniper,[11] who describes her abuse at his hands; Edwinge Danticot, the contemporary novelist is flown in from

Haiti by Bessie Coleman (1892–1926), first African American woman airplane pilot, to report on the impact of Hurricane Ivan on her country. Oprah Winfrey enters to broadcast an Amber Alert for Precious Doe, the child who disappeared unnoticed by Florida Child Protective Services. She also gets to meet one of her idols, Marian Anderson (1898–1993), the great operatic contralto, recent subject of a new biography. As the first act ends, libation is poured for the women of color who died since the last installment of *Kitchen Prayers*, including women in the news between 2002 and 2004, plus all those unknown women who lie in unmarked graves, or who have no graves at all.

The second act begins with a confrontation between Pauline Inuwashurawaho, labeled the "Minister of Rape" during the Rwandan genocide, for her role in encouraging the rape of Tutsi women by Hutu men. Her victims, as well as other victims of rape and genital mutilation, tell their stories. All texts and speeches are taken verbatim from U.N documents of the Rwandan War Crimes Tribunal and from other U.N. reports. African women who were kidnapped and turned into child soldiers also testify. Slavery still exists. Rape is still an instrument of terror. Living women gain insight into their conditions by learning from those who have gone before. Fictional women interact with "real" woman. Poetry, music, and art interact with the prose of historical documents. Though incidents may seem at first disjointed, all are brought together as an indictment of the conditions most women live under today, of our ignorance and apathy in light of those conditions, and an acknowledgement of the presence of history in our daily lives.

The ending includes a celebration of the recently excavated slave burial ground in Manhattan, where remains of ancestors have been recovered. In between, the ramifications of colonial and/or gender oppression as a catalyst for the formation of women's language is explored, with a large helping of irony and humor. The final action by the Prayerful Performers was taken from the women of Swaziland, who, in a traditional show of denunciation of the failure of their leaders to govern wisely, curse them with a show of bare bottoms. The performers moon the audience with their bare bottoms in repudiation of a world overfull of failed leadership. Their Nu Shu is a language of defiant resistance to oppression. As with the other performances in the series, this one was followed by a talk-back session, facilitated by theatre scholars, which gave the audience the opportunity to comment and ask questions. The program, that Dickerson likens to a "scrap book," contains images of most of the women who are named in the performance, and some who are not. These captioned images help the audience keep track of what they have seen and heard.

In July 2006, Dickerson showed the final product of the project, a DVD, "What's Cookin' in the Kitchen? A Planetary Portrait, 9/11/01–9/11/04," at the Black Theatre Network Conference in Louisville, Kentucky. The DVD is designed as an interactive teaching tool that would enable users to use the process to explore other histories. There are two discs: the first provides an overview of the project, including excerpts from the *Kitchen Prayers* performances; the second, in three sections, explains the process of building the scripts, shows the perfomers at work in the process, and includes explanations of the efficacy of the project by theatre scholars Margaret Wilkerson, Harry Elam, and others. It is distributed through the Center for World Performance Studies.

Since completing the project, Dickerson has collaborated with Lynda Gravatt on a one-woman play, *Barbara Jordan: Texas Treasure*, produced at the Alley Theatre, Houston Texas, in 2005. This work is a more conventional performed history, as Gravatt reanimates the pioneering Democratic congresswoman (1936–1996) from Texas, and her call to conscience to her party and her nation.

It is feminist historians and theorists who have first embraced performed scholarship, and Glenda Dickerson is at the forefront of this movement, though her work appears to expand upon the idea by treating more than one event or person at a time, not only in the dimension of history, but, in an inter-disciplinary sense, through the dimensions of folklore, literature, and the arts. It might be said that she is seeking to accomplish in the theatre what Betty Saar accomplished in her collage of Aunt Jemima. Her work as a director is much better known than her work as a playwright, though knowledge of her work is spreading through the academy, particularly among feminist scholars. Her published essays have been a great help in providing information about her work. Her only published script is *Re/membering Aunt Jemima*, her collaboration with Breena Clarke. The scripts of the *Kitchen Prayers* series are available to the public in the Peace Archive, an exhibit based on *Kitchen Prayers* that Dickerson established at the University of Michigan. The rest of her miracle plays and performance dialogs have not yet breathed life beyond the academy, nor existed without her involvement, nor been made available to be performed by other theatres. Dickerson is directing her energy more toward teaching others how to make performance dialogs than in getting those miracle plays and performance dialogs she has already created published. She runs a yearly *Transforming Through Performing* workshop at New York University; she has preserved the *Kitchen Prayers* series on video, and excerpts are available through the "What's Cookin' in the Kitchen?" DVD. Dickerson's forty years of theatrical experience are more than ripe for a dissertation or book length study. She has blazed a trail as a director, theatre practitioner, and postmodern, postcolonial feminist writer.

Dickerson has had a major impact on the theatre artists she has trained and included in her work since her days at Duke Ellington High School. The Prayerful Performers, who spent three years in collaboration on the *Kitchen Prayers* series, were all former students. However, Dickerson's miracle plays and performance dialogs have not yet moved into mainstream theatre. The dissemination of her techniques and ideas are, at present, more apt to be located in the academy.

Notes

1 Sapphire's New Shoe: the Kitchen Table Summit, souvenir program, 29 October 2004.
2 Glenda Dickerson, directing résumé.
3 Dickerson, inspired by John Langston Gwaltney's collection of oral histories of working class African Americans, *Drylongso* (1980), often uses the term in describing her own work.
4 The first was Vinette Carroll, who directed *Your Arms Too short to Box with God* in 1976.
5 Another inspiration for Dickerson came from the book, *The Drama of Nommo* (1972) by Paul Carter Harrison.
6 In Santeria, a New World African religion, an orisha is a conflation of a Yoruba deity and a Catholic saint.
7 Euell includes *I Ain't Yo' Uncle—the New Jack Revisionist Uncle Tom's Cabin* by Robert Alexander, *The Confessions of Stepin' Fetchit* by Matt Robinson, and several other plays in her discussion.
8 A notorious case in which a sixty-six-year-old Bronx grandmother was shot to death by New York City police (1984).
9 The cast changed due to the availability of the performers, who over the series of performances included Sondra Love Aldridge, Rhonda J. W. Bantsimba, Stephanie Berry, Ayana Cahrr, Walonda J. Lewis, Denise Locke, Michelle McCullough, Rhonda Akanke McLean-Nur, Lisa Richards, Maureen Sebastian, Kim Staunton, Tanya Tatum and Erica Tazel.
10 Baartman was exhibited in Europe as a curiosity, even after her death. Her body was returned to South Africa in 2002. Suzan-Lori Parks treats her story in her play, *Venus*.
11 The husband, John Allen Muhammad and his protégé Lee Boyd Malvo, the Beltway Snipers, killed ten people in the Washington D.C. area in 2002.

Works cited

Canning, Charlotte. "Feminist Performance as Feminist Historiography," *Theatre Survey* 45.2 (November 2004): 227–233.

Carlson, Marvin. *Theories of the Theatre*. 2nd. ed. Ithaca, New York: Cornell University Press, 1993.

Carroll, Vinette. *Your Arms Too Short to Box with God* (Music by Mikki Grant; lyrics by Alex Bradford), Lyceum Theatre (Broadway), 1976.

Case, Sue Ellen. *Feminism and Theatre*. New York: Methuen, 1988.

Childress, Alice. *Wine in the Wilderness* in *Black Theatre USA: Plays by African Americans, 1847 to Today*. James V. Hatch and Ted Shine, eds. New York: Free Press, 1996.

Cliff, Michelle "Object Into Subject: Some Thoughts on the Work of Black Women Artists," in *Making Face, Making Soul =Haçiendo caras: Creative and Critical Perspectives by Feminsits of Color*. Gloria Anzaldua, ed. San Francisco: Aunt Lute Foundation Books, 1990: 271–289.

Daughters of the Dust, film directed by Julie Dash, U.S.A. Kino International, 1991.

Dickerson, Glenda. *Ana Bel's Brush: A Live Oak Drama*, 1992.

——*Eel Catching in Setauke*, 1988.

——*Folksay: A Living Exhibit (Talk Story of Style and Substance)*, 1996.

——*Glenda Dickerson is Spreading Lies: A Space Shuttle for Black Women*, 1995.

——*Jesus Christ Lawd Today*, 1972.
——*Magic and Lions*, 1977.
——*Owen's Song*, 1978.
——*Tarbaby, a paradigm for our time*, 1984.
——*The Unfinished Song*, 1970.
——*Wellwater: Wishes and Word*, 1992.
——*Zora and Lorraine and Their Signifyin' Tongues*, 1995.
——"Festivities and Jubilations on the Graves of the Dead: Sanctifying Sullied Space," in *Performance and Cultural Politics*. Elin Diamond, ed. New York: Routledge, 1995: 108–132.
——*Kitchen Prayers: Performance Dialog on 9/11 and Global Loss; Identities on Trial; Sapphire's New Shoe*. Peace Archive, Center for World Performance Studies, University of Michigan, Ann Arbor, Michigan, 2002–2004.
——"The Cult of True Womanhood: Toward a Womanist Attitude in African American Theatre," *Theatre Journal* 40.2 (1988): 178–87.
——"Transforming Through Performing: Oral History, African-American Women's Voices and the Power of Theatre," Fathom: the source for Online Learning, www.fathom.com/feature/122665/index.html 2002.
——"Wearing Red: When a Rowdy Band of Charismatics Learned to Say "NO!" in *Upstaging Big Daddy: Directing Theater as if Gender and Race Matter*. Ellen Donkin and Susan Clement, eds. Ann Arbor: University of Michigan Press, 1993: 153–175.
——(director) "Harambee: For My People." WTOP TV, Washington, D.C., 1975.
——(producer)"What's Cookin' in the Kitchen?" DVD. Ann Arbor: University of Michigan Center for World Performance Studies, 2006.
——and Breena Clarke. *Re/membering Aunt Jemima. In Colored Contradictions: An Anthology of Contemporary African American Plays*. Harry Elam and Robert Alexander, eds. New York: Plume, 1996, and in *Plays by Women of Color: an Anthology*. Kathy A. Perkins and Roberta Uno, eds. New York: Routledge, 1996.
——and Breena Clarke. "The Triune Voice" in *Women in American Theatre*, 3rd. ed. Helen Kritch Chinoy and Linda Walsh Jenkins, eds. New York: Theatre Communications Group, 2006.
——and Alexis DeVeaux. *NO! A Parlor Reading*, 1981.
——and Linda Gravatt. *Barbara Jordan: Texas Treasure*, 2005
Elam, Harry and Alexander, Robert, eds. *Colored Contradictions: An Anthology of Contemporary African-American Plays*. New York: Plume, 1996.
Euell, Kim. "Signifyin' Ritual: Subverting Stereotypes, Salvaging Icons," *African American Review* (Winter 1997): 667–75.
Gates, Henry Louise. *The Signifying Monkey: a theory of Afro-American Literary Criticism*. New York: Oxford University Press, 1988.
Giles, Freda Scott. "In Their Own Words: Pearl Cleage and Glenda Dickerson Define Womanist Theatre," *Womanist Theory and Research* 2.1 (Fall/Winter 1996–1997): 28–35.
——Interview with Glenda Dickerson, 27 January 1996.
——Interview with Glenda Dickerson, 29 July 2006.
Gussow, Mel. "Stage: a Qualified No." *New York Times* (6 June 1981): 14.
Gwaltney, John Langston. *Drylongso: a self-portrait of Black America*. New York: Random House, 1980.
Harrison, Paul Carter. *The Drama of Nommo*. New York: Grove Press, 1972.

hooks, bell. "Talking Back," in *Making Face, Making Soul* =Haçiendo caras: *Creative and Critical Perspectives by Feminists of Color*. Gloria Anzaldua, ed. San Francisco: Aunt Lute Foundation Books, 1990: 209–211.

Hurst, Fannie. *Imitation of Life*. (1933) Reprint. Durham, North Carolina: Duke University Press, 2004.

Morrison, Toni. *The Bluest Eye*. New York: Holt, Rinehart and Winston, 1970.

Parks, Suzan-Lori. *Venus*. New York: Theatre Communications Group, 1997.

——*The Death of the Last Black Man in the Whole Entire World* in *The America Play and Other Works*. New York: Theatre Communications Group, 1995.

Robinson, Matt. *The Confessions of Stepin' Fetchit*. American Place Theatre, 1993.

Shange, Ntozake. *spell #7: a geeche jibara quick magic trance manual for technologically stressed third world people: a theatre piece*. Public Theatre, 1979.

Wolfe, George C. *The Colored Museum* in *Black Theatre USA: Plays by African Americans, 1847 to Today*. James V. Hatch and Ted Shine, eds. New York: Free Press, 1996.

10 "Everybody's talking"
Anna Deavere Smith's documentary theatre

Joan Wylie Hall

The playwright and actress Anna Deavere Smith achieved a national presence in the early 1990s with her solo performances of racially mixed communities at flash point. Crossing ethnic and gender lines, Smith played more than sixty male and female roles in the Obie Award winning *Fires in the Mirror: Crown Heights, Brooklyn and Other Identities* (1992) and *Twilight: Los Angeles, 1992* (1993), her best known works. To create the unconventional docudramas, Smith interviewed community members and others—from scholars to rappers—who became her characters: African Americans and Caucasians, Latinos, Koreans, West Indians, and Lubavitcher Jews. With support from video clips, music, slide projections, and many changes of hairstyle and headgear, she assumed the words, speech rhythms, and body gestures of her notably diverse casts. In portraying a complex range of viewpoints and motivations in these plays and those that followed, Smith says she aimed "to develop a kind of theater that could be more sensitive to the events of my own time than traditional theater could" (*Twilight* xxii). Robert H. Vorlicky compares her achievement to "those of John Lennon, David Henry Hwang, Danny Hoch, and Sarah Jones—other middle- to late-twentieth-century artists who explore the range of representations and possible presentations when one's body and voice are alone on stage" (141).

In a 1993 keynote address for the Association for Theatre in Higher Education, Smith remarked that her "entry into theatre is political. Largely because of my race and gender. I am political without opening my mouth" ("Not So Special" 80). Yet, when a *Salon* reporter asked if Smith's productions are "a form of social activism," her answer was qualified: "Yes, to some extent, but I think I'm more interested in many sides of the story than an activist is" (Goldberg). While Eve Ensler's feminism is on display throughout her solo performances of *The Vagina Monologues* (1996), Smith's reaction to the monologues she speaks in *Fires in the Mirror* and *Twilight* is difficult to infer. Her opinion of specific characters is more apparent in two less famous works, *Piano* (1989) and *House Arrest* (2000); yet, here too, the audience is confronted with an unsettling multiplicity of viewpoints. Smith says she makes an effort "to fall in love" with each person she portrays, "whether they are presidents, high priests, or child murderers, or racists" (*Talk to Me* 136). She also emphasizes that she is "looking at the *processes*" of social problems, not proposing solutions: "I am first looking for the humanness inside the problems, or the crises. The spoken word is evidence of the humanness. Perhaps the solutions come somewhere further down the road" (*Twilight* xxiv).

Because she considers herself an outside observer "who steps in and then steps back out," Smith is reluctant to claim membership in any particular dramatic tradition. Her work is theatre; "but it's also community work in some ways. It's a kind of low anthropology, low journalism; it's a bit documentary," she told Barbara Lewis in one of her first extensive interviews (56). Smith admits to many influences, from Shakespeare, Studs Terkel, and Johnny Carson's *Tonight Show* to the urgent and sometimes humorous complaints she handled as a secretary for KLM Airlines. Debby Thompson suggests that the "most immediate precursor to Anna Deavere Smith's work is that of Adrienne Kennedy, whose 1964 *Funnyhouse of a Negro* takes a highly post-structuralist, anti-Naturalistic approach to character and identity" (128). In the Acknowledgments to her breakthrough drama, *Fires in the Mirror*, Smith singles out a different Kennedy play, *A Movie Star Has to Star in Black and White* (1976), as the one that "dramatically changed my perception of the relationship of language to character"(xv). Smith directed her Carnegie Mellon University students in a production of *Movie Star* in 1979, right around the time she began research for the first installments of her performance series, *On the Road: A Search for American Character*. In the decades that followed, *On the Road* grew to include *Fires in the Mirror*, *Twilight*, and *House Arrest*, as well as *Let Me Down Easy* (2007), a story of disease and recovery that became Smith's first major project of the new century.

Like Kennedy, August Wilson, and Suzan-Lori Parks, Smith thoughtfully explores social and cultural contexts for the modern Black experience. Her multi-play search for American character is reminiscent of Wilson's decade-by-decade representation of twentieth-century African American life. As actress–playwrights, Smith and Parks share an unusual attention to their characters' speech utterances, recognizing poetic lines in the Black vernacular. Smith is unique, however, for embodying such a broad array of characters that she expands notions of race and gender far beyond the typical black–white, male–female binaries. Kimberly Rae Connor suggests that, "by facilitating a radical empathy" through her own performances, Smith allows the audience to share in "a transformative slipping across socially produced identities of race, nation, gender, and class" (178). The survey of her work that follows will emphasize Smith's methods for encouraging an identification with the other that is truly radical. From her earliest performance pieces through the highly successful *Fires in the Mirror* and *Twilight* (both broadcast on PBS), Smith developed a documentary theatre that may finally have strained the limits of the form in *House Arrest*, a play that defied her own great powers of sympathy.

On the road to new communities

Smith's childhood goal in a Baltimore middle-class household with college-educated parents was to become a psychiatrist; but she told David Savran that reading Tennessee Williams's *The Glass Menagerie* and Edward Albee's *Who's Afraid of Virginia Woolf?* made an early impression (242). She attended plays regularly during a study abroad year in London, where Bertolt Brecht's *Arturo Ui* introduced her to a dramatist whose unusual distancing techniques have been cited by commentators on Smith's work (Kushner 248). After graduation from Beaver College in 1971, she drove to California with four friends "to see America and to make sense, each in our own way, of what to do with all the breakage and promise that had been released" by the antiwar movement, the black liberation movement, the women's movement, and the start of the environmental movement (*Talk to Me* 3). Disappointed by the slow progress of cultural change, she enrolled at San Francisco's American Conservatory Theatre to begin a "quest for the 'we' of the new 'we the people' the sixties had promised" (*Talk to Me* 11). A drama assignment helped her to see Shakespeare as "a jazz musician" who improvised on "the given rhythms of his time" (*Talk to Me* 36), as Smith learned to improvise on American rhythms at the end of the twentieth century.

In her epistolary advice book, *Letters to a Young Artist* (2006), Smith tells an imaginary correspondent that "A work of art engenders a conversation" (97). Dialogue occurs at every step of her experimental drama, from preliminary interviews and workshops to the audience discussions that follow many of her one-woman shows. Although Smith's typical play is a sequence of monologues, an intricate exchange takes place in her theatre: between the actress and each real-life character she performs; between characters, whose monologues Smith arranges in conversation with each other; and, finally, between characters and viewers. Aiming to "absorb America," she considers her interviewees' words "the doorway into the soul of a culture" (*Talk to Me* 12). And drama must do more than merely depict the culture. "The real conversations," Smith says, "are the ones that cause change" (*Talk to Me* 40). Throughout the 1980s, Smith received commissions from communities that were attracted by this transformative potential. She says her *On the Road* project evolved "during a time that many institutions were going through identity shifts with regard to gender and ethnicity" (*Fires* xxxiii). As interviewer, editor, and enactor, Smith offered fresh perspectives to civic, academic, and professional groups throughout the country. Carol Martin compares early plays in the series to the "forum theatre" of Augusto Boal, "in which communities enact what is bothering them and often reach, through theatrical actions, decisions about specific alternatives" ("Bearing Witness" 84).

Gender Bending: On the Road Princeton University (1989) is Smith's 50-minute solo performance of excerpts from 25 interviews, most of them conducted with Princeton students, professors, and staff members. In a lively account of the production, Sandra L. Richards observes that Smith offered the Princeton community "a comic, provocative image of itself as it struggles to negotiate differences of gender, race, and class" (35). In the research phase, Smith spoke with 50 people on such topics as "the university's exclusively male eating clubs, assault against women and 'sex-role strain' among female undergraduates, color consciousness among black students, and the paradoxical relationship between hard-line ideologies and the absence of women's girdles in some contemporary societies" (Richards 35). She also drew on her earlier *On the Road* drama, *Charlayne Hunter Gault* (1984), to parallel Hunter Gault's painful experience of integration at the University of Georgia with Sally Frank's attempt to become the first female in Princeton's Cottage Club. Richards suggests that, in separating the Hunter Gault and Frank monologues with a male character's monologue, Smith underscores "certain commonalities" in the young women's gender struggles, despite their racial difference (49). From start to finish, the actress–playwright's physical presence is integral to the power of the production. Carol Martin comments on the remarkable "shape-shifting" facility of the light-skinned, "angular" Smith, who "exposes and represents the structures of racism and sexism while simultaneously using performance as a means to play with the mutability of identity" ("Bearing Witness" 82).

Ironically, her chameleon quality was sometimes an obstacle to Smith's employment. One theatre agent told her that she would "antagonize" clients because "You don't look like anything. You don't look black. You don't look white" (*Talk to Me* 26). A similar encounter is a formative event for Cyprienne, a pediatrics surgeon with an androgynous name in Smith's early play *Aye Aye Aye I'm Integrated* (1983). Staged by the Women's Project and Productions, the two-character drama debuted at "A Festival of Six One-Act Plays" in New York's American Place Theatre from March 20 to April 1, 1984. The director was Billie Allen, who, twenty years earlier, had starred as the tragic Negro Sarah in Adrienne Kennedy's *Funnyhouse of a Negro*. Unlike most of Smith's other work of the 1980s, *Aye Aye Aye I'm Integrated* was not a solo performance. With Seret Scott as the black physician and Elba Kenney as a white nurse, the play relates the doctor's early attempts to break into television and theatre after voicing "Good and Plenty" licorice commercials on radio as a young girl. Smith's allusion to the pink and white-coated candies is typical of the humor in this story about color, race, and gender. Cyprienne recalls her childhood interview with the agent Phoebe, who complains: "I think of a *colored* person as a very *dark* person and this is *not* a very *dark* person this is a very *light* person" (*Aye Aye* 262). Unable to fit Cyprienne into a neat racial category, Phoebe ludicrously tells her to come back when she turns darker. Years later, in an attempt to deepen her color, a teenaged Cyprienne joins a risky research project that makes her look like a victim of liver disease. A year as an exchange student in the Ivory Coast restores her health; observing African midwives inspires her to trade her dream of acting for a career in medicine. Cyprienne clearly achieves a high level of respect and responsibility as an oncologist. *Aye Aye Aye I'm Integrated* is set in the children's ward at the world-famous Sloan Kettering Cancer Center.

In this short drama, Smith complicates a variety of racial, occupational, and gender stereotypes. Cyprienne's father is himself a successful doctor, from a line of Black physicians; the family's white neighbors are friendly and supportive; Cyprienne's best friend is a white boy who studies ballet; her prep school headmistress is an unusually sympathetic figure; Cyprienne's "quarter French, quarter German, half Black" mother worries that the girl is too emotional to be a good actress; the agent Phoebe would gladly represent a dark African American. "In America," she says, "*either* you're Black or White and there's nothing in between" (269); yet, Cyprienne embodies the "in between," as the play's title proclaims. Sites of inclusiveness do exist, but they are off the main path: the hospital pediatrics ward and the elaborate tent Cyprienne created with her friend Roddy as a venue for staging their plays for the integrated neighborhood. Detailed descriptions of the children's "sophisticated costume collection" (259), garnered year-round from garage sales and donations, further reflect Smith's fascination with role-playing and identity formation. Like the contemporaneous *On the Road* dramas, *Aye Aye Aye I'm Integrated* under-scores the complexity of the American character.

Reflections on race and gender in *Fires in the Mirror*

Smith's system of interviewing, editing, and performing has remained a constant of the *On the Road* plays about communities in crisis. Developed through this process, *Fires in the Mirror: Crown Heights, Brooklyn and Other Identities* became her first major production in 1992. Preparing readers for a drama of race and gender, the book cover features Smith in four of her 26 roles. The popular drama premiered at the New York Shakespeare Festival in New York City on May 1, 1992, and was adapted for television's "American Playhouse" the following April. While Smith served as her own director for previous *On the Road* plays, Christopher Ashley directed the two-month New York run of *Fires in the Mirror*; the television performance was directed by playwright George C. Wolfe, author of *The Colored Museum* (1986) and adapter of Zora Neale Hurston's stories in *Spunk* (1989).

The immediate predecessor of *Fires in the Mirror* was a solo piece about racial violence in Crown Heights that Smith staged in December 1991 for Wolfe's Festival of New Voices at the Joseph Papp Public Theatre in New York. On August 19 of that year, seven-year-old Gavin Cato, a Guyanese American, was mortally injured when a local Lubavitcher Hasidic driver swerved onto the sidewalk. Three hours later, in apparent revenge, Yankel

Rosenbaum, a young Jewish scholar visiting from Australia, was stabbed to death. Riots, marches, rallies, and litigation followed. Reaching out to the racially divided community, Smith dedicated *Fires in the Mirror* "to the residents of Crown Heights, Brooklyn, and to the memory of Gavin Cato and Yankel Rosenbaum" (vii). She describes ethnic relationships in the tense New York neighborhood as "the most graphic display I had witnessed of the negotiation of identity" (xxxiii).

Spotlighting this fact, "Identity" is the title of the first of the play's seven major divisions. The first of Smith's characters is Ntozake Shange, who had explored Black women's quest for identity in *for colored girls who have considered suicide/when the rainbow is enuf* (1975). Ryan M. Claycomb considers Shange's choreopoem an outstanding example of "the communal voice on stage," a type of drama in which no single character dominates (97). The form has obvious affinities with Smith's community dramas; she told David Savran that Shange's success at The Public Theater "made it possible for many of us 'colored girls' to come forward" (253). Placing Shange's "Identity" monologue in lead position was "the only possible way to open the door" on *Fires in the Mirror* because Shange "had already opened it for me" (Savran 253).

Titles of the play's next five major divisions are as succinct as "Identity," though only one of them is equally explicit on the drama's social issues: "Mirrors," "Hair," "Race," "Rhythm," and "Seven Verses." Gradually, without reference to the Brooklyn deaths and subsequent riots, Smith lays the foundation for the last and longest of the play's seven sections, "Crown Heights, Brooklyn, August 1991," which comprises the second half of the script. Each of Smith's seven divisions contains from one to fifteen monologues; monologues have individual titles and vary in performance time from under two minutes to about seven minutes. Characters' lines are excerpted verbatim from interviews that often lasted an hour or more. Speeches (with an occasional "uh," "hum," or "nenh") are arranged on the page like free verse, a distinctive feature of Smith's drama. In the theatre, monologue titles, characters' names, and descriptive paragraphs are projected on a screen, recalling one of Williams's stage devices in *The Glass Menagerie*.

In the printed text, a brief paragraph introduces each monologue, establishing character and setting. Three of the 26 characters have a second monologue: the activist minister Al Sharpton; Letty Cottin Pogrebin, one-time *Ms.* editor; and the barrister Norman Rosenbaum, brother of the murdered Yankel. Eight characters are women, and women speak eight of the first fourteen monologues; yet, only one of the fifteen "Crown Heights" monologues is related by a woman. Men are also much more prominent in the violent photographs of city streets that accompany the text. Consequently, the neighborhood women's early comments on home, family, religious practice, and workplace recede in the face of the play's explosive racial and ethnic conflicts.

Some of Smith's monologue titles deliberately arouse expectations about race and ethnicity that are undercut by the narrative. By such juxtapositions, the playwright cautions against trusting immediate impressions. In the historical context of the Holocaust (which Pogrebin and others recall in tragic detail), Rabbi Shea Hecht's title—"Ovens"—seems to refer to Hitler's crematoria. In an earlier monologue, "'Heil Hitler,'" Jewish Community Relations Council director Michael S. Miller says the taunts of Blacks at Yankel Rosenbaum's funeral included "Kill the Jew" and "Throw them back into the ovens again" (*Fires* 86). But Rabbi Hecht does not mention Nazis or concentration camps. Instead, he emphasizes the impossibility of Blacks and Jews sharing meals in their Crown Heights homes. The issue is more complex than simply buying kosher food; Lubavitchers cannot eat food cooked in other people's ovens. Hecht relieves the audience's initial apprehension about his subject; but, once evoked, the image of deadly ovens is impossible to forget. A revelation to most non-Jews, the rabbi's explanation for the impossibility of breaking bread together is matter-of-fact; however, the implications for sharing a metaphorical communion are grave.

Throughout, *Fires in the Mirror* raises a disturbing question: how can radically dissimilar groups form a true community? In his controversial study *Strangers in the Land: Blacks, Jews, Post-Holocaust America*, Eric J. Sundquist suggests that, in this play, "Everything from hairstyles and slang to the observance of holy law demonstrates the near impossibility of tolerating, let along bridging, differences" (497). Smith has been accused of exacerbating the problem in some of her enactments. She acknowledges that a gap necessarily exists between herself and each real-life character whom she represents on stage; and she is well aware of the contemporary controversy over "issues of *who is portrayed*" and who portrays them (*Fires* xxviii). Nevertheless, she speaks about bridge-building—between herself and her characters, but also between factions of torn areas like Crown Heights. Smith hopes tensions might become productive rather than destructive if she can interest people "in moving from one side to the other, in experiencing one hand and the other hand" (*Fires* xxxix). The hope is especially ambitious because of the many internal differences in the Brooklyn neighborhood's Black (Caribbean as well as African American) and White (mainly, but not exclusively, Hasidic) communities.

In his foreword, Cornel West praises *Fires in the Mirror* as "the most significant artistic exploration of Black–Jewish relations in our time" (xvii). Through many voices, Smith trains her listeners to avoid making harsh and uninformed judgments. Her artful guidance is evident early in the play with a sequence of four interviews: the single monologue of the "Mirrors" section and the three "Hair" monologues that follow. In the role of Aaron M. Bernstein, Smith portrays an MIT physicist with expertise in telescopic lenses. Explaining the best way to view stars with minimal distortion, Bernstein repeats the phrases "errors in the construction" and "circle of confusion" (*Fires* 14–15).

This astronomer's "Mirrors and Distortions" interview does not refer to Crown Heights, ethnicity, or race construction; but the playwright is clearly reminding her audience that human lenses are even more liable to misperception than mechanical ones.

The three "Hair" monologues reveal just how closely one's sense of personal identity depends upon others' perceptions, whether the individual is male or female, young or middle-aged, Black or white. Ethnic boundaries become a real circle of confusion for an unnamed Haitian girl, who describes selective mirroring of fashions at her junior high school. Categories of Black, Hispanic, and White are in such flux throughout her interview that the referents for "us," "they," and "you" become impossible to sort out. Affirming that "Black people are into hairstyles" (17), the girl anticipates the next monologue, by the Reverend Al Sharpton; but the third monologue in the "Hair" series reveals that hair is also a concern of Lubavitcher Jews. Sharpton's rationale for straightening his hair is as unexpected as his subject. He promised the R and B singer James Brown, who treated him like a son, always to wear his hair like Brown's, as "a personal family thing" (19). In contrast, Rivkah Siegal, in the monologue "Wigs," admits that, for her, hair is both a personal matter and a very public one. Siegal's distinctions between Jewish women who shave their heads and those who cut their hair very short for the ritual bath become as confusing to outsiders as the Haitian girl's ethnic groupings. As a married woman, Siegal accepts the religious custom and appreciates the opportunity to change her appearance with a variety of wigs; still, she feels deceptive when co-workers admire her hair. Ellipses and dashes in her lines suggest that her very syntax is grappling with realities of gender, ethnicity, religion, and identity.

Steve Feffer concludes that the African American Sharpton and the Jewish Siegal both "feel marked and culturally defined by the cultural obligation that their hair represents" (407). In his essay on *Fires in the Mirror* in a hip-hop context, Feffer also relates Smith's portrayals of Sharpton and Siegal to her larger *On the Road* project. "These two American characters emerge in response to how they are perceived and the identity they assert to negotiate that difference," he says. "A curious community of hair is created in the space of their obvious dissimilarities. The creation of this space is the ultimate goal of Smith's work" (408). Just as she groups monologues on hair to reflect upon identity, Smith arranges other monologues to show further common ground between Brooklyn's Jews and Blacks, including resentment of police activity, love of family, and an emphatic yearning for justice. She leaves it to her audience to grasp the undeniable likenesses that could unite embattled factions.

The play's climactic seventh section, "Crown Heights, Brooklyn, August 1991," shows just how painful it can be for a single neighborhood to negotiate its vast differences. At last, Smith's characters describe the deaths of Gavin Cato and Yankel Rosenbaum and the riots that followed. Smith told Carol

Martin she "thought it would be powerful to have the audience forget about
Gavin" through much of the play ("Anna Deavere Smith" 58). "There's a
way in which the larger powers obliterate the smaller powers even when
those smaller powers are the very reason for our gathering," she explained
(58). In the final series of fifteen interviews, Blacks and Jews angrily call for
justice, blaming each other, the media, police, New York politicians, and the
legal system for the violence in Crown Heights. Most of these characters are
very emotional, as evidenced by monologue titles like "My Brother's Blood,"
"Rage," and "Pogroms." Several lines spoken by Lubavitcher resident
Roslyn Malamud, the only female character in this section, are written in
capital letters. "Chords" is the name of black activist Sonny Carson's speech;
but his focus is discord as he tells Smith he refuses to support "any coming
together and healing of/ America/ and all that shit" (105). In his recent
analysis of Jewish and African American holocaust discourse in the play,
Gregory Jay suggests that Smith "intends audiences and readers to engage in
the same labor of unsettling cross-cultural empathy with loss that she herself
performs on stage; if we do, the result complicates our commitments by challenging the identity politics that influences them" (121). On the other hand,
in evoking the historical traumas of slavery and the genocide of the Jews to
tell their stories, the contrary factions in Crown Heights insist on the uniqueness of their suffering. Such an insistence, says Jay, "may end up being an
acting out that never includes a working through, thus blocking rather than
enabling empathy and justice" (147). For Jay, the playwright's goal of staging a shared experience of pain in *Fires* is threatened by her characters'
emphasis on the exclusive nature of their own ancestral trauma.

  Fires in the Mirror's most poignant monologue comes at the end with
Carmel Cato's "Lingering," spoken at the corner where his son Gavin was
killed. More than the rhetoric of several rabbis and ministers earlier in the
play, Cato's lines—delivered in "a pronounced West Indian accent" (135)—
bear a sense of the holy, even the apocalyptic. Calling for justice, he
describes the death of innocence. Cato did not have the last word in the
play's earliest version; but Smith took the advice of JoAnne Akalaitis, a
director and writer who told her, "When the father speaks the show is over"
(Martin, "Anna Deavere Smith" 52). Smith considers Carmel Cato a
"remarkable man"; she says she "never heard anybody journey in a
language across so many realms of experience" (Martin, "Anna Deavere
Smith" 52). These realms extend to the supernatural as he describes his
terrible premonitions during the week before Gavin died, a dread so great
he could drink only water and could not eat at all. "I'm one of the special,"
he tells Smith; marked by second sight, he is "a man born by my foot," or in
breech position (*Fires* 139). Cato feels empowered by his unusual birth, and
his final line is fearless: "You can repeat every word I say."

  Repeating his words and those of 25 other characters, Smith "oscillat[es]
between identification and difference," says Janelle Reinelt (615).
Reinelt suggests that "It is the bridging of difference which must be enacted,

displayed, performed in order to make visible the possibility of replicating it in ordinary life" (615). In psychoanalytical terms, Molly Castelloe says Smith "functions as a transitional object for the residents of Crown Heights," enabling them to "recognize, despite ethnic differences, the experience of inhabiting many common social worlds" (209, 211). With *Fires in the Mirror*, Smith's documentary drama spoke, for the first time, not simply to a neighborhood but to a nation.

Cultural work in *Twilight: Los Angeles, 1992*

Fires in the Mirror had just opened at the New York Shakespeare Festival when Smith was commissioned to develop *Twilight: Los Angeles, 1992.* This docudrama presents many reactions to the riots that followed the not guilty verdict in the trial of white policemen who beat Rodney King, an African American, during a 1991 traffic arrest. For her one-woman show, Smith conducted over 200 interviews with individuals ranging from King's aunt to Reginald Denny, the white truck driver who was attacked by a group of Black men on April 29, 1992, the day the King verdict was announced. This second major work in the *On the Road* series was produced by the Center Theatre Group/Mark Taper Forum in Los Angeles from May 23 through July 18, 1993, with Gordon Davidson as artistic director/producer. Director was Emily Mann, who characterizes her own plays, beginning with the one-woman *Annulla: An Autobiography* (1977), as Theater of Testimony. George C. Wolfe directed *Twilight* for the New York Shakespeare Festival in March 1994, with Tony Kushner as dramaturge. On April 17, 1994, the Broadway production opened at the Cort Theatre.

Smith played about 25 parts in the Los Angeles and New York versions; but the 1994 Anchor Books edition, which she introduced as a companion work to the stage play, includes over 40 characters. Jennifer Drake believes that "By including such a wide variety of voices and perspectives in *Twilight*, Smith makes a political art based on the democratic ideal of full representation" (166). Pictured on the cover, the dramatist's eyes hold an "ambiguous expression" that, according to Robin Bernstein, "could signal concern, anger, or perhaps an accusation" (132). Following a structure similar to that of *Fires in the Mirror*, Smith groups her monologues into a prologue and several main divisions: "The Territory," "Here's a Nobody," "War Zone," "Twilight," and "Justice." For Berkeley Repertory Theatre's 1996 touring production of *Twilight*, she revised her early solo performances, portraying more than 35 characters in a new two-act format. Adapted by Smith for her 2001 PBS broadcast of *Twilight*, the Berkeley script was subsequently published by the Dramatists Play Service.

In her memoir, Smith observes that the Los Angeles riot following the Rodney King verdict "was one of those events that cause the public to think, as they do from time to time, that race is one of the most important issues our country has to face" (*Talk to Me* 97). Committed to representing the whole community, Smith formed a team of dramaturges whose professions and ethnicities would help her to extend *Twilight* beyond a "black-and-white canvas" (*Twilight* xxiii). Thus, "The Park Family" sequence in the long "War Zone" section presents the trauma of a Korean father, mother, and son in the aftermath of the street attacks. Walter Park's monologue follows an unusually long prefatory note in which Smith describes his modern California home, with its reproduction Louis XIV furniture and its mingling of Eastern and European artwork—a mix that suggests the family's success in crossing cultures. Yet, the permanent brain damage Park suffered during the Los Angeles riots leads his wife to question the promise of America. Describing her husband's twenty years of hard work as a storeowner and his generous contributions to the Compton area, she cries: "Then why,/ why he has to get shot?" (147). For an interview with another Korean business owner, Smith records a phonetic transcription of the conversation provided by the man's son. Alternating passages of Korean and English in her performance, Smith dramatized the very distinctive heritage of a major segment of South Central Los Angeles.

Several characters in *Twilight* reveal the same deep distrust of other ethnic groups recorded in *Fires in the Mirror*. In *Twilight*, Smith told Diane Wood Middlebrook, she "expressly tried to avoid stirring things up," fearing that another riot might break out in the aftermath of a second trial for the accused police officers in the spring of 1993 (189). Black activist Paul Parker believes Reginald Denny's beating would have been ignored if he had been Black, Indian, or Latino; at the same time, Parker is pleased that so many Korean stores were burned: "The Koreans was like the Jews in the day/ and we put them in check" (*Twilight* 175). Mrs. Young-Soon Han, on the other hand, reflects that her people are left out of a society that has recognized the rights of African Americans. In the aftermath of the riots, she fears Blacks and Koreans have too many differences to live together peacefully. With a deep display of emotion, both Parker and Han call for justice. Their bitterness is shared by Hispanic residents. Rudy Salas, a painter, says white teachers typically made him feel inferior because of his Mexican heritage; for fifty years, he has hated white policemen because an early confrontation with four cops left him deaf. Julio Menjivar, a lumber salesman from El Salvador, describes being kicked by both Black and white National Guardsmen during the street violence, even though he was a bystander.

Barraged with a litany of mental and physical anguish, the audience perceives commonalities that the sufferers cannot grasp. Jill Dolan believes that Smith's "political gesture" in both *Fires in the Mirror* and *Twilight* is "to turn these diverse monologues, these discrepant points of view about irresolvable tragedy, into a staged conversation which in itself becomes a utopian performative, a momentary 'doing' of a world in which such interracial, cross-gender, cross-faith, cross-cultural dialogue might be possible" (514). Smith is highly aware of the obstacles to such dialogue.

More than once, she has stated her disappointment that Twilight Bey, whose name inspired the title, never attended the play, not even when it was performed in his neighborhood. For Smith, "The tragedy of both Crown Heights and Los Angeles was that there was no one who could speak across lines. The future will demand that we have people who can" ("Not So Special" 87).

Smith encourages such border-crossings through her selection of parallel passages from her hundreds of hours of interview tapes. Although characters fail to "speak across lines," their words expose their fundamental sameness. Smith reveals identical resentments and longings in a cross-section of cultures. Some speakers share the ideas and imagery of characters whom they would view as antagonists; occasionally, their very words are the same. As the title of Reginald Denny's monologue remarks, there is "A Weird Common Thread in Our Lives." Denny would like to have a house with a room for his riot memorabilia; but "it's gonna be a happy room" with framed expressions of "love and compassion" and no "color problem" (110–11). Staring intensely at the audience, he says, "Lord/ willing, it'll happen" (112). Paul Parker, whose brother was accused of shooting at Reginald Denny, also wants a house with a special room. He will display his clippings and other memories of the riots for his children to see, if he is still here to guide them, "God willin'" (177). The image of a memorial room, the hopeful vision of those who will visit, and the invocation of the divine tenuously link Denny and Parker across their great differences.

With her title image, which is also the title of the penultimate section of *Twilight: Los Angeles, 1992*, Smith connects an even more varied group of speakers, from the Hollywood director Peter Sellars to a former El Salvadoran nun and revolutionary, whose nom de guerre was Lucia (for "light.") In the monologues "Twilight #1" and "Limbo/Twilight #2," the culture critic Homi Bhabha and the gang member Twilight Bey both visualize an in-between state of fuzzy borders; but their views of twilight are not identical. Interviewed on a phone call to England, Bhabha finds twilight instructive because the fading of boundaries allows us to "see the intersections/ of the event with a number of other things that daylight obscures" (233). Interviewed at a Denny's restaurant in Los Angeles, Bey identifies knowledge with the light. With a mythic self-consciousness, he feels "stuck in limbo,/ like the sun is stuck between night and day/ in the twilight hours"; but he stretches toward the "light" of "understanding others" (255). At the end of her introduction to the play, Smith comments, "Twilight's recognition that we must reach across ethnic boundaries is simple but true" (xxvi). As the final speaker, Twilight Bey recalls Carmel Cato at the conclusion of *Fires in the Mirror*; in poetic lines, both describe the loss of innocence and the uneasy state of limbo, of lingering.

Reorganizing history in *House Arrest*

House Arrest (2000) is an even more ambitious work than *Fires in the Mirror* and *Twilight: Los Angeles*, but reviews of this play about politics and the media were less enthusiastic. Based on 500 interviews (twice the number Smith conducted for *Twilight*), the third major installment in the *On the Road* series is divided into two acts, with almost 60 monologues spoken by more than 40 characters. Twelve actors performed an early version at the Mark Taper Forum in Los Angeles in spring 1999; Smith played all roles when *House Arrest* opened on March 26, 2000, at New York's Public Theater, with George C. Wolfe as producer. Even though she crossed genders and ethnicities with her usual skill, the sheer number of parts made it harder for audiences to empathize with individual characters. The fact that several characters are historical figures (Thomas Jefferson, Abraham Lincoln, Walt Whitman, Franklin Delano Roosevelt, and others) deflects from the usual sense of immediacy in Smith's drama. The high proportion of journalists, celebrities, and highly ranked government staff employees in *House Arrest* also makes for less of a human-interest story than those related in *Fires in the Mirror* and *Twilight*. Lacking the central significant event that created such powerful theatre from crises in New York and Los Angeles, the play stretches the documentary form very thin.

Although President Bill Clinton's relationship with the press was Smith's immediate subject, her concerns are much broader than a single administration, as indicated by the subtitle *A Search for American Character In and Around the White House, Past and Present*. Like the earlier play, *Piano* (1989), with which it was published, *House Arrest* also explores nineteenth-century controversies. In her introduction to the two works, Smith describes them as "*reorganizations* of history—interactions *with* history, reactions *to* history, metaphors *for* history" (*House Arrest* xvii). With *Piano*, she says, "I was specifically looking for a time and place in American history in which people of all different races could be in one living room" (xviii). The characters who gather in a Cuban plantation house, during an era of imperial struggle, are of European, African, Asian, and Indian descent. Some have a mixed ethnic heritage, including the young "criollito" Rosa, whose startling performance on her mistress's piano suggests the emergence of a new Cuba. While *Piano* is the most traditional and the least known of Smith's full-length dramas, it resembles the documentary plays in presenting a variety of conflicting perspectives, from the revolutionary fervor of the Congolese-Cuban maid Susanna to the colonial zeal of General Antonio Lopez y Vargas, a racist and a rapist.

House Arrest multiplies the audience's interactions with historical moments, but the brevity of the encounters seriously diminishes their impact. Moreover, Smith's typical objectivity toward her characters received unprecedented challenges in this "Press and Presidency" project. While she established a real rapport with the charismatic Clinton, Jefferson's racist pronouncements seriously threatened her determination to love each character she portrays (*Talk to Me* 133–7). Another challenge was the proliferation of national issues in *House Arrest*, from racial violence and gay pride to child abuse and in-fights among journalists. For Smith, Washington in the

1990s "felt more dangerous than a race riot. It's a bigger, more complicated powder keg that holds among other things the potential for race riots ... and wars and more" (*Talk to Me* 30).

Smith's ongoing concern with matters of race, gender, and power is prominent not only in the Jefferson–Hemings sequence but also in her portrayals of other presidencies. Lincoln's monologue follows a monologue by his wife's seamstress, Elizabeth Keckley, who explains that she purchased her freedom from slavery. The most sympathetic character in the Roosevelt White House sequence is another African American woman in service, the cook Lizzie McDuffie. Black women associated with the Clinton presidency in *House Arrest* rank much higher in the professions than Keckley and McDuffie. Yet Maggie Williams, Hillary Clinton's Chief of Staff; Alexis Herman, U.S. Secretary of Labor; and law professor Anita Hill are grouped in the ominously titled sequence "Sending the Canaries into the Mines." Herman seems to speak for all three when she says that, as a Black woman, she has always felt "you're on the outside looking in,/ trying to bring down the walls ... to be in the room/ to get to the table" (*House Arrest* 94).

"Everybody's Talking," a chapter in Smith's memoir, describes Monica Lewinsky's disruption of Washington's usual "tones of studied nonchalance" (*Talk to Me* 270). Smith wonders if it takes a crisis for people to challenge the status quo and emerge from "complacent language" (*Talk to Me* 270). Certainly, the poetic language and emotional force of *Fires in the Mirror* and *Twilight* were forged from moments of crisis. When *House Arrest* was produced in Los Angeles in 1999, Smith's dramatic team encouraged everybody to talk. By reserving the complete second act for the audience to discuss "what was happening in our country," this early version of the play provided "room for the expression of a possible theater of our time" (*Talk to Me* 266)—a theatre of engagement. For Smith, "The audience, ideally, is a witness and a participant" (*Talk to Me* 228). In a long interview with Kevin L. Fuller and Andrea Armstrong, Smith said she wants people to "experience the length of the differences of our perspectives, and there's so few times that we get to have a room of people engaged in that a lot" (Fuller).

Let Me Down Easy (2007), Smith's latest addition to the *On the Road* series, grew out of interviews with doctors and patients that she first performed as a visiting professor at Yale University's medical school in 2000. Expanding her work on the strength and vulnerability of the body, Smith traveled to several African nations to study the treatment of HIV/AIDS, the aftermath of genocide in Rwanda, and other health crises. In 2005, the premiere at New York's Public Theater was postponed so Smith could interview victims of Hurricane Katrina. Her revised docudrama was to debut at New York's Public Theater in spring 2007, a co-production with Berkeley Repertory Theatre; but further delays have pushed the premiere to January 2008 at the Long Wharf Theatre in New Haven, Connecticut. Like Suzan-Lori Parks's *Venus* (1996), a historical drama about the woman known as the Venus Hottentot, *Let Me Down Easy* explores gendered and racialized conceptions of the body in an international context. Perhaps the best analogue for *Let Me Down Easy* is Mann's Theater of Testimony or Teya Sepinuck's Theater of Witness, genres that rely heavily on individual oral histories of tumultuous times. Like its powerful antecedents, *Fires in the Mirror* and *Twilight: Los Angeles, 1992*, Smith's current documentary theatre confronts her audience with the many voices of trauma, faithfully articulated.

Works cited

Albee, Edward. *Who's Afraid of Virginia Woolf?: A Play.* New York: Scribner, 2003.

Bernstein, Robin. "Rodney King, Shifting Modes of Vision, and Anna Deavere Smith's *Twilight: Los Angeles, 1992.*" *Journal of Dramatic Theory and Criticism* 14.2 (2000): 121–34.

Brecht, Bertolt. *The Resistable Rise of Arturo Ui.* John Willett and Ralph Manheim, eds. New York: Arcade, 2001.

Castelloe, M[olly]. "The Good-Enough Setting of Anna Deavere Smith: Restaging Crown Heights." *Psychoanalysis, Culture and Society* 9 (2004): 207–18.

Claycomb, Ryan M. "(Ch)oral History: Documentary Theatre, the Communal Subject and Progressive Politics." *Journal of Dramatic Theory and Criticism* 17.2 (2003): 95–121.

Connor, Kimberly Rae. "Negotiating the Differences: Anna Deavere Smith and Liberation Theater." *Racing and (E)Racing Language: Living with the Color of Our Words.* Ellen J. Goldner and Safiya Henderson-Holmes, eds. Syracuse, NY: Syracuse University Press, 2001. 158–82.

Dolan, Jill. "'Finding Our Feet in the Shoes of (One An) Other': Multiple Character Solo Performers and Utopian Performatives." *Modern Drama* 45.4 (2002): 495–518.

Drake, Jennifer. "The Theater of the New World (B) Orders: Performing Cultural Criticism with Coco Fusco, Guillermo Gómez-Peña and Anna Deavere Smith." *Women of Color: Defining the Issues, Hearing the Voices.* Diane Long Hoeveler and Janet K. Boles, eds. Westport, CT: Greenwood, 2001. 159–73.

Ensler, Eve. *The Vagina Monologues: The V-Day Edition.* New York: Villard, 2000.

Feffer, Steve. "Extending the Breaks: *Fires in the Mirror* in the Context of Hip-Hop Structure, Style, and Culture." *Comparative Drama* 37.3/4 (2003/2004): 397–415.

Fuller, Kevin L. and Andrea Armstrong. "Media Killers: An Interview with Anna Deavere Smith." *AppendX: Culture/Theory/Praxis* issue 2 (1997). 8 July 2006. www.appendx.org/issue2/smith/index.htm.

Goldberg, Nan. "She, the people: Anna Deavere Smith talks about empathizing with Rodney King, the LAPD and President Clinton." *Salon* (1 November 2000; 12 July 2006). http://archive.salon.com/books/feature/2000/11/01/smith/index.html

Hurston, Zora Neale. *"Spunk": Three Tales by Zora Neale Hurston.* Adapted by George C. Wolfe. Music by Chic Street Man. New York: Theatre Communications Group, 1991.

Jay, Gregory. "Other People's Holocausts: Trauma, Empathy, and Justice in Anna Deavere Smith's *Fires in the Mirror.*" *Contemporary Literature* 48.1 (2007): 119–49.

Kennedy, Adrienne. *Funnyhouse of a Negro. Adrienne Kennedy in One Act.* Minneapolis: University of Minnesota Press, 1988. 1–23.

——*A Movie Star Has to Star in Black and White. Adrienne Kennedy in One Act.* Minneapolis: University of Minnesota Press, 1988. 79–103.

Kushner, Tony. "Why Get Out of Bed?: Anna Deavere Smith." *Tony Kushner in Conversation.* Robert Vorlicky, ed. Ann Arbor: University of Michigan Press, 1998. 245–54.

Lewis, Barbara. "The Circle of Confusion: A Conversation with Anna Deavere Smith." *Kenyon Review* 15.4 (1993): 54–64.

Mann, Emily. *Annulla: An Autobiography.* New York: Theatre Communications Group, 1976.

Martin, Carol. "Anna Deavere Smith: The Word Becomes You: An Interview." *The Drama Review* 37.4 (1993): 45–62.

——"Bearing Witness: Anna Deavere Smith from Community to Theatre to Mass Media." *A Sourcebook of Feminist Theatre and Performance: On and Beyond the Stage.* Carol Martin, ed. London: Routledge, 1996. 81–93.

Middlebrook, Diane Wood. "The Artful Voyeur: Anna Deavere Smith and Henry Louis Gates, Jr., on private life and public art." *Transition* 67 (1995): 186–97.

Parks, Suzan-Lori. *Venus.* New York: Dramatists Play Service, 1998.

Reinelt, Janelle. "Performing Race: Anna Deavere Smith's *Fires in the Mirror.*" *Modern Drama* 39 (1996): 609–17.

Richards, Sandra L. "Caught in the Act of Social Definition: *On the Road* with Anna Deavere Smith." *Acting Out: Feminist Performances.* Lynda Hart and Peggy Phelan, eds. Ann Arbor: University of Michigan Press, 1993. 35–53.

Savran, David. "Anna Deavere Smith." *The Playwright's Voice: American Dramatists on Memory, Writing and the Politics of Culture.* New York: Theatre Communications Group, 1999. 237–62.

Shange, Ntozake. *for colored girls who have considered suicide/when the rainbow is enuf.* 1975. Reprint. New York: Scribner, 1997.

Smith, Anna Deavere. *Aye Aye Aye I'm Integrated. Here to Stay: Five Plays from the Women's Project.* Julia Miles, ed. New York: Applause, 1997. 253–71.

——*Charlayne Hunter Gault* 1984.

——*Fires in the Mirror: Crown Heights, Brooklyn and Other Identities.* New York: Anchor, 1993.

——*Gender Bending: On the Road Princeton University* 1989.

——*House Arrest: A Search for American Character In and Around the White House, Past and Present* and *Piano* in *Two Plays.* New York: Anchor, 2004.

——*Let Me Down Easy* 2007.

——*Letters to a Young Artist.* New York: Anchor, 2006.

——"Not So Special Vehicles." *Performing Arts Journal* 50/51 (1995): 77–89.

——*On the Road: A Search for American Character* 1983.

——*Talk to Me: Listening Between the Lines.* New York: Random House, 2000.

——*Twilight: Los Angeles, 1992.* New York: Anchor, 1994.

Sundquist, Eric J. *Strangers in the Land: Blacks, Jews, Post-Holocaust America.* Cambridge, MA: Harvard University Press, 2005.

Thompson, Debby. "'Is Race a Trope?': Anna Deavere Smith and the Question of Racial Performativity." *African American Review* 37.1 (2003): 127–38.

Vorlicky, Robert H. "'Imagine All the People': Hip Hop, Post-multiculturalism, and Solo Performance in the United States." *Crucible of Cultures: Anglophone Drama at the Dawn of a New Millennium.* Marc Maufort and Franca Bellarsi, eds. Brussels: Peter Lang, 2002. 141–50.

Williams, Tennessee. *The Glass Menagerie.* New York: New Directions, 1999.

Wolfe, George C. *The Colored Museum.* New York: Grove 1988.

——(adapter). *"Spunk": Three Tales by Zora Neale Hurston."* Music by Chic Street Man. New York: Theatre Communications Group, 1991.

11 Digging the Fo'-fathers
Suzan-Lori Parks's histories

Debby Thompson

in memory of Rajiv Bhadra

> History is time that won't quit.
> (Suzan-Lori Parks, "from *Elements of Style*," 15)

Foolhardy as it is to attempt to encapsulate Suzan-Lori Parks's aesthetic in three words, I offer the phrase "Digging the Fo'-fathers." This phrase gets at the primary activity of Parks's plays—digging—as well as at their radical ambivalence towards the material that gets dug up. The resurrection and re-membering of histories—painful and pleasurable, factual and fictional, literal and figurative, simultaneously—are both the form and content of Parks's operating theatre. Playfully signifying on American and Western history through African American accents, Suzan-Lori Parks performs archeologies and genealogies on contemporary racial discourses and identities. Below I want to sketch out potential archeological readings of Suzan-Lori Parks's plays, starting by reading my title phrase Parks-style, then by exploring her aesthetic of digging in relation to Foucault's archeological project, and finally by digging the discourses of her 1996 play *Venus*. First, though, I offer a brief genealogy of Suzan-Lori Parks's emergence.

Digging Suzan-Lori Parks

The mass of Parks's plays can be seen as History Plays, not in the classical sense of representing the life of a stately or heroic figure, but in the sense of attempting to "locate the ancestral burial ground, dig for bones, find the bones, hear the bones sing, write it down" (Parks, *America* 4). While official American histories may say to African Americans and others, "once upon a time you weren't here" (Drukman 67), Parks is writing histories that imaginatively fill the spaces of "The Great Hole of History"; she writes into and out of the absences—or "abscesses" (Drukman 67–8)—of history, where history's "abscesses" play out like Derrida's *aporia*. Rather than attempting to recover what "really" happened, Parks is interested in what might have happened, as well as in how things might have happened differently.

She's more interested in the myths of history than in "actual" history, in how history came to be created and how it functions in the present. So her plays can't be contained in linear plot progressions; rather, "[t]he immediate experience of Parks's characters is more like that of Ralph Ellison's Invisible Man, who sees history not as an arrow or a spiral but as a boomerang, for which one had best 'keep a steel helmet handy'" (Garett 6).

Playwriting started for Parks when, in a fiction writing class with James Baldwin at Mount Holyoke College in 1983, her mentor suggested that she write plays. Her first major play, *Imperceptible Mutabilities in the Third Kingdom*, won an Obie in 1990 for Best New American Play. In Hilton Als' summary, it is "a series of dense scenes about black life from slavery to the present, linked by the metaphor of the natural sciences" (Als 78). This early work resembles that of Adrienne Kennedy, whose plays "are highly experimental, surrealistic nightmares of young black women (and men) struggling with questions of identity and self-worth in a white, prejudiced world" and "stage the harrowing territory of the subconscious, a chaotic world of shifting times, locations, and selves" (Kolin xi). *Imperceptible Mutabilities*, which premiered at BACA Downtown Theater in 1989, began Parks's working relationship with director Liz Diamond.

Parks's next full-length play, *The Death of the Last Black Man in the Whole Entire World*, is described in her "New Dramatists" website entry as "[a]n historical dreamscape of death, and non-religious resurrection." Structured like a classical Greek play, the basic story consists of two main characters: Black Man with Watermelon and Black Woman with Fried Drumstick. The Black Woman, widow of the (last) Black Man, performs "Hoodoo" to bring about her husband's returns. Meanwhile, he is killed again and again, in a variety of different ways—falling off a building/ slaveship, electrocution, hanging, lynching—only to be resurrected again and again. The Overture, Panels II, IV, and the Finale consist of a Chorus of strands of historical discourses and cultural mythologies: Lots of Grease and Lots of Pork; Yes and Greens Black-eyed Peas Cornbread; Queen-then-Pharaoh Hatshepsut; Before Columbus; Old Man River Jordan; Ham; And Bigger and Bigger and Bigger; Prunes and Prisms; Voice on thuh Tee V. The Chorus performs the Last Black Man's re-mem-burial service. Alice Rayner and Harry Elam, Jr. explain that the Chorus exists because the legacy of the black man:

> must be preserved into the future. The other figures of the play, who
> represent spirits of black people already deceased, prevent him from
> passing over into their world until the significance of his life and his
> history is passed on to Black Woman, the only "living" character in the
> play. Because of this "unfinished business," Black Man exists in a
> liminal space between the living and the dead. He is dislocated,
> caught in a continual "Middle Passage." In addition, Black Man with
> Watermelon's plight reflects the current dislocation, fragmentation, and

disillusion that Cornel West terms the "postmodern condition" of contemporary black America (Rayner & Elam 451).

Risking the resurrection of negative images and stereotypes, Parks "challenges and satirizes these stereotypes and questions their origins" (Rayner & Elam 453). In *Death*, strands of history—and in particular strands of historical discourses about African Americans—also reappear again and again like the return of the repressed, killed off only to be reborn.

The rhythm of resurrection and re-death, of simultaneous burial and exhumation, recurs again in *The America Play*, a play which most embodies what Parks calls "the digger motif" (Jiggetts 310). In Act I, the Foundling Father, presumably a black man, a gravedigger by trade, goes out West to replicate an amusement park (known as "The Great Hole of History") that he saw back East on his honeymoon. In his lesser, supplementary hole, the Foundling Father imitates Abraham Lincoln at the moment of his death and, for a penny, allows spectators to play Booth and "shoot" him. When he decides to quit the profession, he buries all the relics of his hole of history. He may or may not have been shot for real, as Abraham Lincoln, at the end of Act I. In Act II, his wife and son (Lucy and Brazil, respectively) dig to unearth the relics of the Foundling Father to re-member him. At the end of the play, the Foundling Father reappears (perhaps as a living ghost) and is put on display as Abraham Lincoln in his coffin.

We are ghosted by a history that won't stay buried. *The America Play*, which has scenes with titles such as "Archeology" and "Spadework," continues the project of digging through history, not to recover what "really happened," but to realize the power of its replications in the present. For us in the present, histories are always already replications.

As Parks's career has "progressed" (to use an inapt term for such a nonlinear playwright), her plays have become increasingly more coherent, with more distinct plots and characters (rather than the "figures" of earlier plays), but her ambivalence about history and about identity, particularly African American identity, remains. Her 1996 play *Venus* (which I will discuss at length below in relation to her digging aesthetic), examines the story of Saartjie Baartman, a South African woman brought to Europe in the early 1800s and displayed as an anthropological curiosity due to her steatopygia (a condition in which fat accumulates around the buttocks). Directed by Richard Foreman in 1996 at Yale Repertory Theatre, the play performs an autopsy and revivisection of historical constructions of black female embodiment.

Parks's play *Topdog/Underdog* has even more recognizable characters: Booth and Lincoln, played by Mos Def and Jeffrey Wright, respectively, in the 2002 Broadway production at the Ambassador Theatre, directed by George C. Wolfe. As the characters' names suggest, this play returns to the motif of a black man playing Abraham Lincoln (in a kind of reversal of the blackface tradition), as well as to the motif of a black man being shot at repeatedly, and to the larger motif of black men being constantly under fire and endangered. *Topdog/Underdog* presents a study of the minute and minute-by-minute psychological and micropolitical shifts in the relationship between two brothers, whose plays for power are ongoing but unreliable, as unreliable as the card game con artist that Booth aspires to be. "Topdog" and "underdog" are not stable identities but positions constantly being negotiated in unpredictable ways. This play brought Parks center-stage into the theatre world; it appeared on Broadway and won a Pulitzer.

Other plays include her "Red Letter Plays": *In the Blood* and *Fucking A*, which re-imagine Hawthorne's Hester Prynne as a black abortion provider. Parks's latest project is *365 Days/365 Plays*, which, as its title suggests, consists of 365 mini-plays, written one per day for a year, from November 13, 2002 to November 12, 2003. These plays will be performed at multiple sites throughout the country from November 2006 to November 2007 (Walat).

Throughout Parks's plays, for all their variations and mutabilities, certain motifs recur: the "digger motif"; continuing death and resurrection; burial and excavation; the inevitable return of repressed history and its compulsive repetition; the frustration of the linear progress narrative; the instability of identity; the interrelations between spectacle, spectatorship, and surveillance; the filling of the abscesses of history; and an aesthetic of signifying on, appropriating, and re-citing the discourses of fo'-fathers past and present.

Digging the Fo'-fathers

Hilton Als, in a recent article in *The New Yorker*, calls Parks "one of the few in the popular theatre to fully exploit the power of spoken black English" in plays which are "multi-layered, historically aware, and linguistically complicated" (Als 74). "Exploit" is a good word for Parks's aesthetic; she doesn't replicate Black English, she rummages through it for exploits, gems of telling puns and wordplays. This wordplay, which tells the truth but tells it slang, is nowhere more telling than in Parks's "Fo'-fathers," a term which occurs in *The America Play* first as "foe-father." The Black English pronunciation of "fore" gives the word a more "multi-layered" and "historically aware" meaning than its white counterpart.

The America Play circles in the first half around "The Foundling Father," a "digger by trade," who impersonates Abraham Lincoln at the moment of his death while customers play at shooting him. In the second half of the play his survivors dig to both resurrect and bury him. The play itself digs through "The Great Hole of History" (or "an exact replica" of it) for remnants of the past: "Mr. Washingtons bones," "uh bust of Mr. Lincoln carved of marble," "thuh lick-ed boots," "several documents: peace pacts, writs, bills of sale, treaties, notices, handbills and circulars, freeing papers, summonses, declarations of war, addresses, title deeds, obits, long lists of dids," as well as medals "for bravery and honesty; ... for standing tall; for standing still ... For makin do ... For bowin and scrapin. Uh medal for fakin ..." (*America* 185–6). Buried under cultural mythologies of America's "fore-fathers" are the remains of the "lesser knowns," the "foundlings," the orphaned possibilities that can only be recovered with labor. Parks's plays reanimate the "forefathers" of American and Western history, most especially the frequently recurring Abraham Lincoln, as well as Washington, Columbus, Queen Hatshepsut, Georges Cuvier (as The Baron Docteur in *Venus*), and others. These forefathers of history have had ambiguous relations with African American history: they represent both lineage and rupture; they are both fore-fathers and foe-fathers. They are also, as Brazil in *The America Play* indicates, "faux-father(s)" (184), sometimes fake or inauthentic, sometimes downright false, crooks and liars, as are the dominant narratives of cultural lineage and evolution.

In some plays, we are given extensive genealogies of forebears, most notoriously in the genealogy of Ham in *The Death of the Last Black Man in the Whole Entire World*. As Ham recites his family tree ("Histree" or "Ham's Begotten Tree" [*America* 121]), the text moves from an Old Testament-like list of "begots" into a blackface minstrel performance ("HAM BONE HAM BONE WHERE YOU BEEN ROUN THUH WORL N BACK A-GAIN" [123]) into a slave auction ("SOLD!" [124]). The genealogy of modern constructions of Africans in America contains ancient biblical narratives of children of Ham, the commodification of black bodies that the religious discourse justifies, and stage performances mimicking and reifying white anxieties and desires about black men and women. Such genealogies trace not only the official fore-fathers but also the foundling and wayfaring discourses left out but still wandering through.

In the pseudo-Black vernacular of Parks's characters, "fore-fathers," "foe-fathers," and "faux-fathers" are one, their three-pronged meanings all bound up in one utterance like tines on a fork. Spectators might hear one or another word first, but with the persistent repetition and revision—what Parks calls "Rep & Rev" (*America* 9)—of the word, meaning accumulates and shifts. In Parks's aesthetic, Black vernacular itself is a "Rep & Rev" of standard American English (SAE), or, in Henry Louis Gates' term, a "signifyin'" on its antecedent dialect. Black vernacular brings out meanings of which the host dialect may not be aware. The white forefathers are, in Black dialect, always already foes as well as fakes, not true fathers. If Black dialect is a supplement to SAE, then the supplement is more accurate, more authentic, than the original. The truth is in the play. Parks's wordplay not only celebrates Black dialect but unearths embedded dialectics.

In her plays, Parks "digs" these fore-foe-faux-fathers, along with the discursive formations of which they are metonymic. Digging is a major activity on Parks's stages. In fact, in one of her very first plays, written as an undergraduate, she "had a lot of dirt on stage which was being dug at," but was told, "you can't have dirt on stage" (Jiggetts 310). A Suzan-Lori Parks play has dirt on stage—a lot of dirt, and a lot of digging. Act II of *The America Play* contains scenes entitled "Archeology" and "Spadework."

"Spade" is a derogatory slang word for an African American. Calling a spade a spade, Parks's provocative plays go on the offensive to do the work, necessary for African American historical recovery, of digging for meanings behind words, for their (unofficial) etymological histories (or would-be histories). *The America Play* is populated by diggers: The Foundling Father, Lucy, Brazil. In addition to physical, on-stage digging, Parks's stages are riddled with characters identified with digging—The Negro Resurrectionist of *Venus*, for example—and with acts of dis-re-membering.

Parks's characters, and the plays themselves, perform archeologies, both literal and figurative. "Diggiddy-diggiddy," a common scat refrain in Parks's plays, announces rhythmically an aesthetic of digging. Along with physical historical remains (a statue, wooden teeth, a rock with writing under it, pickled genitals, freedom papers), Parks digs discourses.

"Digging" emerged in Black vernacular (and is now standard in American spoken dialect more generally) as a word for liking or enjoying or understanding: "You dig?" But the word, like that three-pronged fork, can also be an instrument for stabbing and jabbing. To "take digs at" something is to poke it and critique it. Parks's plays dig the fo'-fathers.

Digging through history, enjoying history, and taking digs at history, Parks's plays can all, in a sense, be seen as history plays. In a postmodern era, in which history is a question of ruptures, replicas and simulacra, rather than of coherent world views, in which the classical genres of drama are inadequate, where tragedy has become trite, where comedy has turned over to the farce of repeated history, Parks writes the only kind of history plays now possible: deconstructive histories, which sweep up tragic and comic traces in an archeological dig.

"Diggidy-diggidy-diggidy"

The terms "archeology" and "genealogy" should bring to mind the structuralist/poststructuralist project of Michel Foucault. Although Foucault never performed a genealogy of race, or even of gender (except as a secondary effect of sexuality), his model of genealogy and archeology is one that is not only useful for understanding the work of Suzan-Lori Parks, but one that she herself, in her plays, is engaged in—and not only in the literal sense of on-stage characters digging through rubble and reciting lineages. Parks's plays do to race in America what Foucault's *History of Sexuality* did to sexuality: it "dis(-re-)members" the ruptured strands of discourse that produced contemporary knowable identities.

In his *Archaeology of Knowledge*, Foucault develops an archeological method of excavating histories of knowledges and their rules of formation. This method assumes first that knowledges are not inevitable from the start, nor are they eternal, but are rather "discursive formations" with histories. An archeological history is a matter of 'treating discourses ... as practices that systematically form the objects of which they speak" (*Archaeology*).

For example, examining "race" as a discursive formation allows us to see it not as a given but as a subject of knowledge, a subject formed by discourses. As "disciplines," such "structures of knowledge operate as disciplinary regimes," or as what Foucault elsewhere refers to as "Power/Knowledge." As Arnold Davidson reminds us, an archeological approach may turn up discontinuities in knowledge systems that seem to be unified, and continuities among seemingly discontinuous systems:

> If one sets out to describe the historical trajectories of the sciences in terms of anonymous rules for the formation and production of statements, then what looked continuous from some other perspective may very well appear radically discontinuous from this perspective. Problems of periodization and of the unity of a domain will be almost entirely transformed by the archaeological method. One will find, for example, that new kinds of statements which seem to be mere incremental additions to scientific knowledge are in fact only made possible because underlying rules for the production of discourse have significantly altered. However, the method of archaeology also makes possible the discovery of new continuities, overlooked because of a surface appearance of discontinuity (Davidson 223–4).

For example, modern heterosexual love, which may look very different from empiricist medicine, may, when dug into, expose continuities with its seeming opposite. Genealogy, though a somewhat different project than archeology in its primary attention to "modalities of power" over "systems of knowledge," converges with archeology, Davidson suggests, in "disturb[ing] what is considered immobile, fragment[ing] what is thought to be unified, and show[ing] the heterogeneity of what is taken to be homogeneous" (Davidson 225).

The disciplinary formations of knowledge of the body—knowledges that create the body as a subject to be studied—operate as "biopower." The "subjects" of study produced within discursive regimes of biopower that Foucault studies include the madman, the criminal, the homosexual, with their objects being madness, criminality, and sexuality. The racial subject and "race" itself as an object of discursive formation are not sites where Foucault himself conducted archeologies or genealogies. They have, however, been rich sites for fruitful digging by an array of theorists and historians of race and gender, many directly influenced by Foucault. A sampling includes Anthony Appiah, David Theo Goldberg, Noel Ignatiev, Eric Lott, Anne McClintock, David Roediger, Jana Sawicki, and Ann Laura Stoler.

And Suzan-Lori Parks. Her plays, I'm asserting, are themselves performing an archeology of race, and especially of African American female identity as a subject-position. Race, in the work of the theorists above and of Parks, is by no means a given; it's not a pre-existing biological category which then accrues historical meaning and political valence. Race itself can be treated as a "discursive formation," an object of biopower, a construct of disciplinary structures of knowledge (and hence of power). Parks's plays perform an archeology of race, digging through layers of sediment.

"Visibility is a trap"

For the remainder of this essay I have chosen to explore Parks's archeological performances through the specific example of her 1996 play *Venus*, which I will explore in some depth. First performed at the Yale Repertory Theatre under the direction of Richard Foreman, the play is structured around the real-life story of Saartjie Baartman, a native of what is now South Africa, who was taken by the Dutch brother of her employer (The Mans Brother and The Man, respectively, in *Venus*) to England in 1810 for exhibition. (My main source of information about the life of Saartjie Baartman [and I suspect Suzan-Lori Parks's as well] is Stephen Jay Gould's essay, "The Hottentot Venus," which, when it appeared in his 1985 collection *The Flamingo's Smile*, aroused new interest in the subject.) Suzan-Lori Parks invents the character of the Mother–Showman as the agent who displays Saartjie Baartman as a freak in a freak show; her (purportedly) unusually large buttocks excited great interest among European spectators. A humanitarian society pressed for Baartman's release, but Baartman stated in court that she was not being restrained. She next traveled to Paris and continued to excite European spectatorial interest. She also aroused the interest of Georges Cuvier (The Baron Docteur in *Venus*), a French anatomist, who performed an autopsy on her after her death in 1815. Parts of her body, including her genitals, were preserved in formaldehyde ("in a pickle," as Parks puts it) and displayed in the Paris Musée de l'Homme. In 2002, her remains were returned to her native home in the Gamtoos Valley of South Africa.

Venus shows the creation of current cultural discourses about black women's bodies and the way we see them. This creation is in no way an evolution to a more and more refined, humanitarian, organic whole, as an Enlightenment narrative might have it, but a series of interventions and epistemic shifts, with traces of rupture and exclusion. Parks's play itself begins with an "Overture," in which, after The Venus "revolves" like a museum piece on display, the main characters introduce to the audience first "The Venus Hottentot," then themselves and then each other by their cast role descriptions: "The Chorus of the 8 Human Wonders"; "The Man, later/The Baron Docteur"; "The Negro Resurrectionist"; "The Brother, later/The Mother-Showman! Later/The Grade-School Chum"; "The Chorus of the Spectators"; "The Chorus of the Court." (Left out for now is "The Chorus of the 8 Anatomists.") After all of these introductions on the part of other characters, and after all these characters then reintroduce "The Venus Hottentot!" she speaks for the first time, introducing herself by the term already prescribed (or pre-scripted) for her: "The Venus Hottentot" (2). That is (to cast it in Althusserean terms for the moment), we see a theatrical representation of The Venus being hailed into subjectivity by discourses that precede her. Her agency follows.

In "The Re-Objectification and Re-Commodification of Saartjie Baartman in Suzan-Lori Parks's *Venus*," Jean Young laments that "Parks's historical deconstruction presents a fictitious melodrama that frames Saartjie Baartman as a person complicit in her own horrific exploitation; Parks depicts her as a sovereign, consenting individual with the freedom and agency to trade in her human dignity for the promise of material gain" (Young 699). Young argues instead that "Baartman was a victim, not an accomplice, not a mutual participant in this demeaning objectification" (Young 700). I'm suggesting, though, that the play encourages us to see Venus less as a character than as a discursive formation. Venus is, from the start, discursive. It's not that she doesn't have agency, but that that agency is created within and through the very discourses that make her subject-position possible from the start. Note that a common refrain is the question, never answered, "Do I have a choice?" While a realistic documentation of the kind Young supplies might well show Saartjie Baartman to be brutally victimized, Parks's interest is not in Venus the person but in Venus the subject, Venus the discursive formation.

The Overture introduces, in a synchronic slice, an array of discontinuous, rupturing discourses presented in a scene and style that is itself disruptive, rupture-ridden, nonprogressive. These strands of discourse include those of commerce and commodification, religion and morality, science and medicine ("I look at you, Venus, and see:/ Science."), and modern romantic love, among others. A Chorus member offers, as if hawking wares:

> Thuh gals got bottoms like hot air balloons.
> Bottoms and bottoms and bottoms pilin up like
> like 2 mountains. Magnificent. And endless.
> An ass to write home about.
> Well worth the admission price.
> A spectacle a debacle a priceless prize, thuh filthy slut.
> Coco candy colored and dressed all in *au naturel*
> she likes when people peek and poke. (7–8)

Figuring Venus's body as a landscape, the Chorus member's cartography equates Venus's "mountains" with territory to be colonized. Discursive frames war with each other: Venus is a landscape, a freak, a prize, a consumable good (chocolate), and a peep show. The Negro Resurrectionist concludes the scene:

> Tail end of our tale for there must be an end
> is that Venus, Black Goddess, was shameless, she sinned or else
> completely unknowing of r godfearin ways she stood
> totally naked in her iron cage.

> She gaind fortune and fame by not wearing a scrap
> hidin only the privates lippin down from her lap.
> When Death met her Death deathd her and left her to rot
> *au naturel* end for our hot Hottentot.
> And rot yes she would have right down to the bone
> had not The Docteur put her corpse in his home.
> Sheed a soul which is mounted on Satans warm wall
> while her flesh has been pickled in Sciences Hall. (8–9)

Note here the mixture of religious and scientific discourse rubbing uneasily against each other and revealing their faultlines.

The Overture gives a synchronic slice of the various discourses whose traces can be found in the presentation of Saartjie Baartman as The Venus Hottentot. The course of the play proper charts them out diachronically to show an array of discourses—imperialist, spectatorial, legal, medical—disrupting and overtaking one another while still bearing the traces of their predecessors.

As the Overture foreshadows, the early scenes (numerically the highest because the play's scenes are numbered in reverse, counting down to one) show "The Girl" (not yet "The Venus") in southern Africa, in the early 1800s, "deciding" to travel to England as an "African Dancing Princess" in order to "make a mint." As the servant of "The Man," the offer from his brother comes from a position of power imbalance and implied coercion, as is indicated by the very name "The Man," the colloquial Black English synecdoche for white men of power beyond question. She asks for the first time, but certainly not the last, "Do I have a choice?" (17). Under the illusion of choice, she is as much contained in the discourse of colonization as the Dutch colonizers. Just as The Man and The Brother instinctively see The Girl, like the land, as raw material to be exploited, they present England to her in the same vein, as a place whose "streets are paved with gold" (15), from which to extract riches to bring back to the motherland. A discourse of colonialism frames the decisions, as well as the illusion of free will, of all three characters.

In England the prevailing discourse reproduces what Foucault has called (in other contexts) a "Society of the Spectacle," one that could also be formulated as a shift from the spectacular to the specular, without entirely displacing the spectacular. This spectacular discourse is not unrelated to the discourse of colonialism, but neither is it synonymous. It is not *simply* colonialism by other means, or even not *simply* slavery by other means.

In *Discipline and Punish* Foucault lays out a long historical shift, in European thought, from a "Society of the Spectacle" to a "Society of Surveillance." A similar shift is unearthed, in microcosm, in *Venus*. The discourse of spectacular display of The Venus in the earlier scenes is covered by other discourses—religious, legal, medical, romantic—while still bearing its trace.

Within the discourse of a society of the spectacle is the trace—or perhaps concurrence, collaboration, corroboration—of a moralistic Christian taxonomy. One of the 8 Human Wonders is, according to the Mother–Showman:

> one step closer to the monkeys.
> Uh Fireman who dines on flame.
> He claims thuh Devil his creator
> but really hails from thuh Equator. (32)

In this spectacular display of the fire-eater, anthropological, religious, and imperialist discourses intermingle, while remaining disparate. The anthropological, evolutionary model of human descent from a common ancestor with other primates flickers into a religious discourse of human creation by a "creator" and a moralistic discourse of good and evil, which flickers into a discourse of exploration and cartography. Of The Venus herself the Mother–Showman says:

> Come on inside and allow her to reveal to you the Great and Horrid Wonder
> of her great heathen buttocks.
> Thuh Missing Link, Ladies and Gentlemen: Thuh Venus Hottentot:
> Uh warnin tuh us all. (43)

The reference to "the missing link" of the evolutionary model of human emergence combines a scientific discourse with one of freak show, the display of exotica of explorers. It also combines with a religious sermon against heathenism.

Christian moral taxonomies, freak show display, and colonialist discourse, all bearing traces of each other, also ghost the legal discourse which seeks to displace them, and all—more importantly for the purposes of this essay—ghost our present conceptions of race, which seek to be scientifically neutral, free from the mythologies of religion and colonialist supremacy. When she is taken to court as both victim and criminal, is both rescued from enslavement and accused of indecency, The Venus pleads:

> Good good honest people.
> If I bear thuh bad mark what better way to cleanse it off?
> Showing my sinful person as a caution to you all could,
> in the Lords' eyes, be a sort of repentance
> and I could wash off my dark mark.
> I came here black.
> Give me the chance to leave here white. (76)

This plea comes after it has been revealed that The Venus has been baptized. Baptism has hailed her into a religious discourse that casts her as sinful. The moralistic narrative of cleansing oneself of sin maps onto the legalistic narrative of crime and rehabilitation. Both of these narratives employ an even older structuring metaphor wherein blackness is negative and whiteness is positive. All of these discurvise narratives lie as remains underneath modern concepts of race, here seen in production.

The fact that The Chorus of the Court is played by the same cast as The Chorus of the 8 Human Wonders as well as The Chorus of Spectators would seem to suggest a continuity between freak show and the Law, between spectacle and surveillance, with one transforming into the next as easily as the members of the Chorus transform their roles. This view could be seen to be supported by the Negro Resurrectionist's repeated iterations of the statement, "The year was 1810, three years after the Bill for the Abolition of the Slave-Trade had been passed in Parliament. Among protests and denials, horror and fascination the show went on"(77).

One could read the showing of The Venus as a form of slavery by other means, a de facto slavery simply called something else. When "The Court grants the writ of *Habeas Corpus*" and demands to "Bring up the body of this female" (73), this act could be seen as simply transferring ownership of Saartjie's body from slave-owner to employer-owner to the Law, under whom she becomes a subject. However, in such a transfer, the very notions of ownership and subjection change hands. The Court asks The Venus, "Are you here of yr own free will/or are you under some restraint?" (75), to which The Venus can only reply, "Im here to make a mint." In this moment, discrepant discourses can't accommodate each other. The legal discourse of "free will" vs. "restraint," furthermore, is unable to accommodate the question of subjectivity within a discourse that both enables and limits it. Agency for such a subject is not either/or. Hence "the Court rules/ not to rule" (78).

The Chorus of the Court soon turns into the Chorus of the 8 Anatomists as Saartjie changes subjecthood from the Mother–Showman to the Baron Docteur, who essentially buys her. The spectacle moves from freak show to court to "the anatomical Theatre" (91) where, during the intermission, the Baron Docteur "dis(-re-)members" The Venus. In the ensuing scenes, his amorous exploration of her body is simultaneous with a scientific exploration. After the Baron Docteur bribes her with chocolates and protestations of love while expressing his true desire to make a name for himself, The Venus offers, "You could discover *me*" (108). As an "Anatomical Columbus" (124), he writes in his medical notebook statements such as:

> Her movements had rapidity and came unexpected calling to mind well, with all respect to her, the movements of a monkey. Above all, she had a way of pushing out her lips just like the monkeys do. (109–10)

This "Anatomical Columbus" logs his scientific observations much as an explorer would log his discoveries of the flora and fauna of new lands. Medical exploration, too, creates a cartography, mapping out alien bodies and placing them under its power-knowledge. Medicine, again, is not simply colonization by other means, but nor are they opposites. Empire and empiricism share a common will to order.

The Baron Docteur pre-empts charges of exploitation by stating, "She submitted to these examinations as willingly as a patient submits to his doctors eyes and hands" (110). For Venus, as for the prisoner in the Panopticon, "[v]isibility is a trap" (Foucault, *Discipline* 200). Under medical examination, she's spectacle all the more, but differently so. A patient's submission to a doctor's eyes and hands is so naturalized, at this point, that nobody would think of calling it exploitation. On the contrary, such surveillance is understood as humanitarian beneficence, for the patient's own good.

The medicolonial discourse of discovery, exploration, and exploitation is further intertwined with discourses of romantic love. Throughout the play, Venus's story is interrupted by a play-within-a-play, "For the Love of the Venus." In this play, a young (European) man is bored with his Bride-to-Be, as his fantasies stray towards "something Wild" (48) and, in particular, "something called 'The Hottentot Venus'" (49), whom he hasn't been able to get out of his head since he saw her on display. To win back his desire, the Bride-to-Be masquerades as the Hottentot Venus, successfully winning his pledge of eternal love.

The Bride-to-Be's masquerading as the Hottentot Venus only obscures the fact that "the Hottentot Venus" was always already a masquerade, and that Saartjie Baartman masquerades as The Venus. Venus finds, when she attempts to remove the masquerade, though, that she is granted no subject-position outside of that role. Other characters, like the Bride-to-Be, depend on the reality of The Venus, in relation to whom they define themselves. The Europeans need to assign The Venus the role of "wild Love" through and against which they can formulate their "romantic love." If there weren't a Hotttentot Venus, it would have been necessary for the European characters to invent one.

At several points in the play, the Baron Docteur watches the play-within-the-play. In his protestations of love to The Venus, he even cites from the play, "My love for you is artificial/Fabricated much like this epistle" (102). This prefabricated discourse of romantic love arises from a play which arises from colonialist discourses. Here we see the discourse of modern romantic heterosexual love in the process of formation as it incorporates earlier and contemporaneous discourses of medicine, exploration, jurisprudence, and freak show. Foucauldian archeology can uncover ways in which one discourse which poses as the opposite of another may (also) be genealogically related. The history of romantic heterosexual love is a history of colonization and commodification.

This archeology of romantic heterosexual love is condensed in "A Brief History of Chocolate," the antepenultimate scene (Scene 3, 155–6). Parks's archeological aesthetic can be seen in its most condensed form in this tour-de-force monologue scene. Ostensibly a historical account of the development of chocolate, it is also an archeology of discursive formations of black women, with whom, the monologue suggests, chocolate has become discursively and imagistically aligned. Through chocolate have circulated discursive strands of geographical conquest and imperialism, of Christianity, of commerce, and of medicine. Just as all of these discourses have produced and regulated chocolate, they have simultaneously produced and regulated black women and discourses of race. To the extent that black women are imagistically equated with chocolate, the production of chocolate is the production of race materialized. Venus herself, eating the chocolates the Baron Docteur has given her, asks him, "Do you think I look like/ one of these little chocolate Brussels infants?" (105) and comments on the chocolates that share her name, "*Capezzoli di Venere.* The nipples of Venus. Mmmmm. My favorite" (105). The traffic in chocolate has become a kind of gift exchange, a gift in exchange for a woman's body. Symbolically, chocolate is the equivalent of the woman's body for which it is being exchanged. If black and brown bodies in cacao-growing regions have been subjugated in order to produce chocolate and subsumed under the product, European women also become objectified under the sign of chocolate. While the gift's history has been lost for most of its consumers, that history still underwrites the consumption of chocolate. Underlying a seemingly simple (if guilty) pleasure is a massive history of discourses.

As with chocolate, so with Venus: she's not just a unique anomaly but a product of complexly intersecting discourses, and an index of these discourses. Digging (up) and resurrecting Venus unearths these discourses. Both modern romantic heterosexual love and modern conceptions of race bear (bare) the traces of imperialism, exoticism/ primitivism, commerce and currency, religion and medicine. Venus's final appeals for romantic love before (and even after) she dies—"Miss me Miss me Miss me" (160), "*Kiss* me *Kiss* me *Kiss* me *Kiss*" (162)—would not provide the escape she seeks; the discourse of romantic love entraps her more than any other.

"A digger by trade"

Parks archeologizes not only modern conceptions of race, science, and romantic heterosexual love, but also of theatre itself. The 8 Anatomists, like the Baron Docteur, in the act of exploring Venus's body, turn aside to masturbate, just as the Chorus of Spectators earlier masturbated to the spectacle of Venus. This recalls the stereotypical joke about how, in an earlier and more censored era, young boys often discovered female bodies in *National Geographic* magazine displays of topless African women, which they would masturbate to. Condensed in this joke, though, is an anxious awareness that scientific (medical and anthropological) discourse is not (only) the opposite of pornography, but (also) its counterpart. The African woman is, in both discourses, rendered an object of primitive and shameful (to Westerners) desires projected onto her. She becomes an image of the sexual abundance that must be repressed to maintain Western civility. The medical gaze, if not itself voyeuristic, shares a specular structure with pornography's voyeurism.

After the Anatomists measure The Venus, the Baron Docteur states:

> That's plenty for today and Im sure our lovely subjects
> all exhausted.
> Put yr hands together, Sirs.
> Show The Venus yr appreciation. (120)

At this, the stage directions say, "[t]hey applaud politely" in their medical theatre, as an audience would applaud for the performers at the end of a play. Not only is the play digging medical discourses and discovering religion, imperialism, and freak shows, but it's also archeologizing modern theatre and discovering all of these discourses and more. Ultimately the play is an Archeology of Theatre—as is much of Suzan-Lori Parks's work.

Contemporary theatre, in a society of surveillance, resembles the museum more than the spectacle. (Even Richard Foreman's productions, of which the first production of *Venus* is one, however much they are known for their "spectacular" nature, are more investigations, inspections, explorations, interrogations than they are carnivalesque festivals.) The contemporary director is a kind of curator of cultural imagery. Particularly when theatre offers up one cultural race to the gaze of another we can see its found(l)ings in earlier discourses of anthropology and its predecessors, exploration, imperialism, and empiricism. George C. Wolfe's play *The Colored Museum* blatantly enacts this formulation. Venus's near final lines, closing her summation of her life off in a couplet (before unraveling the couplet's tidiness by her final line, "*Kiss* me *Kiss* me *Kiss* me *Kiss*" [162]), are: "Loves soul, which was tidy, hides in heaven, yes, that's it/Loves corpse stands on show in museum. Please visit" (161). Much as spectators may shudder, by the end of the play, at the prospect of visiting this poor woman's remains in a museum and subjecting her to further gawking and scrutiny, we have, in effect, done just that over the course of the last two hours: this play is a visitation of Venus's remains.

The Negro Resurrectionist, who reads many of the "historical extracts" throughout the play, is himself "a digger" who "used to unearth bodies" (150) but now works as a "Watchman," watching imprisoned "criminals" such as Venus at the end of the play. (Her last lines before she dies are directed to the Resurrectionist as Watchman: "*Dont look at me*/don't look ..." [159].) His job is to watch in perpetual, inescapable surveillance. The antepenultimate lines, recited by all of the characters, are "Diggidy-diggidy-diggidy/Diggidy-diggidy-diggidy-dawg!" (162). As I've been suggesting, those lines are not just percussive jazz riffs or scatting—though they are this, too—but invocations to dig. Coming just after The Venus's invitation to visit the museum of her remains, this summation of the play asks us to dig the fo'-fathers.

If I have spent an inordinate amount of space here reading *Venus*'s digging aesthetic in chronological detail, I have done so as a model of approaches to other Parks plays as well, all of which engage in and reward archeological approaches. Parks's plays self-consciously theorize their own and their audience's embodiments of surveillance culture. Contemporary theatre—or at least Suzan-Lori Parks's theatre—bears the traces of medical and anthropological gazes, as well as of the objectifying and exoticizing gazes of imperialism. These discourses are the genealogic relatives of contemporary racial configurations and, in particular, of black female subjecthood. Theatre itself, in its modern forms, is a symptom and an agent of disciplinary regimes of race and gender. If we have shifted from a society of the spectacle to a society of surveillance, our theatre has too. Our current theatres of surveillance are analytical; they act as anthropological, sociological, even scientific studies of human behavior. Parks's play, however meta-discursive and meta-theatrical, is also, necessarily, a theatre of surveillance, including surveillance over black female sexuality and subjectivity. It digs into "The Great Hole of History." *Venus*, like the museum that (until recently) displayed Saartjie Baartman's remains, is complicit in the subjection/ subjecthood of its subject. Parks's play, too, places a black woman—one who pleads, "Dont look at me"—on display for exhibition and analysis. The play is an unearthing of discourses creating black female subjectivity, but it also (necessarily) occupies and reproduces those discourses. Her audience's gaze is directed by spectators of freak show and court, by the medical and anthropological gazes, and by a male gaze objectifying and romanticizing beauty. Parks's history plays don't simply dig through prior discourses, including discourses of theatre, but also resurrect and reanimate these discourses.

The ultimate "forefathers" are the discourses of knowledge that create us as subjects, and through which we perform ourselves. Our current power/knowledge structures have been constructed in the wake of prior discourses or epistemes, which they both displace and subsume, both define themselves in opposition to and are defined by. Prior discourses are, hence, both true and false, both remote ancestors and incestuous bedfellows, both opponents and unfaithful lovers. They are faux/fore/foe fathers (and mothers, sisters, and brothers). A theater that "digs" its "fo-fathers" enjoys them, understands them, unearths and resurrects them, takes digs at them, and performs archeologies upon them, all at once.

Works cited

Als, Hilton. "The Show-Woman: Suzan-Lori Parks's Idea for the Largest Theatre Collaboration Ever." *The New Yorker* (30 October, 2006): 74–81.

Appiah, Kwame Anthony. *In My Father's House: Africa in the Philosophy of Culture*. London: Oxford University Press, 1993.
Davidson, Arnold I. "Archaeology, Genealogy, Ethics." *Foucault: A Critical Reader*. David Couzens Hoy, ed. New York: Basil Blackwell, 1986.
Drukman, Steven. "Suzan-Lori Parks and Liz Diamond: Doo-a-diddly-dit-dit. An Interview by Steven Drukman." *The Drama Review* 39.3 (T 147) (1995): 56–74.
Foucault, Michel. *The Archaeology of Knowledge*. London: Tavistock Publications, 1972.
——*Discipline and Punish: The Birth of the Prison*. Translated by Alan Sheridan. New York: Vintage Books, 1979.
——*The History of Sexuality, Volume I: An Introduction*. Translated by Robert Hurley. New York: Vintage Books, 1980.
Gates, Jr., Henry Louis. *The Signifying Monkey: A Theory of African-American Literary Criticism*. New York: Oxford University Press, 1988.
Garrett, Shawn-Marie. "The Possession of Suzan-Lori Parks." *American Theatre* (October 2000): 22–6, 132–4.
Goldberg, David Theo. *Racist Cultures: Philosophy and the Politics of Meaning*. Oxford: Basil Blackwell, 1993.
Gould, Stephen Jay. *The Flamingo's Smile: Reflections in Natural History*. New York: W. W. Norton & Co., 1985.
Jiggetts, Shelby. "Interview with Suzan-Lori Parks." *Callaloo* 19.2 (1996): 309–17.
Ignatiev, Noel. *How the Irish Became White*. New York: Routledge, 1996.
Kolin, Philip C. *Understanding Adrienne Kennedy*. Columbia: University of South Carolina Press, 2005.
Lott, Eric. *Love and Theft: Blackface Minstrelsy and the American Working Class*. New York: Oxford University Press, 1993.
McClintock, Anne. *Imperial Leather*. New York and London: Routledge, 1995.
Parks, Suzan-Lori. *The America Play and Other Works*. New York: Theatre Communications Group, 1995.
——*The America Play*. In *The America Play and Other Works* 1995. 157–99.
——*The Death of the Last Black Man in the Whole Entire World*. In *The America Play and Other Works* 1995. 99–131.
——"from *Elements of Style*." In *The America Play and Other Works*. 6–18.
——*Fucking A*.
——*Imperceptible Mutabilities in the Third Kingdom* 1990.
——*In the Blood*.
——*Topdog/ Underdog*. New York: Theatre Communications Group, 2002.
——*Venus*. New York: Theatre Communications Group, 1997.
Rayner, Alice and Elam, Jr., Harry. "Unfinished Business: Reconfiguring History in Suzan-Lori Parks's The Death of the Last Black Man in the Whole Entire World." *Theatre Journal* 46 (1994): 447–61.
Roediger, David. *The Wages of Whiteness: Race and the Making of the American Working Class*. London: Verso, 1991.
Sawicki, Jana. *Disciplining Foucault: Feminism, Power, and the Body*. New York: Routledge, 1991.
Stoler, Ann Laura. *Carnal Knowledge and Imperial Power: Race and the Intimate in Colonial Rule*. Berkeley, CA: University of California Press, 2002.
——*Race and the Education of Desire: Foucault's History of Sexuality and the Colonial Order of Things*. Durham, NC: Duke University Press, 1995.

Young, Jean. "The Re-Objectification and Re-Commodification of Saartjie Baartman in Suzan-Lori Parks's *Venus*." *African American Review* 31.4 (1997): 699–708.

Walat, Kathryn. "These are the Days: Suzan-Lori Parks's Year of Writing Dangerously Yields 365 Plays." *American Theatre* (November 2006): 26–31, 81–3.

Wolfe, George C. *The Colored Museum*. New York: Grove Press, 1988.

12 An intimate look at the plays of Lynn Nottage

Sandra G. Shannon

Critically acclaimed African American playwright Lynn Nottage (1964–) spent much of her adult life sequestered within the ivory towers of academia— surrounded by books and censored by all of the regulations associated with this environment. Like Lorraine Hansberry, she grew to adulthood enjoying a comfortably middle-class lifestyle yet, also like Hansberry, she was able to transcend this world to find art in the noble struggles of the voiceless, nameless and less fortunate. In 1982, she received her diploma from New York's High School of Music and Art in Harlem and subsequently enrolled at Brown University where she received her B.A. Degree in 1986. Without interruption, she went on to receive her M.F.A. in playwriting at Yale School of Drama in 1989.

But the disturbing look on the faces of physically abused women pushed Lynn Nottage to become a playwright and to accept that she needed time to interface with the real world. By gradual degrees, she became a full-time playwright in the 1990s after spending four years at Amnesty International. Opportunity finally knocked in the form of a commissioned monologue for a musical entitled, *A ... My Name Will Always Be Alice*, a vignette written at the request of Michael Dixon, literary manager of Actors' Theatre of Louisville. By 2007, Nottage had written, workshopped, staged, and/or published nearly ten plays while steadily expanding her repertoire. Her published works include *Poof!* (1993), an escapist piece that shows the surprising results of a battered woman's wish for her husband to disappear; *Mud, River, Stone* (1998), a tough lesson for an African American couple seeking thrills in Africa to reenergize their pampered and essentially boring lives; *Las Meninas* (1989), a dramatization based on the true story of love, lust, and lies within the court and in the bedroom of Louis XIV; *Intimate Apparel* (2003), a very private glimpse into the life of a thirty-something year old African American seamstress who takes a bold chance at finding love; *Becoming American* (2003), a five-to-ten minute comedy in which a distant instructor indoctrinates a group of outsourced African telephone operators on how to appease American customers; *A Stone's Throw* (2004), a ten-minute play based upon a reworking of Sophocles' classic tragedy *Antigone* follows the deadly repercussions of a tabooed love affair between an African woman and a married man; *Crumbs from the Table of Joy* (2005), a 1950s coming of age story for a young African American girl who refuses to be defined by societal conventions; *Por'knocker* (2005), an explosive political satire involving a "failed" act of civil disobedience carried out by a culturally diverse group of would-be revolutionaries; and *Fabulation, Or the R-education of Undine* (2006), a social satire and "comeuppance tale" about a comfortable middle-class African American woman's self-discovery, ironically during the course of bouts with poverty, despair and an unexpected pregnancy.

In many ways, Lynn Nottage became a playwright out of necessity. After experiencing, in succession, the deaths of her mother of Lou Gehrig's Disease in 1997 followed by the birth of her daughter Ruby, Nottage turned to writing intricately layered dramas of "restless searchers," "forgotten people," "alienated folks," "mismatched souls," "unlikely lovers," and "odd couples."[1] Her efforts to give voice and agency to the least likely are byproducts of her own family members' reticence. She recalls, for example, a grandmother whose chronic paranoia is manifested in her abnormal tendency to hide valuable photos in odd places around her home. As the self-made custodian of her family's history, Nottage saw in the idiosyncrasies of her elderly relative a challenge to preserve her family's stories by embedding them in her plays. For example, the untold story of one of her distant relatives found form in a play that is based loosely upon her Barbadian great-grandmother, who, in 1904, immigrated alone to New York and found work as a seamstress, with particular skill in making frilly, sensual undergarments for the city's elite. Her signature play, *Intimate Apparel*, mirrors the suppressed, displaced passions of Ethel Boyce, who dared to love and lose before returning to a life as a spinster. As Nottage explained in an article written for *The Los Angeles Times*, "It has taken me the act of writing a new play to rescue the members of my family from storage ... If my family hadn't preserved our stories, and history certainly had not, then who would?"[2]

Nottage credits her own curiosity—what she calls the "what if" factor—and a healthy obsession for research as inspirations for her growing body of dramatic works. These factors, along with the indelible imprint left by childhood memories of her mother, a constant hankering for excursions, keen powers of observation, and a healthy imagination have placed her in the forefront of a new generation of black female playwrights. As Randy Gener observes, "In her plays, as in her life, Lynn Nottage is an intrepid traveler. With a keenly perceptive eye and an unerring ear for dialogue, as well as a healthy appreciation for the unusual, the absurd and hilariously ironic, she will go anywhere and try just about anything to make the theatrical experience full and rewarding."[3]

Unlike relationships that exist individually and collectively among August Wilson's cycle of ten plays, Nottage's works do not engage in intertextual conversations. Her not-so easily classified new matrix of plays resists neat structuralist groupings; each play introduces a completely isolated set of circumstances, and each play is packaged in a form underscoring its individuality.

Director David Sullivan, who participated in the Roundabout Theatre Company's production of *Intimate Apparel*, observes, "I don't think there's necessarily a Lynn Nottage voice. She can go from the abstract world to the satirical. She can also create a thoroughly researched piece."[4] Despite the distinct nature of Nottage's individual plays, each tends to focus upon one or more of the playwright's recurring themes:

- rescuing voices from history
- discovering silencing between the lines
- black women defining themselves
- race, multiculturalism, and diversity
- escaping reality.

Perhaps one of the most important themes in Nottage's dramas is her emphasis upon retrieving lost or suppressed history, particularly that of African American women. In *Las Meninas* (1989), Nottage performs the work of an archivist, painstakingly researching and resurrecting little known, forgotten, or ignored moments in history in order to give a voice to those women who have been marginalized. The play, which takes its title from the famous Velazquez painting, dramatizes a romantic relationship between two outcasts: Queen Marie-Thérèse, the unhappy wife of King Louis IV of France and an African dwarf named Nabo. A blatantly philandering King Louis XIV demoralizes his queen Thérèse by flaunting his African mistresses in front of Thérèse and by avoiding sexual contact with her at all cost. Humiliated, the Queen begins confiding in a dwarfed African man who was presented to her as a gift. The two get along just fine—so much so that a physical relationship develops between them. A child is born to them bearing a striking resemblance to its African father. The King, who is, of course, incensed, orders Nabo's execution and banishes his child to a convent. The Queen, delirious over this turn of events, goes insane.

In *Las Meninas*, Nottage adopts a metanarrative approach while dramatizing the true story of cruel indifference that plagued the marriage of this royal pair. Serving in the role as narrator of the affair to which the court of Louis IV went to great lengths to suppress is Louise Marie-Thérèse—the illegitimate daughter of the Queen and her African gift and the very focus of the play's conflict. Decades after her unwelcome birth into royalty, this African woman of mixed racial parentage, as narrator, offers a retrospective on notorious past secrets of the court that forced her into a nunnery and that ultimately drove her mother insane. Now, years later, she reclaims her story and her identity, all while remaining sensitive to her mother's misery in marriage.

In addition to rescuing characters from history and giving them voice, Nottage studies what she calls "the space between the lines";[5] that is, the innermost thoughts of marginal characters whose voices remain muted and whose stories have been deemed irrelevant by those around them who wield more power. Such is the case of Esther, a lonely black seamstress living and working in New York at the turn of the twentieth century. As the Hebrew name suggests, this Esther—not to be confused with August Wilson's elderly matriarch in *Two Trains Running* (1990), *Gem of the Ocean* (2003), and *Radio Golf* (2005)—is a woman of faith, courage, and caution, combined with resolution. She epitomizes the dutiful, docile and obedient servant. Single, 35, African American, and living alone in New York in 1905, Esther is all but resigned to a life without romance, intimacy, marriage and children. Nevertheless she is still more fortunate than most black women of her time in her situation. She has a rare talent in making intimate undergarments for New York's elite.

In *Intimate Apparel* Nottage highlights the silence between the lines that exists during the pre-Freudian era of the early 1900s when there were no means of grappling with the hidden workings of the subconscious mind. "The story is in the behavior" Gener observes.[6] Examining the play through psychoanalytic lens, critics easily discover that it is rife with sexual tension—sexual tension contained in the love letters exchanged between George and Esther as well as sexual tension projected onto exquisite undergarments in Esther's shop. Because of societal taboo, the obvious physical attraction between Esther and her Jewish fabric supplier cannot extend beyond the sensual, near orgiastic stroking of a rare piece of fabric, nor can it progress beyond Esther's fussing over a missing button on Marks's shirt or his longing glances at her. A tidal wave of safely guarded emotions occurs in the expressionistic gestures or silences between the lines in *Intimate Apparel*. Nottage shows that the emotions and desires of this "Unidentified Negro Seamstress" are no different from those of most of her clients. It is the complex, layered emotions conveyed in silence and indirection that garner the play much of its acclaim.

Most recently, Nottage has begun to explore several now-familiar themes in her work, especially those that have to do with rescuing voices from history, discovering silencing between the lines and black women defining themselves. "How far will you go to find a play?" she asks in "Out of East Africa," an intriguing account to her impromptu transatlantic research trip.[7] The answer to her question was made clear in several whirlwind trips to the continent to explore new dramatic territory. While there in the summer of 2004, she tapped a mother lode of raw material centered on the testimonies of oppressed, sexually abused African women. Her most recent play project entitled *Ruined* is inspired by what she witnessed during these excursions. As she recalls in this graphic narrative of her experiences, "I'm trying to find a human way of dramatizing these women's experiences that will provoke thought."[8]

A Stone's Throw also mirrors conflict in the daily lives of oppressed African women. The play, which as part of a multiple-authored five-play package represents Nottage's contribution to the 2004–2005 season of the Women's Project,[9] is based upon a reworking of Sophocles' classic play *Antigone*. Here, as in the majority of Nottage's plays, one finds a fresh and complex modern woman who is not afraid of her convictions. Undoubtedly inspired by one of several of Nottage's brief stints in Africa and her concern for breaking the silence of African women, this ten-minute play follows the deadly repercussions of a tabooed love affair between an African woman and a married man.

Like her literary foremothers, Nottage concentrates on black women in self-defining roles. Black female characters in her plays buck the system to boldly assert their individuality or undergo painful journeys that end in self-discovery. In her plays *Crumbs from the Table of Joy* (2005) and *Fabulations, Or the Re-Education of Undine* (2006), two black female characters take distinctly different paths that lead to psychological liberation and an affirmation of their identities. Nottage reveals that the correlations between these plays are not coincidental, indeed referring to them as "bookends."[10]

At the center of Nottage's memory play *Crumbs from the Table of Joy* is the 17-year-old African American girl Ernestine Crump, who is on the verge of womanhood in an essentially womanless home. She and her sister are being raised by an adoring but naïve father who is ill prepared to share the rites of passage that his young daughters must undergo as they grow into young women. Set in the 1950s, the family moves to New York after the devastating death of their mother. A fiercely independent Ernestine excitedly readies herself for an imminent high school graduation and, while doing so, faces choices that would lead her outside the comfort zone of the 1950s social environment. In *Fabulations, or the Re-Education of Undine*, Nottage reverses the black woman's path toward self-discovery. Undine Barnes Call-es is a successful, militant, progressive African American businesswoman, who, after a series of unfortunate events and reversals of fortune, winds up alone, unemployed, pregnant and scared. A well-educated and highly motivated socialite, she is arrested for heroine possession when busted on charges of purchasing heroine; it was for her grandmother. A once fairytale marriage turns into a nightmare when she discovers that her calculating and opportunistic Argentinian husband has depleted her bank account and disappeared. But ironically Undine seems to rise out of the ashes of her circumstances—even triumphing—all the while questioning herself and seeking advice from the audience to find answers as to who she really is and who she is destined to be.

Lynn Nottage prides herself in her representations of race, multiculturalism, and diversity in her plays. She asks, "Can a writer cross cultural boundaries. ... I certainly hope that I am permitted to source the different aspects of myself. And those aspects may come across as a white male or an Asian woman or a Latina."[11] To some extent, one can sense Nottage flexing her artistic muscles along these lines in *Las Meninas*, but perhaps more obviously so in her plays *Por'knockers* and *Mud, River, Stone*. The conflict of the political satire *Por'knockers* involves a group of would-be revolutionaries who conspire and succeed at bombing a building to draw attention to their muddled cause. It also features a panhandler in a prolonged search for gold in a rain forest.

According to Nottage, *Por'knockers* was inspired by a television documentary about a man on a quest for the por'knocker, the name given to "a miner who usually goes off by himself in search of gold, and he can stay out in the jungle for months, if not years, until he finds his fortune."[12] Fascinated by this image and somewhat bored after the success of *Crumbs*, Nottage pondered to find a way to make drama out of this one man's ritual. "I began thinking about the state of African-American politics and how, certainly in the 1980s, there hadn't been one leader or philosophy that generated tremendous excitement. Why were we, in a sense, still panning for our gold? Who are the modern-day por'knockers?"[13] Though perhaps not immediately obvious, *Por'knockers* is a tribute to diversity and a challenge to the practice of making blanket assumptions about any one race, culture or ethnicity. Toward this end, Nottage not only diversifies her cast of characters in terms of gender, race, and class, but she also tries to diffuse assumptions that members of certain racial and ethnic groups are automatically like-minded.

Mud, River, Stone, a tough lesson with near-tragic results for a thrill-seeking African American couple in war torn Africa, was a commissioned work for a multicultural organization called The Acting Company. In this affluent couple's quest for a novel experience, they go off the beaten path and find what appears to them to be a lovely hotel in the middle of chaos. When the rains set in and turn relentless, they become marooned and finally come to realize that their four-star hotel is an all but deserted fortress in the midst of an impoverished, war torn town. While *Por'knockers* grew out of a documentary that intrigued her, Nottage explains that the idea for *Mud, River, Stone* sprang from "an article in *The New York Times* about a town in Mozambique where, for a period of time, everyone who passed through was taken hostage by soldiers." This became the framework for this next play, which explores the explosive mixtures of tribal war, colonialism, and diverse cultural identities. Nottage's focus upon the classic search for identity continues in *Mud, River, Stone* as she forcefully juxtaposes Africans with African Americans. In doing so, the playwright—who had not once visited Africa before writing this play—underscores the complex, interrelated struggles of this motley multicultural group.

Becoming American (2003), like *Poof!*, typifies Nottage's forays into the gray areas between fantasy and reality. Under the guise of a naturalistic setting, flavored with modest amounts of humor, she presents a scenario that, upon closer examination, reveals some very disturbing realities about what the construct of "American" signals from an international perspective. A snapshot labeled *Mount Rushmore, South Dakota, 1969*, featuring one of America's most enduring landmarks and one of this country's most recognizable symbols of American nationalism, was chosen by organizers of the 2001–2002 Humana Festival as the inspiration for a playwriting experiment that led to an anthology of seventeen original works. Nottage joined this group of seventeen talented playwrights with a provocative take on race and nationalism inspired by the four stone-carved busts of former United States presidents perched atop this popular national landmark. A nameless instructor located in a classroom a world away in Africa uses a tape-recorded voice of an American as a teaching prop to educate his African students on ways to suppress their Africanness, for fear that they may repel his company's American clients: "Don't panic. Do you say I'm from Accra, Ghana to John from San Antonio? John who thinks Africa is a country and India a small reservation in New Mexico that he drove through when he was a boy."[14]

By her own admission, Nottage found her voice as a playwright in writing *Poof!*, a popular piece whose conflict concerns an abusive husband who is unintentionally zapped into oblivion for mistreating his wife. *Poof!* is uncanny in its universality—that is its ability to cross cultural boundaries and resonate among all women in abusive relationships. In writing this play, however, Nottage was careful that abused women not be given the message that homicide was an option for confronting violence leveled against them. Instead, through imaginative willpower, she gives them agency in initiating other more civil and more reality-based ways to negotiate intolerable relationships. On the surface this short, fantasy-driven play reveals the duality of Nottage's writing. On one level the play intimates a level of despair among battered women that has been never before considered. On another, its whimsical tone is prone to draw laughter.

Lynn Nottage now stands as one of the most respected and most produced African American female playwrights of the twenty-first century. The beautifully textured and layered meaning in her work place her right alongside the best, brightest and most promising writers of her time. Though her journey as a playwright often meant going it alone, she now acknowledges a kinship with a community of African American women playwrights such as Dael Orlandersmith, Ntosake Shange, Kia Corthon and Suzan-Lori Parks. Drawing upon comedy, spoof, political satire, memory, myth, fantasy, expressionism, and metatheatre, for example, she conveys her characters' stories in forms that are as different as the women whose lives she brings to the stage. Nottage celebrates African American women in a myriad of voices and characters with a style that simultaneously situates her in the company of a continuum of African American female playwrights and distinguishes her as one of the most refreshing and promising new voices among contemporary dramatists.

Notes

1 Randy Gener. "Conjurer of Worlds." *American Theatre* 22 (October 2005): 24.
2 Lynn Nottage, "Lives Rescued from Silence." *Los Angeles Times* (13 April 2003): E37.

3 Gener, 23.
4 Director David Sullivan's comments about Lynn Nottage appear in Randy Gener's "Conjurer of Worlds." In *American Theatre* (see page 144 in the above reference).
5 John Istel, "Perfect Fit': An Interview with Lynn Nottage." Front & Center Online: the Online Version of Roundabout Theatre Company's Subscriber Magazine (Winter 2004): 3. www.roundabouttheatre.org
6 Gener, 144.
7 See Nottage's detailed account "Out of East Africa" in *American Theatre* 22, No. 5 (May/June 2005): 26–7, 66–8. Here she provides graphic details of her excursion to Africa where she discovered stories of sexual abuse among African women that literally took her breath away.
8 Gener, 23.
9 The Women's Project was founded by Julia Miles in 1978 in response to the lack of opportunities for women in theatre. The group has staged over 120 productions, 450 readings and workshops, and published 10 anthologies of produced plays. It also nurtures emerging artists through its outreach programs and its award-winning, curriculum-based arts education program.
10 Gener, 144.
11 "Lynn Nottage: An Interview" by Alexis Green in *Women Who Write Plays: Interviews with American Dramatists*. New York: Smith and Kraus, 2001.viii.
12 Ibid, 349–50.
13 Ibid, 350.
14 Lynn Nottage, "Becoming American," in *Snapshot: A Dramatic Anthology*. New York: Playscripts, Incl, 2003: 61.

Works cited

Gener, Randy. "Conjurer of Worlds." *American Theater* 22 (October 2005): 22–24, 144–145.
Green, Alexis. "Lynn Nottage: An Interview." *Women Who Write Plays: Interviews with American Dramatists*. New York: Smith and Kraus, 2001.
John Istel. "'Perfect Fit': An Interview with Lynn Nottage." *Front & Center Online: the Online Version of Roundabout Theatre Company's Subscriber Magazine.* (Winter 2004): www.roundabouttheatre.org
Nottage, Lynn. *Becoming American*. In *Snapshot: A Dramatic Anthology*. New York: Playscripts, Inc., 2003.
——*Crumbs from the Table of Joy and Other Plays*. New York: Theatre Communications Group, 2004.
——*Fabulation, Or the R-education of Undine*. In *Intimate Apparel, Fabulation: Two Plays*. New York: Theatre Communications Group, 2006.
——*Intimate Apparel, Fabulation: Two Plays*. New York: Theatre Communications Group, 2006.
——*Las Meninas*. In *Crumbs from the Table of Joy and Other Plays*. New York: Theatre Communications Group, 2004.
——"Lives Rescued from Silence." *Los Angeles Times* (13 April 2006): E37.
——*Mud, River, Stone*. In *Crumbs from the Table of Joy and Other Plays*. New York: Theatre Communications Group, 2004.
——"Out of East Africa: The Show Must Go on for Uganda Orphans and Batwa Pygmies in the Wake of Cross-Border Violence, Civil Wars, Disease and Devastation." *American Theatre* 22, No. 5 (May/June 2005): 26–27, 66–68.

——*Poof!* In *Crumbs from the Table of Joy and Other Plays*. New York: Theatre Communications Group, 2004.

——*Por'knockers*. In *Crumbs from the Table of Joy and Other Plays*. New York: Theatre Communications Group, 2004.

——*Ruined* (forthcoming).

——*A Stone's Throw*.

Wegener, Amy. "Developing Snapshot." Foreword. *Snapshot: A Dramatic Anthology*. New York: Playscripts, Inc., 2003, 8.

Wilson, August *Two Trains Running*. New York: New American Library, 1990.

——*Gem of the Ocean*. New York: Theatre Communications Group, 2006.

——*Radio Golf*. New York: Theatre Communications Group, 2007.

13 An interview with Lynn Nottage

Sandra G. Shannon

Lynn Nottage describes her more than a decade-long journey as an African American female playwright as "a circuitous one, filled with typical frustrations, moments of epic disappointment and some surprising successes."[1] Following her phenomenal—albeit nonlinear—rise to prominence since the early 1990s, Nottage remains ambitious in her efforts to place even more dramatic focus on the many untold stories of African and African American women. From spending countless hours in the New York Public Library researching women's often unspeakable experiences, to jetting off to African villages in search of stories from traumatized rape victims, Nottage appears to have no limit in how far she would go to find dramatic material. I caught up with her at Baltimore, Maryland's Center Stage Theatre for the June 2006 opening of *Crumbs from the Table of Joy*. Nottage, who knew well my mission, was eager to discuss her work at length and most accommodating.

SS: I read in an interview that it was not until you had put the last punctuation mark on *Poof!* that you decided that playwriting was what you wanted to do. How has this play changed your life?

LN: I was working at Embassy International at the Press Office, so I was handling major media. I made a decision that when I graduated from the Yale School of Drama to leave playwriting because I had gone straight through in my education from first grade until graduate school without interfacing with the world, and so I felt like I needed to have a much more expansive experience. I felt as though everything that I had done up to then had been filtered through academia. I knew that I wanted to write plays, but I didn't feel qualified. *Poof!* led me.

SS: And you had already written some that were like closet plays —

LN: Yes, I had been writing plays, and I was a writer. But I didn't embrace the notion of being a writer because I felt as though I don't have things to write about. I haven't lived my life.

SS: Where did you get the premise for this play? It's seems like a Franz Kafka *Metamorphosis* mixed with a little of Douglass Turner Ward's *Day of Absence*.

LN: I can tell you exactly where. I was sitting at my desk and our advertising person said, "Come and see these photographs!" This woman had taken photographs of women the moment they entered the battered woman shelter. It was that moment of crisis, and she had captured it and wanted us to do something at Embassy International. But because it wasn't within our mandate, we couldn't do anything. But I was so incredibly moved to respond immediately. And so I looked at these images and I went into my office and *Poof!* came out of that. *Poof!* was a woman who has been battered for many, many years, and it's the moment when she discovers her voice and is able to say "No, I'm not going to take it anymore," that moment women experienced when they walked into that shelter and said, "No, I'm not going to take it anymore." And out of that comes the idea, what could a woman do if she really had all of the power in the world? She'd turn the man into dust and sweep him under the rug. Nonviolently. She'd say, "Stop it." And he would disappear. And so that's how *Poof!* was born. It's a woman being able to stop it and the man disappears.

SS: You credit your mother's gaze as the impetus for your work. Would you explain?

LN: My mother was an incredible woman—very intense, very intelligent, very spirited, and very passionate. And she had a look—and in my memory I still talk about a look she had that could communicate a great deal. It could tell you if you had said too much. It could tell you "I'm proud of you". It could communicate pain. It could communicate joy, and I feel like I found all of what I needed to write about through the filter of her eyes—the way she looked at me and the way I looked back at her.

SS: You have said that your plays were born in an orange colored kitchen with a group of women sitting around a mod Formica counter and that your mother's gaze became your looking glass. How did your studies at the Yale School of Drama contribute to the quality of your work and maybe provide a third level of inspiration?

LN: That's such a complicated question because my time at Yale was difficult and unfortunate. I was just very depressed during much of it. I didn't feel supported as an artist. I was only the second African American woman to come through the program as a playwright, and the woman who was the first who was there; they were in the process of trying to push her out. And so I didn't think that it was a terribly hospitable environment for me to be. I felt like I was fighting to be there rather than feeling —

SS: Was it a case against your gender or race?

LN: I think it was certainly both things. The combination of race and gender made it complicated. And then one of the other frustrations of being there is that the actors have their plays produced, and they have a ready-made ensemble there. But as an African American playwright, you don't have your cast. And so you are constantly being asked to make concessions to cover the acting pool.

SS: You graduated from the Yale School of Drama in 1989. Were you there when Lloyd Richards was there?

LN: Yes.

SS: Did you work with him or take classes with him?

LN: I didn't so much because of the way the departments were divided. As playwrights, we took our playwriting classes, and weren't permitted to take directing courses or designing courses. There wasn't a whole lot of fluidity among departments. But he was the dean, and he brought in great playwrights like Athol Fugard and August Wilson. We could sit in and watch rehearsals, actually meet these playwrights and talk to them, and be part of the process. One of the first shows that I ever worked on was *The Piano Lesson*. I dressed Rocky Carroll and Sam Jackson and got to watch that play as it was being developed through all of its drafts until it finally got to the stage.

SS: Did you know Lloyd Richards? I remember you've said that you did not have a very close relationship because of the circumstances. I remember it was said that he was absent from his office a lot.

LN: I don't even know that he particularly liked me. He was quite busy. He was nurturing August Wilson. I felt terribly unsupported. I think he was quite offended by my first play. Then after that, he kind of gave up on me as a writer.

SS: What was the play?

LN: It was my first-year project, and I wanted to write something that was very provocative. Granted all of my plays when I was there, I felt, were extremely provocative. And that's just the age that you go through when you want to confront your parents. And he was my artistic parent.

SS: You have claimed that your plays are not "kitchen sink dramas." I think it was a headnote for *Intimate Apparel*, which was included in *Colored Contradictions*, an anthology, edited by Harry Elam and Robert Alexander. Is that anything like George Wolfe's "mama on the couch" kind of drama or just totally opposite?

LN: No. It's different. I don't totally reject "kitchen sink dramas" because I think, for me, they are very important. Kitchen sink dramas are very naturalistic plays that were written in the 1950s that took place in the kitchen or in the living room and generally had one or two sets. They were a specific kind of family drama which played out family crises. I don't think my plays are entirely naturalistic, and that's why I don't want them to be played naturalistically. Some of my plays are expressionistic and not naturalistic.

SS: I want to ask you about Girta [from *Crumbs from the Table of Joy*]. What is she doing in this play? She begs for a kind of elaboration. She doesn't fit the fabric.

LN: I like to have surprising elements in my plays. I want people to be lulled into thinking that this is a certain kind of play and then be surprised. When I wrote *Crumbs from the Table of Joy*, I wanted it to be an allegory about the journey that African Americans took from the South to the North. And one of the things that we experienced when we got here was this cultural clash because we were forced to engage with white people in a way that didn't happen in the South. African Americans didn't move folks into our homes, but I wanted to do it in a bold way. So that is why Girta is there. It's the kind of conversation that I wanted to have with integration—how integration impacts with their lives, and on what it says about where we went from there.

SS: Of course, August Wilson claims not to have done any research for his plays, but you've spent hours in the New York Public Library doing research. How does research in the library transfer to a character?

LN: Well, it's the joy of discovering my characters. And I like to know the period times. I want to know what they wear. I want to know the price they paid for food at the supermarket or in the store. I just like all of those delicious details that you get through research that I couldn't organically bring because I'm not there. And granted they may never ever make it into the play, but, for me, research is educating myself, and every time I go on the journey of writing a play, I see it as going to graduate school. I'm going someplace I've never been before. When I did *Crumbs from the Table of Joy*, set in the 1950s, before I was born, I thought "Let me see all of the movies. Let me do the research. Let me read the *Communist Manifesto*. Let me educate myself about the period, and then I will write the play."

SS: Do you consider yourself in the tradition of black female playwrights or are you striking out doing something different or is it both?

LN: It's both. I feel like I am very much in the tradition. I grew up reading the novels of Alice Walker, Toni Morrison, Alice Childress, and Louise Meriwether. That's my literature. That's what I read when I was a child. And so, those are the people who taught me to love writing and to want to be a writer. And so I feel that I am a part of that tradition.

SS: Your plays try to get at women's realities. What are some of those realities and what do you say about them? Do you "write between the lines" or "expose what is between the lines?"

LN: I am concerned about telling stories about women whom I knew in a way that touches audiences. Is it entirely realistic? I don't know, but I feel that there are truths there. And I feel that so many of our stories haven't been told. So in the case of *Intimate Apparel*, I wanted to bridge the gap between women at the turn of the nineteenth century and at the turn of the twentieth century. They were very focused, very hard-working women, and because of the choices that they made, they were being punished, which I think is what's happening to a lot of African American women today who have taken a career path. Look at

Condoleezza Rice. She is a prototype of a certain kind of African American woman who has excelled, but there is a price she has paid for that.

SS: Your fellow playwright Shay Youngblood portrays black women, in works such as *Shakin' the Mess Outta Misery*, as "Big Mama" prototypes. Do you have a comparable way of describing your black female characters?

LN: I didn't because I did not have Big Mamas in my family. I do have a prototype, Lily from *Crumbs*. She is a woman that I know very well. She's a woman who exists in my family. I come from a family of very large personalities of women who were striving for great things and worked very quietly to achieve them.

SS: You create some very powerful metaphors to communicate women's realities: a sewing machine, lingerie, the motion pictures, and expressionistic images in *Crumbs*, such as the graduation dress and the twitching leg. What are you attempting to convey through these images?

LN: With the cinema, it's escape. How does one escape? Where does one go when one retreats into darkness and darkness then becomes light. It's the moving image. And so that's escape. One of the repeated images I use in many of my plays is sewing, the assembling of a garment. It's that you can take something from nothing and create something quite magnificent and beautiful. You have to start with these very raw, basic materials. And so I am very interested in how one assembles something. You can assemble a patchwork quilt, or you could turn something into a corset that then becomes constraining, or you could turn something into a wedding gown or a graduation gown and that becomes a sign of liberation. And so I'm interested in how fabric is transformed and in the woman's relationship to fabric and her own transformation.

SS: The paradox is so beautifully drawn out in *Intimate Apparel*. This woman is putting together lingerie for another type of person that she cannot imagine herself being.

LN: The paradox of the image, for me, is that while she was also creating the corset—which was used to confine and to constrict—she was part of her own destruction.

SS: Which contemporary black female playwrights do you admire and why?

LN: I admire them all. I love something about all of the playwrights. I love Dael Orlandersmith because of the lusciousness of her language, and I see her very much in the tradition of Ntozake Shange—these choreopoems where you kind of lose yourself in the language and in the imagery. I admire that Kia is doing stark, political plays that force you to confront them when you are sitting in the audience. And there's Suzan-Lori Parks constantly playing with form and surprising us in the places that she goes and asking us to think about the architecture of the play, not just the content. I admire them all! I host this barbecue called

"Sister Barbecue" and invite all African American women dramatists to come.

SS: At the center of your plays are black women. Where do you position black men?

LN: Women are my focal point. But I feel like this question is similar to something August Wilson was also asked: Where are the black women in your plays? I deal with the black woman because I feel we have been marginalized for so long that it's time for us to be center stage. The black male is there, but I am telling a story of the black woman. It's my story, and I don't feel like I have to tell this story of the black male. August Wilson told that story. I don't want to tell it again.

SS: Some writers such as Toni Morrison and the late August Wilson admit that their characters crowd into their heads. And I remember you commenting on this. They demand agency and voice. Have any of your characters been conceptualized this way?

LN: I write my plays totally in my head. I think this is why I do more research. As I'm researching, I'm writing. And so when I finally sit down to write, the writing process is very quick. I feel as if I know these characters. I know their journeys. I've told their stories. I've visited the highs and the lows. I know where it's going to end.

SS: In one of your interviews you indicated that in *Intimate Apparel*, you were specifically interested in space between the lines. (See John Istel's interview with Nottage, "Perfect Fit," in the winter 2004 online version of *Roundabout Theatre Company's Subscriber Magazine*).

LN: Well, no. It's the silence. I was interested in the silence between the lines—what's unspoken.

SS: Would that be the case for all of your plays?

LN: I think more so in *Intimate Apparel* because of the time period, the Victorian Age, during which: *one*, we didn't have the language of psychoanalysis to express everything that we're feeling; *two*, there was a lot that wasn't permitted to be said; *three*, it was in an age with far fewer cross-cultural conversations. People could exist in the same space but not have certain kinds of conversations. So I was interested in what was communicated without the words.

SS: So, with your research and with filling in the gaps, you're creating this reality. Maybe not creating it but giving it voice. It's been there. It just needs to be teased out.

LN: Yes, it's been there.

SS: Have you gotten to a point in your career when you can look back on what you've done and describe a particular aesthetic that is what and who do you write about, and how do you go about writing about them?

LN: I'm trying to think and go deeper into my mind to find out what all of my plays have in common. A lot of them deal with self-definition, race—about having a conversation on race and multiculturalism, which I feel people in my generation had to have much more so than, say, people from August

Wilson's conversations. And I think that's why my characters probably have more diversity in them than his. Perhaps, his plays do because I feel like the world is slightly more diverse than the world he grew up in.

SS: Do you mind people calling you a black female playwright?

LN: Well, I am! I don't mind them calling me that as long and they're not marginalizing me by calling me that. It's really interesting because when I first began writing, the reviews always referred to me as African American female playwright Lynn Nottage. And I know now the reviews say just "playwright."

SS: Do they also try to compare you with somebody, thinking that they're giving you a compliment?

LN: Yes, they did back then. I was compared to Lorraine Hansberry, Tennessee Williams. I use to get these comparisons because of *Crumbs from the Table of Joy*, which is a memory play, not necessarily because of the writing of it but because of the language that's slightly expressionistic. But it bothered me when I was called an African American female playwright, and I felt being diminished in that context. But it doesn't bother me because that's what I am. As long as you're not diminishing me or marginalizing me or dismissing me. And I felt like sometimes it was dismissive. It was like saying "Oh, I don't need to read this review because it's an African American playwright."

SS: You come at history in a number of ways—your own personal family history and also our cultural history. In particular, what is it you're trying to do with that? I know August Wilson says that he is rewriting history. What are you doing with history?

LN: I feel that I am rescuing our voices from history. We, as African American women, don't see ourselves in the history books. We don't see ourselves in the literature, unless, of course, we're serving the cold refreshments or nannying the children. And I think we play a much greater role. And so I feel like I have to constantly go back and say "Wait a minute. I'm here!"

SS: What scripts are you working on now?

LN: I am writing a play based upon interviews I've been doing in Africa with Congolese refugee women who've been the victims of gender specific human rights abuses.[2] In particular, I'm looking at how rape has become one of the primary tools of war. My issue of passion is to try to get us as African American women to focus on the plight of African women and figure out a way to use the power that we have to empower them. So my play is about a group of women who, because they have been raped and because they have been damaged by rape, have banded together for the community.

SS: What do you think the most pressing things are that black women writers ought to be doing? It appears that you are already doing what they ought to be doing.

LN: Far be it for me to say what any writer should do. But I think we should somehow be engaging the culture we live in, commenting on it and helping people to understand. And just have a conversation with culture. Sometimes I believe I have not been as good about keeping that conversation going. With this play [*Ruined*] I hope to shed some light on what's going on in Africa, not because I feel that we always have to do it, but I think we are artists and can create things that are beautiful. Like Tyler Perry, we can create things that permit us to escape because I think escape is a very important theme. But I feel like I'm such a schizophrenic because, on one hand, I believe that we should be writing these plays and actively engaging culture. On the other hand, I feel like we should be writing plays with myth. When I get home from my job in a token booth in New York City, I should go and be able to see myself cast in a role that's fun and irreverent and delightful. I don't necessarily want to see that play [*Ruined*] about me being raped. So we have to have both of those things.

SS: You have gained the respect of theatre critics for dramatic works that feature African American women. What do your male playwright colleagues have to say about your work in general?

LN: I don't know, and I don't care. I honestly don't know.

SS: Do you read reviews?

LN: I do, but I am a masochist. I am. I enjoy the good, the bad, and the ugly. "Bring it on!"

Notes

1 "A Play By Play Special Tribute: Contemporary Female Playwrights." *TDF Play by Play* 10.4 (2006): 2.
2 The play referenced here is *Ruined*, Nottage's response in play form to widespread cases of rape among African women in war torn Sudan and Democratic Republic of the Congo. For more details on Nottage's trip and her interactions among the locals, see her account "Out of East Africa" in the May/June 2005 issue of *American Theatre*.

Works cited

Elam, Harry and Alexander, Robert, eds. *Colored Contradictions: An Anthology of Contemporary African American Plays*. New York: Plume, 1996.
Kafka, Franz. *Metamorphosis*. New York: Bantam Classics, 1972.
Nottage, Lynn. *Crumbs from the Table of Joy and Other Plays*. New York: Theatre Communications Group, 2004.
——*Intimate Apparel, Fabulation: Two Plays*. New York: Theatre Communications Group, 2006.
Ward, Douglass Turner. *Day of Absence*. In *Black Theatre U.S.A.* Hatch, James V. and Shine, Ted, eds. New York: The Free Press, 1996.
Wilson, August. *The Piano Lesson*. New York: Plume, 1990.
Youngblood, Shay. *Shakin'the Mess Outta Misery* in *Colored Contradictions: An Anthology of Contemporary African American Plays*. New York: Plume, 1996.

Index

Suzan-Lori Parks: A Casebook
(Casebooks on Modern Dramatists)
Edited by Alycia Smith-Howard and Kevin J. Wetmore Jr

Suzan-Lori Parks: A Casebook is the first major study of this Pulitzer Prize-winning playwright's works, from *Topdog/Underdog* to *Venus* and *The America Play*. The essays in this volume provide contexts for Parks's work to date, including Shawn Marie Garrett's analysis of Parks's first major play, *Imperceptible Mutabilities of the Third Kingdom* and Parks herself, discussing in interview the process of creating her 365 project internationally.

Parks is neither easy to pigeonhole, nor easy to summarize, but her work in the theatre (and now in film and fiction) have proven to be some of the most dramatically exciting writing in the United States today. This volume seeks to understand how, within this wide variety of Parks's work, the similarities and differences demonstrate an artist who paints a unique portrait of the United States, both past and present.

ISBN10: 0-415-97381-3 (hbk)
ISBN10: 0-203-93728-7 (ebk)

ISBN13: 978-0-415-97381-6 (hbk)
ISBN13: 978-0-203-93728-0 (ebk)

Available at all good bookshops
For ordering and further information please visit:
www.routledge.com

Martin McDonagh: A Casebook
(Casebooks on Modern Dramatists)
Edited by Richard Rankin Russell

This book represents the first collection of original critical material on Martin McDonagh, one of the most celebrated young playwrights of the last decade. Credited with reinvigorating contemporary Irish drama, his dark, despairing comedies have been performed extensively both on Broadway and in the West End, culminating in an Olivier Award for the *The Pillowman* and an Academy Award for his short film *Six Shooter*.

In **Martin McDonagh: A Casebook**, Richard Rankin Russell brings together a variety of theoretical perspectives – from globalisation to the gothic – to survey McDonagh's plays in unprecedented critical depth. Specially commissioned essays cover topics such as identity politics, the shadow of violence and the role of Catholicism in the work of this most precocious of contemporary dramatists.

ISBN10: 0-415-97765-7 (hbk)
ISBN10: 0-203-93585-3 (ebk)

ISBN13: 978-0-415-97765-4 (hbk)
ISBN13: 978-0-203-93585-9 (ebk)

Related titles from Routledge

A Sourcebook on African-American Performance: Plays, People, Movement (Worlds of Performance)
Edited by Annemarie Bean

A Sourcebook on African-American Performance: Plays, People, Movements is the first volume to consider African-American perform-ance between and beyond the Black Arts Movement of the 1960s and the New Black Renaissance of the 1990s.

A Sourcebook consists of writings previously published in *The Drama Review* (TDR) as well as newly commissioned pieces by notable scholars, writers and performers including Annemarie Bean, Ed Bullins, Barbara Lewis, John O'Neal, Glenda Dickersun, James V. Hatch, Warren Budine Jr., and Eugene Nesmith. Included are articles, essays, manifestos and interviews on:

- theatre on the professional, revolutionary and college stages
- concert dance
- community activism
- step shows
- performance art previously published in TDR

The volume also includes the plays *Sally's Rape* by Robbie McCauley and *The American Play* by Suzan-Lori Parks, and comes complete with an Introduction by Annemarie Bean.

ISBN13: 978-0-415-18234-8 (hbk)
ISBN13: 978-0-415-18235-5 (pbk)
ISBN13: 978-0-203-18221-5 (ebk)

ISBN10: 0-415-18234-8 (hbk)
ISBN10: 0-415-18235-2 (pbk)
ISBN10: 0-203-18221-9 (ebk)
Available at all good bookshops
For ordering and further information please visit:
www.routledge.com

Theatre Histories:
An Introduction
Edited by Philip B. Zarrilli, Bruce McConachie, Gary Jay Williams and Carol Fisher Sorgenfrei

'This book will significantly change theatre education'

Janelle Reinelt, *University of California, Irvine*

Theatre Histories: An Introduction is a radically new way of looking at both the way history is written and the way we understand performance.

The authors provide beginning students and teachers with a clear, exciting journey through centuries of European, North and South American, African and Asian forms of theatre and performance.

Challenging the standard format of one-volume theatre history texts, they help the reader think critically about this vibrant field through fascinating yet plain-speaking essays and case studies.

- Among the topics covered are:
- representation and human expression
- interpretation and critical approaches
- historical method and sources
- communication technologies
- colonization
- oral and literate cultures
- popular, sacred and elite forms of performance.

Keeping performance and culture very much centre stage, *Theatre Histories: An Introduction* is compatible with standard play anthologies, full of insightful pedagogical apparatus, and comes accompanied by web site resources.

ISBN13: 978-0-415-22727-8 (hbk)
ISBN13: 978-0-415-22728-5 (pbk)

ISBN10: 0-415-22727-5 (hbk)
ISBN10: 0-415-22728-3 (pbk)

Available at all good bookshops
For ordering and further information please visit:
www.routledge.com